CONIECTANEA BIBLICA · NEW TESTAMENT SERIES 10

STEPHEN WESTERHOLM

JESUS AND SCRIBAL
AUTHORITY

CWK GLEERUP

CWK Gleerup is the imprint for the scientific and scholarly publications of Liber
Läromedel Lund.

ISBN 91−40−04642−7

© Stephen Westerholm
Doctoral Thesis at Lund University
Studentlitteratur ab
Lund 1978

To My Parents

Preface

My thanks are due primarily to my dissertation adviser, Professor Birger Gerhardsson, both for welcoming me to Lund and for the benefit of his suggestions and encouragement at each stage of my doctoral studies. His thorough acquaintance with the subject matter of this dissertation has been a great asset in its preparation. Thanks must also be expressed to Professor Evald Lövestam and the members of the New Testament seminar at the University of Lund, with whom various aspects of my work have been discussed.

That all those to whom thanks are due cannot be named here is obvious; but I would like to mention specially the Swedish Institute, which provided me with a scholarship enabling me to pursue my studies in Sweden from September 1974 until May 1977; Rev. G.B. Griffiths and friends from Calvary Church, Toronto, for the interest they have taken in my studies; and, of course, Gunilla, to meet whom was obviously the "real" reason for my coming to Sweden!

My interest in biblical studies was undoubtedly inspired by my parents' love for scripture. Their encouragement and love have supported me throughout. To them, with thanks, this book is dedicated.

Lund, February 1978
Stephen Westerholm

Contents

Introduction

According to a well-known distinction drawn by Josephus, the Sadducees recognized as valid only those regulations which were written in the law of
Moses, whereas the Pharisees "transmitted to the people certain regulations
handed down from the fathers" (Ant. 13.297). Interpreted strictly, this means
that Sadducaic scribes had no mandate to create binding law of their own,
but only to interpret and apply what was written in Torah.[1] On the other
hand, we shall see in the course of our study that Pharisaic scribes not
only transmitted traditional laws not found in scripture, but even added to
their number; and the regulations they adopted were held to be as binding
as those found in scripture.

Our study will be concerned, first, to elucidate this phenomenon by which
scribal law was added to scriptural, and treated on the same level; second,
to examine Jesus' view of scribal authority and define his position on the
contemporary issue. To this end, Part One, after attempting to answer the
question who the Pharisees were and to characterize their law, discusses
the makers of Pharisaic law (first the scribes themselves, then the assemblies in which laws were adopted) and the nature and scope of their authority. Part Two begins with Jesus' view of two areas central to Pharisaic law
(tithing and ritual purity), then takes up other areas (sabbath, oaths, and
divorce) in which his attitude towards scribal regulations is also more or
less explicit. The final chapter notes briefly further passages in the gospels which shed light on our subject before drawing conclusions and suggesting their implications for our understanding of Jesus' ministry as a
whole.

The treatment of many questions in the first part is necessarily a summary
one; the historical development of Pharisaic law and institutions is largely
left out of the picture. The attempt is instead made to provide a concise
description of the character of Pharisaic law, and of those men and institutions which may help to illuminate Jesus' relations with the Pharisees. Too
often in the discussion of those relations, details of Pharisaic law are
cited as examples of scribal pedantry or legalism's burdensome yoke without
any attempt being made to penetrate to the rationale behind their law. Yet
it is not only our picture of the Pharisees which suffers in the process;

1

Jesus' own understanding of the will of God cannot properly be appreciated until the position of his partners in the dialogue is grasped. The first part of our study is intended to provide the background for such an understanding.

Part Two may aptly be described as a crossbreed: aspects of two frequently discussed subjects - Jesus and the Pharisees,[2] and Jesus and the law[3] - are taken up, though neither subject is treated exhaustively. In the former case, little is said of the Pharisees' reaction to the proclamation of Jesus, nothing of their possible role in his trial and death; our only concern is with material which illustrates Jesus' view of the authority of their scribes. In the latter case, many aspects of Jesus' understanding of the law are scarcely mentioned: the primacy of the love commandments, for example, and four of the six antitheses of the Sermon on the Mount. Still, what is said here by way of illuminating Jesus' view of scribal law is an important part of that larger subject, and worthy of careful study in its own right.

The one who would depict Jesus' view of the sabbath or divorce is soon made aware of the fact that he is not entering previously uncharted waters. Somewhat less travelled, perhaps, are the areas of tithing, ritual purity, and oaths, but the literature is still plentiful. Some justification may be needed for proceeding with the investigation. First, it is hoped that our study of the nature of Pharisaic law and scribal authority will shed new light on Jesus' conflicts with the Pharisees. Second, in bringing these subjects together and treating them under the common theme of Jesus' view of scribal authority, we will discover that they illuminate each other and provide answers which the treatment of any one of them in isolation could not provide. Third, the attempt is made to draw on studies relevant for our subject which are often overlooked in N.T. discussions, where the sole supporting reference for a point of Pharisaic law is often drawn from Strack-Billerbeck. While the monumental achievement of that work is not to be denied, its limitations in tracing historical development, and hence in identifying that which is of direct relevance to the gospel debates, have long been recognized; in any case, studies in the field of Pharisaic-rabbinic law did not cease with the publication of that great commentary (1922-1928). One aim of this study has been to fill in a few bibliographical gaps by drawing on some important but largely overlooked contributions to our subject.

Before we begin our study, however, an account must be given of the use made of the historical sources.

B. THE SOURCES

Our concern in Part One is not with the view of the law in "Palestinian Judaism", but with the specifically Pharisaic view; further, it is not with what we, by applying formal or dogmatic criteria, may be inclined to label "Pharisaic" (as, for example, when we distinguish what is Pharisaic from what is apocalyptic, [4] or use the term as a synonym for "legalistic"), but with what might be labelled "Pharisaic" by Jesus' contemporaries in that it reflected the characteristic interpretations or practices of a recognizable group within society. The nature of the Pharisaic movement will be examined more closely in Chapter I; but already it should be evident that material for our study cannot be drawn indiscriminately from the Qumran texts, the O.T. Apocrypha and Pseudepigrapha, or even from Philo. These texts may be cited by way of comparison, and perhaps to show that a point of law attested in rabbinic literature had some currency in the pre-70 period; but they are not sources for Pharisaic law. [5] For the latter our primary sources are Josephus, who in fact says little about the subject; the accounts in the synoptic gospels of Jesus' dealings with the Pharisees, where we are confronted with all the problems involved in assessing their historical value; and rabbinic literature.

The critical evaluation of rabbinic sources - certainly a prerequisite for tracing in detail the historical development of Pharisaic law - has only begun. That, however, is not a sufficient reason for abandoning our project. Virtual certainty on a number of points is already attainable; on all points, it will never be. What can be done in a study of this sort is to confine the evidence used to the earliest rabbinic sources: thus, Mishnah and Tosefta, as well as the tannaitic midrashim, are the primary sources; the Palestinian and Babylonian Talmuds, and, in particular, the beraitot they contain, take a secondary place; and later literature is, for all practical purposes, ignored. Further, in the discussion of individual points of Pharisaic law, material is used for which the sources themselves make the claim that they depict the pre-70 period, usually by naming sages who lived at that time, or the schools of Shammai and Hillel, which were then active. These principles have been my guidelines. If, on the one hand, I occasionally depart from them, and, on the other, I do not argue more rigorously for the historicity of the rabbinic materials I do cite, it is because our primary interest here is in the general character of Pharisaic law. Thus the

main argument is not crucially affected if certain details represent a somewhat later development.

The difficulties involved in using the gospels as historical sources are
well known. A comparison of Mt. 15:1-20 with Mk. 7:1-23 (two accounts of the
handwashing dispute), or of Mt. 19:3-9 with Mk. 10:2-12 (accounts of the debate on divorce) shows immediately that we are not dealing with transcriptions of a discussion. The progression of the dialogues is different in the
two accounts. What in one account is an objection raised by the Pharisees
(Mt. 19:7) is, in the other, their simple response to a question put by
Jesus (Mk. 10:3f.). Moreover, the wording in the two accounts differs, even
on some essential matters (compare Mt. 19:9 and Mk. 10:11f.); and so on.

This is only as it should be. The evangelists were writing, not for twentieth
century historians interested in an exact account of what actually was said,
but for Christian communities with their own interests and needs. The question of what Jesus was really like, what he really said and did, cannot have
been a matter of indifference for the early Christians; but the satisfaction
of their interest on that point evidently did not require word-for-word
transcriptions of the dialogues, and it is clear that the evangelists felt
free to alter the wording of a saying transmitted to them, or even to introduce additional material, in order to emphasize certain elements in the
tradition with special significance for contemporary needs. Moreover, the
perspective from which the evangelists viewed the events of Jesus' life was
different from that of the disciples during his ministry. The Master from
Nazareth was now the crucified, risen, and exalted Lord. Such a change in
perspective could not but affect the way in which events were portrayed.
This is why the gospels are not only sources for the life and teaching of
Jesus, but also witnesses to the situation and thinking of the Christian
communities within which they arose, and whose needs they were intended to
meet.

But this makes the task of the historian, eager to know what Jesus himself
said and did, a difficult one. His first problem is this: how are the various adaptations through which the gospel material has passed to be pen-
etrated, and the tradition uncovered in its earliest ascertainable form? To
solve this problem, certain tools of gospel research have been devised:
literary, form, and redaction criticism may be mentioned. Since they are
well-known tools, I will not pause to account for them here. One note should,
perhaps, be added. A majority of scholars are of the opinion that Mark's

gospel has been used as a source by Matthew and Luke, and thus represents an
earlier form of the tradition in cases where the accounts are parallel. This
opinion is by no means uncontested; but in the parallel accounts dealt with
in this study, I find no conclusive reason for rejecting, and many reasons
for supporting, the majority opinion. Some of these reasons will be indicated in the course of our study. Hence, where parallel accounts do exist,
Mark becomes the starting-point for our investigation.

But, assuming that the tradition in its earliest ascertainable form is before
us, problems still remain: Does the tradition even in this form accurately
reflect Jesus' words and deeds? Or were the views represented in the tradition first made explicit in the early church, and the apparently historical
settings first created at a later date? The tendency in current gospel research is to despair of reaching certainty on this point and, perhaps as a
reaction against the uncritical use of sources shown by former generations
and non-scholars of our own, to advise scepticism wherever the matter is in
doubt. Given the climate prevailing in scholarly circles, it might be thought
presumptuous to attempt to depict the views of Jesus on any subject.

To the subject of our study, however, that judgment does not seem applicable.
When we have finished subtracting from the gospels what can be attributed
to the Jewish legacy and the church's creativity; when due allowance has
been made for the liberty of preachers, the inspiration of prophets, changed
conditions, a new perspective, and the alterations (theological or pedantic)
of gospel editors, certain things still remain: among them is a picture of
Jesus who offends his contemporaries by associating with disreputable people
and taking liberties with the sabbath laws; further, a Jesus who prohibits
divorce and the use of oaths. The basic historicity of these elements in
the gospel records is almost axiomatic in contemporary research, and with
good reason. Somehow their presence in the bedrock of the gospel tradition
must be explained. How are we to account for the fact that, within a few
years of Jesus' life, the picture of him keeping company thought scandalous
by contemporary standards was firmly rooted in the tradition? No adherent
is likely to have painted the Master in that way, were it not that any other
depiction falsified known facts. The notion that he took liberties with the
sabbath command is similarly so much a part of the bedrock of tradition
that it scarcely permits any other explanation than that it corresponds with
historical reality. At any rate, such an explanation must be provided by the
one who thinks the notion false. To the extent that such activities can be

shown to violate scribal norms of Jesus' day – and it is part of our task to examine this question – the foundation has been laid for a study of Jesus' view of scribal authority.

Thus our study has its base in elements of the tradition whose historical accuracy is almost axiomatic. But how are we to decide if a given logion in the gospels is "authentic" (i.e. a reproduction, at least in essentials, of Jesus' words, and hence reliable evidence for his views)?

(i) One criterion which has been used in a number of cases relevant to our study is that of "dissimilarity": we may attribute to Jesus statements which cannot have their origin in Judaism or the early church, especially where there are indications that the church found the formulation too radical for its liking.[6] But judgments of uniqueness have at times been premature; given our ignorance of many aspects of Judaism and the early church, they can never be certain. Further, it must be emphasized that we dare not confine the evidence for the views of Jesus to statements with which the early church was not in agreement. Presumably he was not such a failure as a teacher that he never succeeded in communicating his views to his disciples and convincing them of their rightness. Hence, if our picture of Jesus, to say nothing of our picture of the early church, is not to be hopelessly distorted, other criteria must be applied as well. Still, the "criterion of dissimilarity" has some value when used to establish authenticity and not non-authenticity, and when qualified by an acknowledgement of the uncertainty attending any assessment of uniqueness.

(ii) A more useful, though often overlooked indication of a saying's authenticity is any sign that it has generated, or been the object of, further reflection, or that it has been applied to situations arising within the early church. This takes into account the inherent probability that Jesus did impress something of what he had to say on his followers, and that they regarded his words as authoritative. Especially is this to be reckoned with where the saying in question is concise, rhythmic, and formulated to provoke further thought: indications that we are dealing with words which the Master of the mashal intended to be remembered and pondered.[7] The criterion here proposed we may call that of "pregnant speech".

(iii) This brings us to the "criterion of style": where material judged to be authentic exhibits idiosyncracies of speech, the presence of these characteristics in other sayings can be used as an indication (though of course not in itself a proof) of authenticity.[8]

(iv) Further, the "criterion of coherence" enables us to move from texts
shown by other means to be authentic and to state with some probability that
sayings reflecting views consistent with this material are also authentic.[9]
Of course, sayings consistent with Jesus' teaching could have been added
within the early church. Where, however, the saying in question displays
a creative application in a new setting of the same inner logic which came
to expression in material acknowledged to be authentic, we may fairly conclude that Jesus is the source of the new application as well.

These are among the criteria which may be used for establishing that a saying of Jesus in the gospels is authentic. But the historian's task is not
complete when he has isolated the earliest form of a unit of tradition and
applied the criteria of authenticity to it. It is a desideratum for the
historical study of the gospels that satisfactory criteria for establishing
non-authentic material be formulated and applied as well. An example will
illustrate the need.

In the course of this study, we will have occasion to deal with sayings in
the gospels whose authenticity has been rejected by various scholars because
similar statements may be found in literature deriving from other milieus
than first century Palestine. It is thus assumed that the early church drew
upon these other traditions and attributed the results to Jesus. It should
be obvious that, in the absence of critically defined criteria for classifying material as secondary, unstated and unsatisfactory criteria have
filled the vacuum. Either it is supposed that Jesus can only have said what
no ear has otherwise heard nor heart imagined (a tenet dubious as dogma and
horrendous as history); or that Jesus, who lived in Palestine, cannot have
expressed views corresponding to those found in other milieus (which wrong-
ly presupposes that similar ideas cannot spring up in different milieus,
and, where a Hellenistic milieu is in question, often fails to take into
account the evidence for the influence of Hellenistic culture in Palestine);
or that a saying in the gospels is so much more likely to reproduce, e.g.,
Hellenistic-Jewish tradition than words of Jesus that, wherever the former
alternative presents itself, it is to be preferred to the latter (an unwarranted scepticism towards the gospel tradition, since a satisfactory
Sitz im Leben Jesu for the transmission of sayings to the disciples has been
shown).[10] Whatever the criterion used, it has had two unfortunate results:
it has removed from the evidence a potential witness for the views of Jesus;
and, by positing contact between the early church and traditions from other
milieus, it has led to a reconstruction of the development of early church

thought for which the text in question provides no certain evidence.

It must be remembered that sayings in the gospels are historical sources: either they reflect views made explicit by Jesus himself, in which case the community which transmitted those views, while probably sharing them, cannot be credited with their development; or they reflect views developed within the Christian communities responsible for the gospels, perhaps drawing on other sources than the words of Jesus. Yet, whereas in the former case criteria have been formulated for defining what part of the material can be used to ascertain the views of Jesus, and scholarly reserve if not scepticism is advised in the assessing of the evidence, in the latter case, acceptable critical standards for the admission of evidence have not been defined, and hypothetical reconstructions outside the discipline of proper historical research are frequently offered. The result is inevitable: the field of investigation undisciplined by adequate criteria encroaches on the preserve of the disciplined, and claims for its own use historical evidence which the latter was too cautious to appropriate. It is thus symptomatic of contemporary research that, whereas few dare to make statements about the life and teaching of Jesus, creative reconstructions of the theological development of the early church abound, at times with little other support than gospel materials designated non-authentic by the use of inadequate criteria.

Hence there is a need for a clear definition of criteria by which authenticity can with some certainty be rejected; the tradition in question may then be used as a witness for developments within the church, but only in an indirect, negative way for the views of Jesus (i.e. it is unlikely that even secondary material could find a place within the gospel tradition if Jesus was known to have expressed the opposite view). The following criteria are proposed, and will be used in the study which follows.

(i) A unit of the gospel tradition may be considered secondary if it can be shown to presuppose conditions improbable for Palestine at the time of Jesus but existing in at least one of the milieus within which the gospel tradition was transmitted or for which it was recorded. This we may call the "criterion of altered milieu". A special case may here be mentioned, though its use requires great caution: where scripture is cited according to the LXX, and the argument of the passage is dependent on a reading peculiar to that version, the passage in question may be considered secondary. This assumes, of course, that Jesus did not know and use the Greek translation of the O.T., but this assumption, in spite of the evidence for the usage of Greek in Palestine,[11] is probable enough. But there are other dangers which must be borne in mind. The fact that the LXX rendering is given in the gospels may of course be explained by the assumption that Jesus cited a Hebrew text, but that, when the tradition was rendered in Greek, the familiar LXX form was reproduced. Hence it must be shown that the argument of the passage depends on a reading peculiar to the LXX text before it may be classified as secondary. Further, the Qumran texts have demonstrated that the Hebrew O.T. text was not yet fixed at the time of Jesus, and that, at times where the LXX differs from the Massoretic (Hebrew) text, a variant Hebrew text supporting the LXX was known in Palestine;[12] and the Aramaic Targum tradition must be reckoned with as well. Only when we are able to exclude the possibility that Jesus was citing a Hebrew or Aramaic tradition differing from the M.T. but agreeing with the LXX can we safely classify a text as secondary.

(ii) We have argued above that a saying which the tradition indicates has been made the object of further reflection, or applied to problems within the early church, may be considered authentic (criterion of pregnant speech). This suggests, of course, that where the gospel tradition shows such further reflection and application, it may be considered secondary; hence we may speak of a "criterion of derivative speech". Still we must remember that Jesus could have summarized his teaching on a given point in a pregnant mashal which has been carefully transmitted, and then himself developed its implications for his disciples; in such a case, the gospels may reflect the essence (though probably not the very formulations) of his exposition.[13]

(iii) The study of the stylistic idiosyncracies of the various evangelists sometimes enables us to say with some certainty that a saying has been formulated by the editors of the gospels. More problematic is the question whether we are dealing with an ad hoc formulation, or one based on some earlier tradition. The classic illustration is of course to be found in the gospel of John, in which the discourses of Jesus often show the stylistic characteristics of the Johannine tradition to such an extent that we must attribute their present form to the Johannine school, but the question to what extent the discourses are built on earlier, possibly authentic, tradition is very difficult to assess.

(iv) A unit of the gospel tradition may be considered secondary if it can be shown to be incompatible with the views of Jesus (as defined on the basis of material meeting criteria of authenticity), but consonant with the views of some element within the early church which had a part in the formation of the gospel tradition ("criterion of incompatibility"). To this criterion, too, a word of caution must be added: historical figures were not necessarily freer of self-contradiction than we are today. Different contexts often demand that different aspects of an issue be emphasized; the "contradiction" which results may be formal rather than essential. Moreover, a speaker may answer "Yes" and "No" to the same question because the question is not clearly focussed in his mind at the time of speaking; here we may speak of a real contradiction, but one of which the perpetrator is unaware. We are all guilty of contradictions of both sorts; and we must not demand of historical figures a consistency which we ourselves cannot maintain, especially where (as in the case of Jesus) neither what they had to say nor the sources presenting it were systematically conceived.

There will, of course, be cases where a unit of tradition cannot be shown to be either authentic or secondary by the criteria mentioned. The investigator should make the uncertainty of such cases clear. He is still free to exercise his educated judgment, but the material in question should serve his reconstruction of history only as a support for results reached on other, more solid grounds.

One further complication must be noted. We have to this point assumed that the historian of the life of Jesus is called upon to exercise judgment only over the earliest ascertainable form of the tradition. If, then, Matthew's account of an incident is dependent on that of Mark, the historian concerned with Jesus need only consider Mark. This procedure often leads to the view that Matthew has "rejudaized" the tradition, that he has toned down the radicalness of Jesus' break with Judaism, even made him to appear "legalistic". But this is not the only possible explanation. An illustration will make the point clear.

Two men listen to a symphony. Afterwards, A, who has a layman's interest in music, describes the work for other musical laymen. B, who is a professional musician, hears A's report and, impressed by its vigour, passes it on, but feels called upon to alter parts of it in the process. For him, it is not quite accurate to say that the whole orchestra began quietly; only the woodwinds were playing. According to A's report, a beautiful trumpet melody came "about half-way through"; B agrees that it was beautiful, but notes that it came at the beginning of the third movement; and so on. Obviously, B's report, though temporally further removed from the event, is the more accurate description. He is an expert on the subject.

A certain parallel exists with the relationship between Matthew and Mark. Mark may come first, but Matthew is the expert in the Jewish scriptures, Jewish custom and law. He may not be falsifying Mark's account when he introduces technical distinctions and qualifications. Perhaps his standards, and the standards of his readers, require a precision which Mark had neither the interest nor the capacity to match. Should we not rather follow the expert's account?

But, of course, the parallel is not exact. Neither the first evangelist (whom, for convenience, we call Matthew) nor the second (whom we may call Mark) were present at the events they describe. Nor does it seem likely, in most cases at least, that when Matthew "corrects" Mark, he does it on the basis of any independent account of what happened.[14] Certainly the instincts he brings to his task are those of an expert in Jesus' milieu, and we must not lightly dismiss his modifications; he may well be right. But the correct procedure would still seem to be to begin with the earlier account, perhaps raising at a later stage in the investigation the possibility that the learned revisions of Matthew may better correspond with historical reality.

These are the principles underlying the following attempt to depict Jesus' view of scribal authority. If the picture that results is found convincing, it may serve to confirm their rightness. If it is not, the fault need not lie with the principles.

PART ONE
THE MAKERS OF HALAKHAH
Chapter I
The Pharisees and their Law

Before we undertake a study of the creators of Pharisaic law, certain pre-
liminary questions as to the nature of the Pharisaic movement and its laws
must be considered. The discussion here is meant to provide a framework for
the study of Jesus' view of scribal authority; hence there is no need to
trace diachronically the development of the Pharisaic movement and its laws,
and we may content ourselves with a synchronic survey of the situation at
the time of Jesus. Probably people of his day knew little about Pharisaic
origins;[1] still, they evidently had no problem in identifying Pharisees in
their midst. What marked them out? As for Pharisaic law at the time of Jesus,
we must of course draw on sources which depict a later development of that
law. Nonetheless, the careful use of the sources does allow us to define
some of the presuppositions and characteristics of Pharisaic law at the beginning of our era.

A. THE PHARISEES

In Josephus as well as the N.T., the Pharisees (Φαρισαῖοι) are commonly referred to as an αἵρεσις.[2] The word is generally translated "sect", but
Josephus clearly has in mind the technical meaning, "a philosophical
school".[3] He refers to the Pharisees as one of the Jewish "philosophies"
(Ant. 18.11), compares them to the Stoics (Life 12), and frequently uses
the language and ideas of the philosophical schools in describing them.

That Josephus here accomodates the nature of his subject to his non-Jewish
readers is only a partial explanation. Modern scholars have pointed out very
real similarities between the Pharisees and the philosophical schools.[4] In
this connection, it must be remembered that adherence to one of the philosophical schools of his day was not only a means of acquiring knowledge; it
meant also the adoption of a way of life.[5] Josephus himself says that,
after investigating the various Jewish <u>haireseis</u>, he "began to govern (his)
behaviour (πολιτεύεσθαι) in adherence to the <u>hairesis</u> of the Pharisees"
(Life 12).

It would appear, then, that a Pharisee was one who patterned his conduct after certain norms, a kind of Pharisaic code.[6] According to Josephus, the Pharisees were the most accurate interpreters of the ancestral laws, and their strict life-style reflected their interpretations (cf. Life 191; War 1.110; 2.162). This is confirmed by the N.T. Paul, in discussing his background, writes that, "according to the law", he was a Pharisee (Phil. 3:5). Acts 26:5 refers to the Pharisees as the "strictest" haíresis of the Jewish religion, which again suggests their careful observance of a defined code. The disputes between Jesus and the Pharisees in the synoptic gospels witness as well to a Pharisaic concern that certain regulations be observed. Whatever else may be said of the Pharisees,[7] they were a group recognizable in practice by their adherence to certain norms; the nature of those norms will be examined below.

When we turn to rabbinic sources, the problem of identifying the Pharisees is an acute one. It is clear enough that the Judaism of these sources is, in large measure, the outgrowth of pre-70 Pharisaism. This is indicated not only by points of contact with the beliefs and norms of the Pharisees as they are reflected in the N.T. and Josephus, but also by the fact that men called Pharisees in the latter sources (e.g. Gamaliel, Acts 5:34; Simon b. Gamaliel, Jos. Life 191) are recognized as authoritative teachers in rabbinic literature. Thus, with some justification we may cite the statements and decrees of the pre-70 masters and schools mentioned in rabbinic literature as evidence for Pharisaic law. But do the Pharisees as a group appear in rabbinic literature? If so, under what name?

The obvious answer, that they were the perushim (פרושים), is only partially correct, and, besides, not nearly so informative as we could have wished. Not only the similarity of the name with the Φαρισαῖοι,[8] but also the opposition of the perushim to the צדוקים (Sadducees) on numerous points of law,[9] and their separation from the am ha-arez because of a concern for ritual purity (cf. M. Hag. 2.7) make it clear that the perushim, at least in some contexts, are identical with the Pharisees of Josephus and the N.T. Pharisees and Sadducees are rivals in both the latter sources, and the N.T. clearly attests a Pharisaic concern for ritual purity. However, in other contexts those described as perushim are certainly not the Pharisees,[10] and, in any case, the term plays a surprisingly insignificant role in rabbinic texts.

More fruitful for our purposes are certain references to haverim (חברים)

or "associates", i.e. members of a havurah, "association".[11] A number of
factors point to some close relation between the Pharisees and the haverim.
The haverim were those who had taken upon themselves the obligations of observing special standards of tithing and ritual purity (M. Dem. 2.2f.; T.
Dem. 2.2), concerns which we know from the N.T. characterized the Pharisees
(cf. Mk. 7:2-4; Mt. 23:23-26; Lk. 18:12). Moreover, if we allow for a measure
of continuity between the Pharisees and the later rabbinic traditions, the
fact that the regulations for the haverim are contained in rabbinic writings,
and were the subject of discussion and legislation by the recognized authorities of those texts suggests that the haverim were nearly related to the
Pharisees in some way. What we know of the Essenes from Josephus (War 2.137-
-142) and of the Qumran community (1QS 5.7ff.; 6.13ff.) indicates that membership in these groups was undertaken formally and in stages; if the same
was true of the hairesis of the Pharisees, then formal acceptance as a
haver, which also took place in stages,[12] may well have been what was involved. That this was the case is suggested by the fact that the Pharisees
in the N.T. seem to be a clearly defined group, and that Josephus is apparently able to say how many Pharisees there were in the time of Herod (Ant.
17.42): indications that being a Pharisee was not only a matter of holding
certain views or even observing certain practices, but involved entering
the membership of a "closed" community. Finally, M. Hag. 2.7 distinguishes
between the am ha-arez and the perushim, indicating that the clothes of the
former are regarded by the latter as suffering "midras"-uncleanness; this
is reminiscent of the regulation in M. Dem. 2.3, where, however, the am
ha-arez is distinguished from the haver. Apparently perushim and haverim,
at least in this respect, are one.[13]

All this suggests that the Pharisees in our period may be identified with
the haverim; but here caution must be urged.[14] Josephus provides no indication that the Pharisees were specially interested in tithing and ritual
purity; what he does say indicates a group with broader interests and influence than would be true of pious men united only by these concerns. They
are experts in Jewish law (War 1.110; 2.162), are politically active as
advisers of royalty and institutors of laws (War 1.110ff.; Ant. 13.405ff.),
and even have characteristic tendencies in fixing punishments (Ant. 13.294).
Clearly being a Pharisee, at least at one time, involved more than observing
laws of tithing and purity. Admittedly, tithing and purity are areas of interest for the Pharisees of the N.T.; but their interests remain broad,
their activities still include the political sphere (e.g. Acts 5:34; 23:6).

Moreover, traditions of the masters of the Pharisaic-rabbinic stream before 70 do cover a broader range of subjects: especially those of Gamaliel,[15] but also of his son Simeon[16] and (less reliably) of Hillel[17] and even Shemaiah and Avtalyon.[18] The same is true of the disputes between the houses of Hillel and Shammai[19] and those between the Pharisees and Sadducees.[20] Finally, as Alon notes in an important and suggestive article,[21] there are many indications that Pharisaic leaders were actively involved in politics right up to the end of the Bar Kokhba rebellion. The spheres in which the Pharisees moved were thus much more extensive than would be indicated by the requirements for membership in a havurah.

How, then, are we to relate the Pharisees to the haverim? It would appear that, while the Pharisees were interested in all areas of Jewish life, the negligence of the masses in two particular areas (tithing and ritual purity) led to the forming of the havurot within which Pharisaic views on these subjects could be carefully observed.[22] Presumably people who would not call themselves Pharisees might adopt Pharisaic practice on these points and become haverim; on the other hand, we cannot prove that every Pharisee joined a havurah. The terms "Pharisee" and "haver" are thus not synonymous; but the regulations of the havurot represent Pharisaic views on the subjects of tithing and ritual purity, and are an important element in the study of Pharisaic law.[23]

B. THE EXTRABIBLICAL LAW OF THE PHARISEES

As we have seen, Josephus describes the Pharisees as the most accurate interpreters of the ancestral laws. Usually he speaks of the "ancestral laws" without defining them more closely; at times, however, it is clear that he is thinking specifically of the laws of Moses. For Josephus, these laws are recorded in the books of Torah. He relates how one of his foes took the (written) "laws of Moses in his hands", then told a crowd to "look at the ancestral laws" which Josephus was about to betray (Life 134f.). Elsewhere he tells of two teachers who protested against a golden eagle which Herod had raised over the temple gate "contrary to the ancestral law" (Ant. 17.150f.); they explained that it was less important to observe Herod's decrees than "the laws which Moses, at the prompting and teaching of God, recorded (γραψάμενος) and left behind" (17.159). In fact, the prohibition of images (cf. Ex. 20:4) is often at stake when the "ancestral law(s)" is (are) violated (War 1.649f.; 2.192-195; Ant. 18.263f.; cf. Life 65; Ant. 15.276f.); other biblical precepts spoken of in similar phrases include the commands of circumcision (War 1.34), sabbath observance (Ant. 14.63), and capital punishment for adultery (Ant. 7.131). Repeatedly Josephus speaks of Moses as recording the laws (Ant. 3.213, 286, 322; 4.194, 196f., 302), and he can even speak of the Septuagint as a translation of "the laws of the Jews" (Ant. 12.20). Josephus evidently knows nothing of the rabbinic doctrine by which there are two Torahs, one written and one oral, both given by God to Moses. For him, the Mosaic law is written.[24]

He does, however, point out that it is characteristic of the Pharisees to regard certain extrabiblical regulations "handed down from the fathers (ἐκ πατέρων διαδοχῆς)" as binding. The origin of these regulations is not defined more closely.[25] From what has been said, it will be clear that Josephus himself does not regard them as Mosaic nor show an awareness that such a claim was made. This is confirmed by the controversy with the Sadducees over the validity of these regulations. If the Pharisees had contended that these traditions were given by God to Moses, the Sadducees, who did not accept them as binding, would have been compelled to contest the point. But nothing is said of such a dispute. Instead we find them disputing, not the origin of the tradition, but only its binding character (Ant. 13.297).

We meet the same extrabiblical tradition of the Pharisees in the N.T., clearly in "the tradition of the elders (ἡ παράδοσις τῶν πρεσβυτέρων)" of the handwashing dispute (Mk. 7:3, 5), probably in Paul's expression "the traditions of my forefathers (τῶν πατρικῶν μου παραδόσεις)" (Gal. 1:14). The reference, here (cf. also Acts 22:3:, 28:17) as in Josephus, to the tradition as coming from the "fathers" gives us a glimpse of the religious weight which the tradition had for the pious Jew. From the time of the Maccabees, when syncretism was a danger and everything foreign was suspect, what came from the "fathers" was precious and carefully preserved (cf. 1 Macc. 2:19f., 50f.; 2 Macc. 4:15; 4 Macc. 18:5, etc.).[26] The Pharisees, as the champions of such a tradition, could certainly count on popular support. Yet, again, we must note that the claim is not raised that the tradition came from Sinai.[27] When Jesus condemns this "tradition of men" (Mk. 7:8), his choice of words, echoing Isa. 29:13, is clearly polemical: the human tradition is set against the divine command. Still, he does not seem to be arguing that a tradition which the Pharisees regard as divinely revealed is in fact only human; rather, he takes up the phrase "tradition of the elders" used in the accusation against his disciples (v. 5), points out the obvious (if, in this context, painful) fact that the "elders" are "men",

and contests ascribing to this human tradition a binding character and allowing it to supersede the "word of God" (v. 13).

In this gospel pericope, the regulations of the Pharisees are thus portrayed as coming from men; indeed, the Pharisees and scribes are here credited not only with observing (v. 8) and transmitting (v. 13) a tradition
"from the fathers", but also with formulating it and applying it casuistically: "But you say, 'If a man...'" (v. 11); "you no longer permit him..."
(v. 12). Not inappropriately, Jesus speaks of it as "your tradition" (vv. 9,
13).

That Pharisees were involved in the shaping and applying as well as the
transmitting of the tradition is clear from other passages in the gospels as
well. In Mt. 23:2-4, the "scribes and Pharisees" are said to issue statements
of what is to be done, to "bind burdens heavy and hard to bear and place
them on men's shoulders". In Mt. 23:16-18, they appear as the creators of a
casuistic law of oaths. Disputes involving the Pharisees frequently concern
the lawfulness of questions left vague or untouched by scripture: plucking
corn (Mk. 2:23f. par.) or healing (Mk. 3:1-6 par.) on the sabbath; legitimate grounds for divorce (Mk. 10:2 par.); paying tribute to Caesar (Mk.
12:14 par.). In these cases, we see that the Pharisees were not content to
leave to the judgment of the individual that which scripture states ambigu-
ously, or in terms only of general principles, or which, in fact, scriptural
legislation does not cover. These areas became subjects of Pharisaic legal
disputes and legislation. The result was that there grew up not only Pharisaic exegesis of scripture, but a tradition going beyond the text of scripture, defining clearly and concretely what was lawful and what was forbidden.

The N.T., like Josephus, provides no clear evidence for the view that this
tradition had its origin in the divine revelation at Sinai. Certainly there
are indications that the Pharisees claimed to be faithful to Moses. According to Mt. 23:2, the "scribes and Pharisees sit in Moses' seat". This probably takes up the claim found in rabbinic texts (cf. Sifre to Deut. 17:9-11)
that the sages derive authority to decide legal matters from Torah. Still,
the passage in Mt. does not say that the extrabiblical traditions of the
Pharisees have been handed down from Moses; on the contrary, the "heavy
burdens" which their laws constitute are attributed to the scribes and
Pharisees themselves: "they say", "they bind", "they lay on men's shoulders".

In John's gospel, we meet the claim that the Pharisees are "Moses' disciples" (9:28); they are said to "put (their) hope in him" (5:45). But

17

again, the claim is not explicitly made that the extrabiblical laws of their tradition come from Moses. Indeed, in John 5 it is the Pharisees' devotion to the Mosaic writings which is spoken of: Jesus insists that, while they "search the scriptures", they do not in fact believe what Moses wrote, since he "wrote of me" (vv. 39, 46f.). The reference to the Pharisees as Moses' disciples in John 9 may be the evangelist's way of saying that the Pharisees are the adherents of the old dispensation, whereas the man born blind, who is Jesus' disciple (9:28), has experienced the "grace and truth" of the new (cf. 1:17).

More suggestive is Acts 6:13f. Stephen is accused of saying that Jesus will "alter the ἔθη ("customs", or "laws") which Moses passed on to us". The difficulty here lies in the understanding of ἔθη. The term may include extrabiblical tradition (as it probably does in Acts 26:3, 28:17); but it need not (cf. Acts 15:1), and the fact that ἔθη here is parallel with "the law" in v. 13 suggests that only the written Torah may be meant. Similarly, in Acts 21:21, apostasy "from Moses" is illustrated by a failure to circumcise and to "walk according to the customs (τοῖς ἔθεσιν περιπατεῖν)". Circumcision is biblical, ἔθεσιν is vague. Hence "apostasy from Moses" need not mean more than a failure to observe the (written) Torah. The verse is not yet a clear affirmation of the belief that extrabiblical traditions are Mosaic in origin.

From Josephus and the N.T., then, we may conclude that the Pharisees regarded as valid an extrabiblical tradition transmitted and, to some extent, created by their leading authorities. There are at best adumbrations of the view that the tradition was given to Moses on Sinai.

Brief mention may be made in this context of several cryptic references in the Qumran texts. The sect of the scrolls has, among its opponents, those who "searched out smooth things" (דרשו בחלקות , CD 1.18; cf. 1QH 2.15, 32, etc.) and "looked out for gaps" (ויצפו לפרצות , CD 1.18f.); they are called "builders of the wall" (בוני החיץ , CD 4.19; 8.12, 18) and "interpreters of error" (מליצי תעות , 1QH 2.14; cf. 2.31; 4.7, 9f.). These opponents are probably to be identified with the Pharisees.[28] Here, too, behind the polemic may be discerned the fact that the Pharisees not only are interpreters of scripture, but also creators of extrabiblical law: "builders of the wall" may well take up polemically the Pharisaic attempt to "make a fence for the Torah" (M. Avot 1.1);[29] and the expression דרשו בחלקות (cf. Isa. 30:10) takes up a favourite verb of the Pharisaic

tradition for the deriving of laws via exegesis from the scriptures (דרש),
and may even offer a pun on their laws (הלכות). As Jesus charges the
Pharisees with making the word of God null and void in order to observe
their own traditions, so the charge is raised in 1QH that they exchange
God's Torah for חלקות (4.10).

When we turn to rabbinic literature, there is clear evidence that a distinction was maintained between regulations which were based more or less directly on scripture and those which were not. In the Mishnah, we find a distinction drawn between the words of the (written) Torah and the words of the
scribes (M. Sanh. 11.3; M. Par. 11.5f.; M. Yad. 3.2), and even indications
of the novel character of some of the latter rulings (e.g. M. Kel. 13.7;
M.T.Y. 4.6). The most graphic statement of the essentially extrabiblical
character of many rules is found in M. Hag. 1.8: "(The rules about) release
from vows hover in the air and have nothing (i.e. in scripture) to support
them; the rules about the sabbath, festive offerings, and sacrilege are as
mountains hanging by a hair, since (the teaching of) scripture is scanty
and the rules many."

The classic division of law into that which has a scriptural base and that
which is traditional is found in the doctrine of the two Torahs, one written
and one oral, both (according to the developed doctrine) given to Moses on
Sinai.[30] A certain heathen is said to have asked both Shammai and Hillel
how many Torahs they had, and received the answer, "Two, one written and
one oral" (B. Shab. 31a). The historical value of the narrative is open to
question.[31] It appears first in a late source, anonymously, and falls all
too neatly into the pattern of stories told to illustrate Hillel's gentle-
ness and Shammai's impatience: when the heathen expresses his disbelief in
the oral Torah, Shammai repulses him, Hillel patiently instructs him further.
Moreover, the same question (improbable in itself) is said to have been put
to other early authorities as well;[32] probably the tradition used this
means to add weight to a favourite distinction of the rabbis. It is thus not
certain that it goes back to Shammai and Hillel.

But, though the doctrine of the two Torahs may not yet have been developed
in our period, it nonetheless seems true that the Pharisees kept their
extrabiblical traditions separate from the books of Moses by insisting on
the oral character of the former[33] and refusing to commit such traditions
to authoritative writings.[34] The material at our disposal which speaks of
the Pharisaic traditions is not little, yet no mention is made of non-bibli-

cal, authoritative writings. That such texts did not exist seems to be implied when Josephus says that the Sadducees "maintain that it is necessary
to recognize those regulations which are written, but not necessary to keep
those handed down from the fathers" (Ant. 13.297). Admittedly, the context
indicates that, by "regulations which are written", Josephus means "written
in the books of Moses"; but the abbreviation is not likely to have been made
if the laws "handed down from the fathers" had been contained in authoritative writings.[35] Moreover, the procedure at Yavneh, where, in the immediate
post-70 period, the traditions from earlier generations were assembled, is
clear: writings were not consulted, as they presumably would have been had
they existed; instead, those with knowledge of the tradition gave oral testimony to what they had heard or witnessed.[36] The rabbinic tradition indicates that this was the procedure when a point of law was in question in
the pre-70 period as well (cf. M. Or. 2.5; M. Sanh. 11.2; M. Eduy. 1.3; 5.
7); even if the historicity of particular events is questionable, it is
likely that the procedure is correctly portrayed. Finally, it is at least
doubtful that the doctrine of the oral Torah could have arisen in the immediate post-70 period if extrabiblical laws had been contained in authoritative writings only a short time before.

Hence, the extrabiblical laws of the Pharisees were kept as a category apart
from scripture; they were nonetheless held to be binding.

C. THE NATURE OF PHARISAIC LAW

In the pages which follow, the word halakhah is used for the casuistic law
of the Pharisees, the plural halakhot for particular regulations.[37]

As Pharisaic law, halakhah describes regulations which were adopted by the
Pharisees but which, in our period at least, were not necessarily the "law
of the land" in any official sense. Yet to describe halakhah as "sectarian"
law may give a false picture both of the intention of the Pharisees and of
the historical reality. The Pharisaic sages intended that their traditions
be observed, not by a closed group within Jewry, but by all Jews. This is
immediately apparent from the fact that their measures dealt with subjects
other than those which were part of the regulations imposed on their closed
groups (havurot); further, we know that they actively propagated their
views and criticized non-Pharisees (such as Jesus and his disciples) for
not following them. Thus only a few regulations prompted by the non-observ-
ance of the masses and specifically directed towards the members of the

havurot can properly be characterized as "party law" in intention. Moreover,
even in terms of the historical reality, Pharisaic halakhah was not strictly
"sectarian": partly because the custom of the masses (_minhag_) was recognized
as a source of halakhah, and partly because, in varying degrees, the Pharisees were able to influence both the practice of non-Pharisees and the
workings of such institutions as the Sanhedrin.[38)]

Further, halakhah is casuistic law.[39)] The categorical imperatives and prohibitions of apodictic law, addressed directly to the hearer and intended
to guide his future behaviour, do not belong to the sphere of halakhah.
Halakhah posits, objectively and in detail, a concrete case and states the
legal consequences.

The basis of halakhah is, of course, the belief that God revealed his will
to Moses on Sinai, that the books of Moses record the laws he revealed, and
that Israel's responsibility is to obey what Israel's God has commanded.
Moreover, a prerequisite for the development of the Pharisaic code was the
understanding of O.T. law as statute, i.e. as made up of prescriptions whose
very wording was binding for legal procedure.[40)] This, of course, is not the
only possible understanding,[41)] as recent discussions of O.T. law have shown.
It has long been recognized that O.T. apodictic law was not intended for
the courts.[42)] Moreover, there are many indications that the intentions of
Deuteronomy were didactic rather than legally prescriptive.[43)] Recently,
the argument has been forcefully made that the legal documents of Torah in
general, though reflecting legal practice, were not intended as law binding
on the courts: features of language, the ideal character of some provisions,
and parallels from other law codes of the ancient Near East point to a religious and literary rather than primarily legal tradition.[44)]

But whatever may be said of the correctness of these latter views, the
Pharisees understood O.T. law as statute.[45)] The books of Moses were seen
as the "constitution", the "supreme legislation" of Jewish law.[46)] The formulas used in their commands were binding; the purpose of halakhah was to
determine exactly what scripture commanded and how the commandment was to
be fulfilled.[47)] We may here note briefly three indications of this understanding of biblical law.

(i) When halakhah was established by the exegesis of scripture, the wording
of the biblical text was often crucial to the law derived. Under R. Akiva,
this was carried to extremes: the interpretation of a single letter, by
rules of exegesis which led to results far from the simple meaning of the

text, was used to determine halakhah (cf. B. Sanh. 51b). But the wording of
scripture was important for legal interpretation long before R. Akiva. To
note but one example, the schools of Shammai and Hillel disagreed as to what
constituted legitimate grounds for divorce because of different understandings of the phrase עֶרְוַת דָּבָר in Deut. 24:1 (M. Git. 9.10).

(ii) Where legal practice is governed by statutory law, cases inevitably
arise in which the strict application of the law comes in conflict with the
demands of equity. It is virtually impossible to formulate a statute which
will satisfactorily cover every possible development. Unusual cases arise
which the original legislation could not foresee; moreover, conditions which
applied at the time of legislation are bound to change, with the result that
what once was "just" may not always be so.

This familiar problem in the application of statutory law confronted the
Pharisees as well.[48] What made the problem specially acute for them was the
view that the "statute" was divinely ordained and hence, by definition, perfect and immutable.[49] It could not simply be set aside. Nor was Pharisaic
thinking inclined to rule according to the "spirit" rather than the "letter"
of the law: such a tendency would inevitably have led to the dissolution of
their legal system, to which the letter of scripture was basic.[50] One alternative often adopted - and a sure token of a statutory understanding of
the law - was legal fiction, by which the letter of the law could be (fic-
tionally) observed while its undesirable consequences were circumvented.[51]
Examples could be multiplied, but here a quotation from a modern authority
on Jewish law will suffice: "Jewish law abounds in legal fictions and devices to circumvent divine law and alleviate its hardships; and there seems
to be no limitation, either in theory or in practice, either express or implied, to scholarly ingenuity in inventing and sanctioning such ever-new
fictions or devices, if and when circumstances are such that the compliance
with divine law is impracticable."[52]

(iii) The point which has just been made illustrates one tendency of
halakhah: to make the law practicable and humane. There was, however, another tendency quite in the opposite direction: to "make a fence around the
Torah" (M. Avot. 1.1; cf. M. Ber. 1.1), i.e. to make regulations stricter
than the laws of Torah, thus guaranteeing that the latter are not infringed.
Note that the intention was not to promote meritorious conduct beyond the
requirements of Torah, but to avoid the consequences of violating the letter
of the written law.[53] Here, too, we have an indication that the wording of

22

scripture was held to be binding law.

Now it is clear that, though the prescriptions of the O.T. scriptures might serve as the foundation on which a casuistic code of law could be built, they could not themselves constitute such a code. Many problems arose for which the scriptures contained no clear precept; other in which, because of a change in conditions, the application of the scriptural precept would have led to results impractical or even inhumane. In some areas, the scriptural precepts were not sufficiently specific; where they were specific, they were not in any case exhaustive. Hence the Pharisees, in treating their traditions as equal in authority to the laws of scripture, were by no means expressing disrespect for the latter; they were only drawing the consequences of their view of scriptural law as statute. Statutes must be applied casuistically; and if comprehensive casuistic law was required, it is clear that the Pharisaic solution was the only workable one: scripture might serve as the basis of the legal code; the intensive study (midrash) of its formulas might add to the corpus of law; but regulations derived from other sources, such as legislation[54] and custom,[55] must also be given normative status.

Thus halakhot derived from such sources were held to be as authoritative and binding as regulations derived more directly from the revealed scriptures.[56] Nothing is more characteristic of Pharisaic-rabbinic law than the combination of an awareness that regulations originate in the debates of the sages and the claim that they are on a level with the law of God.[57] In time this would be explained by the further claim that every detail of the halakhah was revealed by God to Moses (Sifra to Lev. 26:46; B. Meg. 19b), or that every detail was derivable from the text of Torah. This latter view led to the application of well-defined rules of exegesis to the text of scripture in order to find justification for regulations whose real source was another.[58] These developments, however, appear to be later than our period, and are not, in any case, crucial to the Pharisaic understanding of their laws. The crucial idea is rather that God, after revealing himself in the statutes of Torah, has authorized the sages to apply and supplement them (Sifre to Deut. 17:9-11). Josephus, while not claiming that the extra-biblical law of the Pharisees was divinely revealed, does say that it was divinely approved (Ant. 17.41). The same point finds poetic expression in the later legend that, when the sages refused to be influenced in their debate by the echo of the divine voice (bat kol), God rejoiced in heaven and said, "My sons have defeated me!" (B.B.M. 59b)

Thus, for the Pharisees, the will of God was expressed in their casuistic law.[59] The duty of the pious man was to study, and submit to, a divinely approved code of behaviour; in so doing, he submitted to the yoke of God's kingship.[60] On the other hand, the one who violated the code was guilty of sin in the eyes of God, who revealed his will in scripture and authorized the sages to interpret and supplement its ordinances.[61]

In conclusion, however, certain qualifications must be added to this description if distortions are not to arise.

(i) Torah contains commands, and the halakhah developed them casuistically. But Torah is more than commands; moral exhortation and guidance, and the narratives of God's choosing, redeeming, and caring for his people are among the other aspects which must be borne in mind if our view of Torah, or even our understanding of the Pharisaic view of Torah, is not to be distorted.[62]

(ii) It must not be assumed that, in discussing Pharisaic law, we are discussing Pharisaic soteriology. It is questionable if we may speak of a clearly defined soteriology; yet rabbinic literature does attest to a full awareness that divine election and redemption preceded the giving of the commands, and that man's salvation is dependent on divine mercy.[63] Still, once God had taken the initiative to establish a covenant with Israel, Israel's response was to be shown in obedience to its terms. Our concern here is with the Pharisaic understanding of those terms; but it needs to be emphasized that there were other aspects to their view of God's relations with his people.

(iii) The sages recognized that certain activities, while not punishable by the "laws of men" (in this context, the rules of halakhah) were still punishable by the "laws of heaven" (cf. M.B.K. 6.4).[64] In such a case, the letter of the law did not exhaust the divine will. Further, they were aware that a mechanical obedience to the commands did not correspond to the will of God. Exhortations to fulfil the commands out of love, and with the devotion of the heart, occur frequently in rabbinic literature (e.g. Sifre on Deut. 6:5 and 11:13; M. Ber. 2.1; M. Sot. 5.5; M. Avot 2.13).[65] The Pharisees, like any religious group, had their hypocrites; but, at their best, their adherence to the minutiae of halakhah was both accompanied and motivated by a love for the commands of God.

(iv) The Pharisaic-rabbinic tradition does justify certain breaches of the law motivated by zeal for God in times of dire emergency.[66] Normally legal fiction of one kind or another was introduced to preserve at least the sem-

blance of faithfulness to scripture. But this was not always the case. At
times Ps. 119:126 was quoted to support the breach of scriptural law: "'It
is time to work for YHWH: they have made void thy law.' R. Nathan says,
'They have made void thy law because it is a time to work for YHWH'." (M.
Ber. 9.5)

Such occasions were, of course, rare. The norm is for God to be served by
the cheerful study and observance of his commands.[67]

Chapter II
"The Scribes of the Pharisees"

Those who shaped the extrabiblical laws of the Pharisees are commonly called "scribes" (Hebrew, סופרים ; Greek, γραμματεῖς). Who were the "scribes"?

A. TERMINOLOGY

סופר in the O.T. is the usual word for a "secretary", whether of a private (e.g. Jer. 36:26, 32) or an official (e.g. 2 Sam. 8:17; 1 Kg. 4:3; Est. 3:12) figure. The term is also used for a representative of a professional class of "scribes", to whom the writing of documents was entrusted (cf. Jer. 36:23, 26, 32; Ezek. 9:2, 3). But with the appearance of Ezra, a priest (Ezra 7:11) who was also a "diligent scribe in the Torah of Moses" (7:6), a model was created for a scribe of a different sort. Ezra studied the Torah with the intention of putting it into practice, and teaching Israel its statutes (7:10); and he was given legislative and judicial authority to act in accordance with the laws of God (7:25f.).

In Sirach (38:24-39:11), as in Ezra, the "scribe" is not a mere secretary or copyist. Freedom from business affairs permits him to study both the scriptures and the "wisdom of the ancients" (39:1). He is an influential member of the community, participating in its councils and courts. In short, he is not so much a "scribe" as a "sage",[1] both knowledgeable and influential.

The scribes in the N.T. represent a further development along these lines. They are a recognizable group of practitioners[2] who have made of their knowledge of scripture a profession as "biblical teachers, lawyers, administrators, or scribes".[3] Indicative of their professional status are the words Luke sometimes substitutes for "scribes": νομικός "lawyer", "jurist" (Lk. 7:30; 10:25; 11:45f., 52; 14:3; the reading with this word in Mt. 22:35 is not certain); or νομοδιδάσκαλος, "teacher of the law" (Lk. 5:17; Acts 5:34). A significant number (though not all)[4] are Pharisees (cf. Mk. 2:16 par. Lk. 5:30; Acts 23:9), and are thus experts in the "tradition of the elders" as well. We find them engaged in disputes with Jesus on matters of authority (Mk. 2:6f. par.; 11:27f. par.; Mt. 12:38) and practice (Mk. 2:16 par.; 7:5 par.). They exercise great influence as teachers and creators of the casuistic rulings by which O.T. commands are expanded and applied and

new norms are established (Mk. 7:6-13 par.; Mt. 23:2-4; Lk. 11:46). Some of
them are also members of the Sanhedrin, playing a role in the legal proceedings against Jesus (Mk. 14:1 par., 43, 53 par.; cf. Acts 4:5; 6:12). It
is clear that they command the people's respect.[5]

The gaps in this picture of the "scribe", from Ezra to Sirach, and from
Sirach to the N.T., are great. Unfortunately, there is little material from
which we might fill them in. Neither Josephus nor Philo use the term
γραμματεύς in this developed sense of "sage".[6] There is a mention, in the
letter of Antiochus III cited in Ant. 12.138-144, of the "scribes of the
temple" (12.142; cf. 11.128); such a group quite possibly had a role in deciding questions of sacred law which came up in the temple as well as in
keeping the temple scrolls; but they are scarcely the "sages" of the Pharisaic tradition. The identity of the "scribes" in 1 Macc. 7:12 is uncertain.

A number of references in rabbinic literature to the scribes of the early
period indicate a professional class intensively studying the text of the
scriptures, and concerned with its transmission.[7] The word soferim did,
however, come to be used as an equivalent of חכמים , the "sages", or
authoritative teachers, though usually reserved for teachers of the early
period.[8] When the word took on this meaning is, however, a matter of debate. According to a common view,[9] the soferim were the successors of Ezra,
the "Men of the Great Synagogue", until the time of Simeon the Righteous.
During this "period of the soferim", halakhic rulings were made in midrash
form; i.e. they were deduced by the scribes from a passage of scripture to
which they were attached in transmission. The soferim were thus already in
this period the authoritative creators of halakhah. This view, however, has
come under attack.[10] Urbach argues that, though the soferim, as copyists
and expounders of scripture, were indeed concerned with midrash, their
methods were not at first adopted as a basis for halakhah. In the early
period, halakhic rulings were based on the decrees of the recognized authorities, i.e. the high priests, elders and sages, the courts and Sanhedrin.[11]
Scribes were interpreters, sages the makers of the law.[12]

But this clearcut distinction between "scribe" and "sage" is difficult to
maintain. Already in Sir. 38:24-39:11, the "scribe" is essentially a "sage",
dedicating himself to the pursuit of wisdom, influential in the community.
And the N.T. is a clear witness to the teaching and legal authority of the
scribes. We may safely say that, at the time of Jesus, no such distinction
in terminology was maintained. Hence we will speak of (Pharisaic) "scribes"

and "sages" interchangeably in referring to the shapers of the Pharisaic halakhic tradition in our period.

B. THE BASIS OF SCRIBAL AUTHORITY

According to the O.T., priests are the experts in sacred law.[13] It is their responsibility to distinguish between sacred and profane, between clean and unclean (Lev. 10:10; Ezek. 44:23). In addition, they play an important role in the administration of justice. Admittedly, judges in the local courts are drawn from the leading citizens of the towns (cf. Deut. 21:19f.; 22:15, etc.); but particularly difficult cases must, according to Deut. 17:8f., be brought to the city of God's choosing to be tried by "the priests, the Levites (or "the Levitical priests"), and the judge who is then in office".

The part of the laity is thus largely limited to deciding less complicated cases at a local level, though Deut. 17:9 does indicate that a (lay) judge serves together with priests in a court in Jerusalem. It is only natural, then, that Ezra, a scribe with administrative and judicial responsibilities, was a priest, and that the earliest authorities recognized by the Pharisaic tradition were priests.[14] By the N.T. period, however, priests, though represented among the sages, do not seem to have played a dominant role, and it is apparent that the authority of the scribes was not dependent on any priestly status.

Nor was it dependent on prophetic inspiration. It is admittedly an oversimplification to speak of the intertestamental period within Judaism as an interval between the prophetic periods of the biblical past and the eschatological future.[15] Certain prophetic functions were still carried on. Josephus, for example, knows a number of cases where the future is foretold;[16] thus, at least this capacity, traditionally associated with prophecy, was not unknown at the time of Jesus. Even in rabbinic literature, where the weight of an authoritative tradition might be expected to have suppressed all signs of more immediate contact with the Deity, there are references to men maintaining a peculiar intimacy with God, and receiving miraculous answers to their prayers. Though at times such men stood somewhat apart from the sages of the halakhah, the latter dared not denounce them.[17] And, of course, since scripture itself speaks of an outpouring of God's Spirit in the future (Joel 3:1 (2:28)), those learned in the scriptures could not deny the possibility that, at any given time, a true prophet might arise.

Nonetheless, it is characteristic of the Pharisaic view of scribal authority that their sages made no claim to be prophetically inspired. The divine law was primarily disclosed to Moses on Mt. Sinai.[18] In time it would even be claimed that the prophets of scripture could not make any legislative innovations by means of prophecy (cf. Sifra to Lev. 27:34), and that their writings could not be used as a source for halakhah. Though these views were not the rule at the time of Jesus,[19] it is clear enough that the Pharisaic vision, which included both the sufficiency of the Sinaitic revelation and the mandate of the sages, by exegesis and legislation, to apply the Mosaic laws, left little room for prophetic innovation.[20] Even the "echo of the (divine) voice" (bat kol), which rabbinic doctrine knows as prophecy's replacement in proclaiming the divine will (B. Sot. 48b), came to be excluded from halakhic disputes (B.B.M. 59b), and was never a primary factor in the formulation of laws.

The authority of the sages was thus based neither on priestly status nor on prophetic inspiration. Arising at a time when the priesthood still claimed its traditional prerogatives, an authority of a different kind could only have developed gradually, and was certainly not unopposed.[21] But circumstances combined to make the growth of such an authority inevitable. Israel's constitution, the Mosaic Torah, was available to all who could read it. Anyone could take it upon himself to study and become proficient in the laws it contained; indeed, for many it became a religious duty of the first order to study the words of Torah. The priests enjoyed no monopoly on knowledge of the divine laws.

It was of course so, throughout the O.T. period, that new laws had to be made as times and circumstances changed. As long as the laws had no fixed, unalterable form, and as long as the priests were the recognized source for torot, this presented no great problem; it is well known that the O.T. laws as they have come to us reflect, in their various strata, the development of Israel's law. But the need for new laws and new applications of old laws did not cease with the canonization of the Pentateuch; on the contrary, as Palestine entered more and more into the world of the Greeks and Romans, and many Jews showed themselved willing to compromise the distinctive nature of their traditions and to become more or less assimilated to the ways of the heathen, the need to sharply define and punctiliously observe those traditions was increasingly felt by the pious. Unfortunately, the priestly aristocracy in Jerusalem was often among those most prepared to accomodate themselves to foreign influences, and showed an unholy zeal in gaining the

favour of foreign political rulers.[22] Thus they forfeited, in the eyes of
the faithful, the respect which otherwise was attached to their office. The
situation was ripe for a new kind of authority. It was realized in the
authority of the sages, an authority based on their knowledge of the sacred
scriptures and the "traditions of the fathers", and confirmed in popular
opinion by their disciplined lives.[23]

The transition is perhaps most clearly marked in a famous story about
Shemaiah and Avtalyon (B. Yom. 71b). A crowd followed the high priest until
they noticed the two sages, but then turned and followed them. The high
priest resentfully commented on their dubious ancestry: "May the sons of
heathen come in peace!" The reply of the sages suggests the basis for the
change of authority: "May the sons of heathen who do the works of Aaron
come in peace, but may the son of Aaron who does not do the work of Aaron
not come in peace!"

We may assume that justification was sought in scripture at an early stage
for the situation which had arisen. As we have noted, Deut. 17:9 assigns to
"the priests, the Levites, and the judge who is then in office" the task of
deciding disputes. According to rabbinic interpretation (Sifre to Deut.
17:9), "and the judge" indicated that a court was entitled to issue decisions even without a priest or Levite. Cohon finds a Pharisaic answer to
the authority of the priests in Sifre to Deut. 11:22, where Deut. 33:4 is
cited: "'Moses commanded us a law, it is the heritage of the congregation
of Jacob.' It does not say, the heritage of priests, Levites or lay
Israelites, but of the whole congregation of Israel."[24]

The early sages did not necessarily hold any office.[25] They served on local
courts, but were not alone in doing so.[26] At least from the time of
Alexandra, Pharisaic scribes were represented in the Jerusalem assembly
which came to be called the Sanhedrin.[27] Further, certain public officials
were regarded as sages,[28] and their rulings became part of the halakhic
tradition. Serving in such capacities, they were able to make rulings of an
official character. Otherwise scribal authority was in practice that of
teachers and respected public figures. As it was based on knowledge, it had
an unofficial character, and met with all degrees of recognition: from the
haverim-Pharisees, who recognized it; to the ammei ha-arez, who in many
cases respected it; to the Sadducees, who ridiculed it.

From the time of Hillel and Shammai, we hear of Pharisaic schools, where
scholars were trained in the interpretation of scripture and the traditional

laws, and where discussions on disputed points and problems of halakhah were
carried on. Over their disciples, the masters exercised great influence.[29]
From a still earlier period we have the words of Yose b. Yo'ezer: "Let your
house be a meeting-place for the sages; sit at the dust of their feet, and
drink in their words with thirst" (M. Avot 1.4). The need was felt to "ac-
quire a teacher" (M. Avot 1.6, 16; cf. 1.17; Acts 22:3) in order to study
Torah, and that teacher was then held in reverence (cf. M.B.M. 2.11; M. Avot
4.12; M. Ker. 6.9). From the mouth of a teacher, one "received Torah";[30]
but it was important, too, to observe his conduct. He was assumed to have
mastered the halakhah: the testimony of one who had witnessed the conduct
of a recognized halakhic authority was often the means of deciding points
of dispute.[31] The student was thus advised to pay close attention to his
teacher's behaviour, and to pattern his own accordingly. Where the halakhah
had not been fixed and different teachers had different views, it was of
course usual to follow the opinion of one's own teacher.[32]

Both knowledge of the tradition and attendance upon a master were thus virtual requirements for a scholar of the Pharisees. The question remains if
the disciple who met these requirements was recognized as competent in
halakhic matters on the basis of some formal act of authorization. We know
that at a later period authority (רשות) was conveyed by ordination
(סמיכה). Is there evidence that ordination was practised in the time of
Jesus?

C. THE QUESTION OF ORDINATION
1. "Ordination" and "Appointment"?

Before we can answer this question, however, it is important that we define
what is meant by "ordination". Mantel suggests that we must distinguish between the "appointment" (מנוי) of judges and the "ordination" (סמיכה) of
advanced students. In the latter case, the student was ordained manually,
and thus authorized "to teach in public, to decide matters of a legal and
ritual nature, and perhaps also to judge financial cases not involving
fines".[33] Such authorization was sectarian, "under the supervision of the
Pharisees".[34] The Christians had a similar practice.[35] In the former case,
an already ordained sage was appointed by the Sanhedrin to serve as a judge
in a local court or as a member of the Sanhedrin.[36]

This careful distinction does not appear to find support in the texts for
the period of our concern.

(i) The basic text for appointment to the Sanhedrin is M. Sanh. 4.4. Such an appointment must be described as מנוי , not סמיכה , if Mantel's distinction is valid. But the text says that, when a new member is required for the Sanhedrin, "they ordain (סומכין) him from the first (of the three rows of students sitting before them)." Mantel's statement,[37] that the Mishnah here describes two stages, first ordination and then appointment, appears unwarranted.

(ii) J. Sanh. 1.2 does not seem to demonstrate what Mantel derives from it.

> R. Ba said, "At first everyone appointed his own disciples, as when Rabban Yohanan b. Zakkai appointed R. Eliezer and R. Joshua, and R. Joshua appointed R. Akiva, and R. Akiva appointed R. Meir and R. Simeon.... Then they wanted to honour this house and said that any appointment made by the Bet Din without the consent of the nasi is invalid, but any appointment made by the nasi without the consent of the Bet Din is valid."

This text is commonly regarded as dealing with the ordination of scholars,[38] but Mantel suggests that the subject is rather the "appointment" of judges.[39] Such appointments during the temple period were, according to Mantel, made by the Sanhedrin in Jerusalem.[40] Mantel finds in the above quotation both an "innovation" on the part of Rabban Yohanan,[41] and an "implication... that prior to R. Johanan there was a different form of appointment. The change in the system of appointing judges at that time was essential, since at the destruction of the Temple the Sanhedrin lost its governmental power of appointment."[42]

The text does not, however, indicate that R. Yohanan introduced the practice by which a teacher appointed his own pupils, but only cites him as an example of that practice. And that practice is not implicitly contrasted with a still earlier practice (a supposed appointment by the Sanhedrin), but explicitly contrasted with a later one, by which the consent of the nasi was required.[43] And since the immediately preceding statement in the Talmud is, "There (in Babylonia) they call 'appointment' (מנוייה) 'ordination' (סמיכותא)," there is no reason for making two different institutions of them.[44]

(iii) The Sanhedrin, according to Mantel, was made up exclusively of Pharisaic sages,[45] yet it had the power to "officially" appoint judges for local courts throughout the land. Such appointed judges served with non-experts under carefully regulated conditions. But, leaving the discussion on the Sanhedrin till below, we can here simply state that Mantel seems to overestimate Pharisaic power in this period.

The texts do not, then, seem to support Mantel's distinction between "appointment" and "ordination"; nor can we speak of an authorization of ordained judges by a Pharisaic Sanhedrin. Still, in discussing whether or not
"ordination" was practised in the time of Jesus, we will have to be clear
whether the evidence cited refers to authorization to sit on a sanhedrin
or to a more general authorization to teach and issue decisions on matters
of halakhah. [46)]

2. Evidence for Ordination in the Time of Jesus

(a) According to M. Hag. 2.2, the question of whether or not one may "lay
on hands" was disputed by the "pairs" (zugot). But the dispute almost certainly concerned laying hands on a sacrifice on a festival day, and not ordination. [47)]

(b) Newman's monograph on the subject of ordination contains only one indication that it was practised in our period. Leaving open the question
whether or not semikhah had been practised continuously from the time of
Moses, he writes, "The first trace of the resumption, or continuation, as
the case may be, of Semikhah, we find in the time of Rabban Gamaliel Hazaken,
whose title leaves no place for any doubt that Semikhah was conferred upon
him in a ceremonial and official manner."[48)] B. Sanh. 13b is then cited to
the effect that the title "Rabbi" was given in connection with ordination.
However, the only evidence we have for the title "Rabbi" before 70 suggests
that it was at least not yet exclusively used of the ordained.[49)] Besides,
Gamaliel is not titled "Rabbi" but "Rabban", an indication, not that he was
ordained, but that he was regarded as the head (nasi) of the Jewish people.
We may, with Dalman,[50)] suspect that we are here dealing with a title first
given to Gamaliel at a later period; in any case, the title is not evidence
for ordination in this period.

(c) Perhaps more significant is the title "elder" (זקן).[51)] M. Suk. 2.7
speaks of the "elders" of the schools of Hillel and Shammai. Mk. 7:3 mentions the "tradition of the elders", where the "elders" are probably the
authoritative creators and bearers of the tradition. Were these "elders"
ordained? We cannot be certain. Later זקן was used of the ordained,[52)] but
we have no evidence that it had this meaning in our period.[53)]

(d) Lohse states that semikhah as ordination is mentioned only once in the
Mishnah, in M. Sanh. 4.4.[54)] Here ordination is to a seat in a sanhedrin of
sages. The nature of the Sanhedrin will be discussed below. If we may an-
ticipate the results of that examination, it may be thought unlikely that

entrance to the Sanhedrin, which was made up not only of Pharisees but also of Sadducees, and not only of scribes, but also of priests and the lay nobility, was by way of ordination.[55] In any case, the text does not constitute evidence for an ordination by which Pharisaic disciples became competent teachers of the tradition; membership in the Sanhedrin of our period did not imply that.

We may here mention the theory of Ehrhardt.[56] He distinguishes ordination before 70 from that of the years immediately afterwards: the earlier ordination was the solemn ritual of admission to a seat on the Sanhedrin, where the central act was the "seating" and not the laying on of hands; after 70, ordination was performed by a rabbi on his disciples, and was manual. But the passages in which Ehrhardt finds a "seating" without manual ordination (Mt. 23:2; Assum. Mos. 12:2) do not seem to refer to taking a place in the Sanhedrin. The text which does refer to taking a place in the Sanhedrin,[57] besides being of doubtful historical value for our period, does imply the laying on of hands as well as the seating (M. Sanh. 4.4). Furthermore, given that the biblical precedent was Joshua's authorization by Moses, in which the laying on of hands is explicitly mentioned (Num. 27:18; Deut. 34:9), it is difficult to believe that the laying on of hands could have played little or no role in such an act of authorization.

(e) Mantel cites M. Yom. 1.6 as an indication that a scholar had to be ordained in order to teach in public.[58] The passage, speaking of the high priest on the eve of the Day of Atonement, reads: "If he was a sage, he used to expound (the scripture), but, if not, the disciples of the sages used to expound before him." But, aside from the idealized character of the description, it is not certain that "sage" here means one ordained, nor that the principle of exposition stated in this specific case can be made into a general statement about teaching competence. Furthermore, the text does allow for the (unordained) "disciples of the sages" to expound before the high priest if the latter is not a sage, counter to Mantel's hypothesis.[59]

(f) In Mk. 11:28, Jesus is asked by what authority (ἐξουσία) he does "these things", and who gave him the authority. Daube sees behind ἐξουσία the Hebrew רשות in the sense of "rabbinic authority": "Whatever part of his activity it may be that he is required to justify, the reason for the attack is clear: he acts like a Rabbi, like one having reshut, without being properly ordained."[60] If this is the point of the attack, we have here indirect evidence for ordination at this time.

But it seems unlikely.[61] Neither ἐξουσία nor רשות is restricted in meaning to "rabbinic authority".[62] Authority for any act which requires it can be so expressed (Mk. 13:34; Acts 26:12, etc.). This being the case, it is difficult to see how ἐξουσία can mean "rabbinic authority", i.e. authority conveyed by ordination, here. The charge seems to be a sequel to the cleansing of the temple;[63] but even if it refers to another of Jesus' sharply criticized activities (e.g. his conduct on the sabbath, or his disregard of certain regulations regarding ritual purity), it was in all probability not directed against an activity which lacked legitimacy only because he was not ordained. Ordination was never seen as giving the right to violate the laws!

(g) Perhaps the argument most frequently used[64] to show that ordination of scholars was practised in the time of Jesus is based on the adoption of a similar practice by the early church. Jeremias says flatly, "The corresponding custom in primitive Christianity (Acts 6:6, et passim) is a guarantee of the antiquity of this rite."[65]

The argument is valid only if a custom can be found (i) in earliest Christianity (otherwise we have no proof that its Jewish counterpart dates back to the time of Jesus) that (ii) corresponds closely enough to the ordination of scholars to show dependence. These conditions are not met.

The laying on of hands occurs commonly enough in the N.T., but most cases (e.g. in healing, Mk. 5:23 par.; 6:5; 7:32, etc.; blessing, 10:16 par.; and the giving of the Holy Spirit to a new convert without any suggestion that he is at the same time receiving a specific authorization or task, e.g. Acts 8:17-19; 19:6) can be immediately excluded as parallels to the ordination of scholars. A parallel exists only if, in connection with the ceremony, an authority is once and for all conveyed upon a candidate by one already recognized as possessing authority.

Possible passages are Acts 6:6; 13:3; 1 Tim. 4:14; 5:22; 2 Tim. 1:6. Of these, Acts 13:3 can be immediately excluded as a parallel to Jewish ordination.[66] Certainly Paul did not think his authorization came from men (cf. Gal. 1:1), as such an interpretation of Acts 13:3 would seem to imply; in any case, the "prophets and teachers" at Antioch (Acts 13:1) were scarcely in a position to convey it to him;[67] they did not possess an authority he lacked. Besides, both Saul and Barnabas are depicted as active in the church previously (Acts 11:26; 12:25), so that Acts 13:3 can scarcely represent a once and for all authorization.

Lohse accepts Acts 6:1-6 as a Christian parallel to rabbinic semikhah.[68] This depends on a reconstruction of the passage, since an authorization to "serve tables" (vv. 2f.), which is explicitly contrasted with the service of the word of God (vv. 2-4), no matter how similar in ceremony, cannot be regarded as a parallel to rabbinic semikhah.[69] According to Lohse, the ordination was in fact ordination to the office of evangelist.

Lohse supports this contention that the narrative in Acts 6 is to be regarded as a parallel to rabbinic ordination by pointing to similarities with Num. 27:15ff., where Joshua is "ordained" by Moses; this passage was used by the rabbis as the model of their ordination.[70] But the parallel presents difficulties. Why would Luke, while changing the point of the story from an ordination to a preaching ministry to an appointment to "serve tables", deliberately echo the language of the classical text of rabbinic ordination, to which serving tables was no counterpart? We must also, however, note the differences Lohse points out between rabbinic ordination and the ordination of the seven. In Acts 6:6, prayer plays an important part in the ceremony, though it did not in Jewish ordination.[71] The relation of the apostles to the seven is not presented as that of teacher - pupil.[72] Nor is the ordaining done by an individual, but rather by a collegium,[73] if not by the people as a whole.[74] Given these differences, and the fact that the "ordination" in Acts can only be regarded as authorization to teach and preach by an interpretation counter to the text as we have it, it can scarcely be said that we here have proof of an institution reflecting rabbinic ordination.[75]

In the Pastorals, the laying on of hands seems to be connected with teaching (cf. 1 Tim. 4:14 in the context of 4:11-16). At least in 2 Tim. 1:6, it is performed by a recognized authority. And it has been claimed that the phrase ἐπίθεσις τῶν χειρῶν τοῦ πρεσβυτερίου (1 Tim. 4:14) renders the Hebrew סמיכת זקנים [76]

Here, then, we do have a fairly close parallel to rabbinic ordination.[77] Given, however, the widespread use by Jesus and the early church of the laying on of hands for communicating spiritual blessings - and even in the Pastorals it is a χάρισμα which is conveyed (1 Tim. 4:14; 2 Tim. 1:6) - there is no need to assume that a current rabbinic practice has here been adopted. The development can have taken place independently in the church. In any case, the evidence of the Pastorals is too late to constitute proof for the practice among Jewish scholars in the time of Jesus.

(h) That a grave-inscription from Jerusalem, dating probably from the period before 70, contains the word διδάσκαλος is not proof that "Rabbi" was at that time the title of an ordained teacher.[78] Even if "Rabbi" at one time became the title for an ordained teacher, it need not imply ordination in this period. In any case, "Rabbi" as an ordained teacher is a phenomenon of rabbinic Judaism, which has points of contact with Pharisaism of the temple period. The Greek διδάσκαλος is not confined to that tradition. A rabbi may, however inadequately, be described as a "teacher"; a "teacher" (διδάσκαλος) need not be a rabbi. There is no indication that the teacher whose grave-inscription was discovered was in fact a rabbi.[79]

(i) Lohse argues that Assumption of Moses 12:2 can, with some probability, be regarded as proof for pre-Christian ordination.[80]

In Assum. Mos. 11, Joshua, having heard Moses' description of the future, tears his clothes, casts himself on the ground before Moses, and complains of his own inadequacy to guide, foster, and feed the Israelites. He rejects Moses' attempt to comfort him and, in 12:1, casts himself again at the feet of Moses. Then we read: "And Moses took his hand and raised him into the seat before him, and answered and said unto him, 'Joshua, do not despise thyself, but set thy mind at ease, and hearken to my words.'" Moses then assures Joshua that God has foreseen all that will happen, and that God has appointed him (Moses) to be an intercessor.

At best, the statement that Moses took Joshua's hand and "raised him into the seat before him" indicates in this context an encouragement to Joshua to undertake the task given him. Nothing suggests an authorization for that task: no authority, no "spirit of wisdom" is conferred; only comfort. Lohse finds an indication of ordination here because a similar statement in Sifre to Num. 27:19 clearly has that meaning. But in the absence of any indication that ordination is intended in the text of Assum. Mos., we cannot regard it as proof of a pre-Christian practice.

There is thus no clear proof that ordination was practised in the time of Jesus. Evidence for it consists in the use of זקנים , which, however, need not yet be a title for an ordained scholar; in the possibility that ordination to a seat in the Sanhedrin was practised, though the nature of the Sanhedrin in the text speaking of this is problematical (M. Sanh. 4.4); and in the guess that various indications of ordination in a slightly later period may apply already in the time of Jesus.

3. Evidence against Ordination in the Time of Jesus

As evidence against ordination in the time of Jesus, rabbinic tradition suggesting an innovation by Yohanan b. Zakkai may be cited.[81]

The epistle of R. Sherira Gaon[82] notes that the title "Rabban" was first used by Gamaliel the Elder, his son Simeon, and Yohanan b. Zakkai, and that the title "Rabbi" began to be used by the ordained in this period, and dates from the disciples of Rabban Yohanan. But this epistle is far too late to be used as historical evidence for our period.[83]

We have already noted that J. Sanh. 1.2 does not specifically say that Yohanan was the first to ordain his disciples; it only cites him as an example of this practice. Can we conclude that rabbinic tradition did not know of earlier examples?

That assumption may be strengthened by the fact that the title "Rabbi" in rabbinic tradition is generally reserved for a period beginning with the pupils of Yohanan. Moreover, we know that unordained men in the time of Jesus were called "Rabbi" (e.g. Mk. 9:5; John 3:26). Indeed, though Jesus was certainly not ordained by a Pharisaic sage, he often seems to be treated as a teacher on a level with those of the Pharisees: questions concerning the interpretation of scripture, matters of faith and practice are brought to him. He is even asked to adjudicate in the dividing up of an inheritance, quite as a scribe might be consulted (Lk. 12:13). It is apparently only after he displays an indifference to, and, indeed, flagrant violations of, what was held to be valid law; only after he openly challenges current procedures in the temple; in other words, only after he presumes to act in ways no scribe, however influential, would dare to act, that his authority is called in question (Mk. 11:27-33 par.). This suggests that authority in this period was not attached to a formal act of ordination, but was only gradually and quite unofficially acquired with a reputation for learning and (at least as far as the Pharisees were concerned) strict adherence to prescribed practice.

Finally, it may be of significance in this context to note that the masters of the Pharisees in the period before 70 are not on the whole closely tied to specific teachers. It was obviously in the interests of the credibility of the tradition to see those masters as forming an unbroken chain with their teachers before them. Such interests have given rise to the list at the beginning of M. Avot, where the leading sages of each new generation are said to receive Torah from their predecessors. Nonetheless, traditions of the individual masters do not otherwise indicate that they have studied with their predecessors until the case of Hillel.[84] He is said to have studied with Shemaiah and Avtalyon (B. Pes. 66a; B. Yom. 35b). Gamaliel is not said to have studied with Hillel.[85] Whether or not Yohanan b. Zakkai had done so is still disputed.[86] But the situation changes with Yohanan; his disciples are named (M. Avot 2.8), and, as we have seen, he is said to have ordained them.

This, of course, does not mean that the early masters had not studied with sages; that was early regarded as crucial to one's knowledge of Torah. It does, however, suggest that the halakhic competence of the early masters was not based on any act of ordination conferred by their teachers; otherwise a relation with their teachers would presumably have been stressed. That relation is stressed in the later period, beginning with the disciples of Yohanan; and it is first then that ordination is explicitly spoken of.

The evidence does not permit a dogmatic stand either for or against ordination in the time of Jesus. But we may at least say that ordination was not emphasized as a prerequisite for the issuing of halakhic rulings.

We conclude, then, that, in our period at least, the authority of the masters of the Pharisaic tradition to interpret and supplement biblical law was not based on priestly status, nor on prophetic inspiration, nor, apparently, on a formal act of authorization. Rather it was based on their reputation for knowledge of scripture and the Pharisaic tradition, a knowledge gained by studying with a Pharisaic master; and it was confirmed in popular opinion by a life of piety.

At times, of course, the sages differed as to what the halakhah should be. In any case, the rulings of the individual sage did not automatically become a part of Pharisaic law. We must now consider the assemblies in which halakhic debates were held and laws were adopted.

Chapter III
Halakhic Assemblies

We have seen that it was characteristic of the Pharisees that they assigned
to a corpus of extrabiblical law, shaped by sages and distinguished from the
(written) words of Torah, a binding character. We have seen that individual
sages, because of their learning and the impact of their holy lives, exercised a certain influence, especially over their disciples, but even over
others as well. Their manner of living was observed and could be adopted as
a pattern; their teaching and rulings were remembered and practised. Still,
neither their way of life nor their words became automatically a part of
Pharisaic law. At best they could be cited as precedents in the formulation
of rules adopted by the Pharisees.

The question then arises if a central body, an assembly, existed which, by
approving the rulings and opinions of individual sages, could give them a
more binding character for Pharisaic practice. To answer this question, we
turn first to the assembly spoken of in the N.T., Josephus, and rabbinic
sources as the Sanhedrin. Was this assembly a suitable forum for the
issuing of Pharisaic halakhah?

A. THE SANHEDRIN
1. The Nature of the Sanhedrin and its Authority

(a) In the modern discussion of the Sanhedrin, its importance for the
halakhah is often minimized, or even excluded.
(i) Zeitlin, noting that συνέδριον before 70 A.D. means "council", not a
"court of justice",[1] and that a high priest or state official is frequently
said to "assemble" a synedrion,[2] argues that the N.T. and Josephus speak
of a number of different "sanhedrins", having the status of councils constituted to deal with a problem at hand.[3] They are not to be confused with
the religious Bet Din haGadol of rabbinic texts.[4] Hoenig shows that a
synedrion could be a court of law even before 70,[5] but otherwise agrees
with Zeitlin in seeing synedrion in the N.T. and Josephus as used for a
number of such courts, the highest of which is that of the high priest,
none of which is the Great Sanhedrin of rabbinic texts.[6]

Against Zeitlin, it is clear that the Greek texts do speak of "sanhedrins"
which are more than councils summoned to meet a particular need. At times

they are courts of law.[7] Just as M. Sanh. 1.6 distinguishes the Great Sanhedrin of 71 judges from local sanhedrins with 23 (cf. T. Sanh. 7.1), so the
N.T. speaks both of (local) sanhedrins, i.e. lower courts of justice (Mk.
13:9 par.; Mt. 10:17), and "the Sanhedrin", i.e. a supreme assembly which
we find repeatedly involved in judiciary proceedings. That it is said to be
"assembled" may indicate that it did not meet on a regular basis. Still, it
was a defined body with a recognizable membership.[8] Its composition may
have varied from one period to another,[9] but in our period is described in
a fairly consistent way: high priests,[10] scribes, and elders.[11] Moreover,
its membership is broader and of more significance than one would expect of
a temporary council summoned by a high priest. A number of Pharisaic scribes
are a part, including apparently the most illustrious Pharisaic leaders of
their time;[12] the "elders" represent the lay nobility of the land. Thus we
have represented on the Sanhedrin just those elements one would expect in a
national assembly.[13]

(ii) Still, its significance for the halakhah is often minimized by referring
to it as a kind of "political" or "judicial" sanhedrin, and distinguishing it
from a "religious" or "legislative" sanhedrin.[14] These distinctions represent a commendable attempt to do justice to both the Greek and rabbinic
sources, which offer quite different pictures of the Sanhedrin. Unfortunately, those sources speak of a plurality of sanhedrins only to distinguish
lesser sanhedrins from the supreme assembly; they do not distinguish them
as to spheres of competence such as "political" and "religious", or "judicial" and "legislative"; nor can such distinctions be said to be natural to
Judaism of this period.[15] The Sanhedrin we meet in Acts 4-6 is clearly
dealing with religious, not political matters (cf. 4:7, 17f.; 6:12f.;) yet
it is the same body as was involved in the proceedings against Jesus (5:28),
which many of the authors who distinguish a "religious" from a "political"
court think were handled by the latter.[16] Nor does the Mishnaic tractate
Sanhedrin make any such distinctions. The Great Sanhedrin is there seen
primarily as the highest judicial instance (11.2; cf. T. Sanh. 7.1). It is
responsible for trying what we would call religious crimes (e.g. the trial
of false prophets, proclaiming a city to be apostate, 1.5), but also for
sending people out on a "battle waged of free choice" (1.5), i.e. one not
waged in a religious cause (cf. M. Sot. 8.7). Furthermore, it is hardly
likely that a supreme sanhedrin which included the chief priests and the
leading Pharisaic teachers would have been specially responsible for political, not religious matters. The texts are indeed difficult to reconcile;

but we do not come nearer to the truth by speaking of two bodies where they speak of one, and imposing distinctions in areas of competence which they do not recognize.[17]

(iii) Finally, Kennard assigns little significance to the Sanhedrin as a religious, legislative body by describing it as a "provincial assembly", fully loyal to Rome, with representatives drawn only from the wealthy classes (including, admittedly, several wealthy Pharisees), but detested by the main body of the Pharisees and the people as a whole; a different body, a Pharisaic assembly, had more popular influence.[18] As we shall see, there are reasons for believing that a separate Pharisaic assembly did exist. It is correct to distinguish the Sanhedrin of the N.T. and Josephus[19] from such an assembly by recognizing the more "official" status of the Sanhedrin.[20] But the texts do not support a dividing up of the Pharisees into, on the one hand, a small group of wealthy men sitting on the Sanhedrin, and the majority who detested them and it. Kennard sees Shemaiah, Avtalyon, Shammai, perhaps Hillel, certainly Gamaliel, Simeon b. Gamaliel, and presumably Yohanan b. Zakkai as belonging to the former category,[21] men cited in many cases in the rabbinic tradition as halakhic authorities and respected leaders of their day. Urbach's picture is undoubtedly closer to the truth: there was one Sanhedrin, on which some of the sages were represented;

> throughout its existence, the institution was enveloped by an aura of sanctity and supreme authority, and, just as the holiness of the Temple was not impaired in the estimation of the Sages by the High Priests who were unworthy of officiating, so it never entered their minds to repudiate the institution of the Sanhedrin, or to set up a rival to it in the form of a competing court, even if they did not approve of its composition and even if they opposed the High Priests and their entourage. They endeavoured rather to exercise their influence, and to introduce their rulings and views even into the ritual of the Temple service and into the Sanhedrin's methods of operation.[22]

(b) We may, then, speak of the Sanhedrin as the supreme assembly of the Jews in matters of religious, civil, and criminal law. Moreover, its authority was, on the whole, recognized by both Romans and Jews.

(i) The Romans were wise enough to leave the administration of Jewish affairs largely in Jewish hands.[23] Especially when Judaea was given provincial status (6 A.D.),[24] the high priest and the Sanhedrin of which (as we shall see) he was the head were the recognized administrators of the province in matters not handled by lower officials on the local level or reserved for the procurator.[25] Roman officials were admittedly free to intervene in the proceedings of the Sanhedrin, and were not bound to follow

its decisions.[26)] Still, there is plentiful evidence of their recognition
and even sponsorship of that body. Its head, the high priest, was appointed
by the Romans (Jos. Ant. 20.249); matters of Jewish law, including civil
and criminal cases, seem routinely to have been left to it (cf. John 18:31).
According to Josephus, the emperor Claudius addressed the council (i.e.
Sanhedrin) in a letter: "Claudius... to the rulers, council, and people of
Jerusalem..." (Ant. 20.11).[27)] The procurators and kings are seen dealing
with the "high priests and council" (War. 2.331, 336), even assembling them
(Ant. 20.202[28)]). The Roman tribune consulted the Sanhedrin (Acts 22:30;
23:28). Roman recognition of the Sanhedrin imparted to its decisions a kind
of official character.

(ii) On the other hand, Jewish recognition of the authority of the Sanhedrin
was little influenced by the recognition given it by the Romans. After the
death of Herod the Great, the official jurisdiction of the Sandedrin was
limited to Judaea.[29)] Still, Jews outside the province seem to have submitted to its authority.[30)] This is apparently the conclusion to be drawn
from a number of traditions and texts, even though details are probably at
times unhistorical. Hillel's authority is purportedly recognized by the
Alexandrians in a dispute concerning marriage contracts (T. Ket. 4.9). Acts
assumes that Jews in Damascus (9:1f.) and Rome (28:21) were to some extent
subject to Jewish authorities in Judaea. Especially was the diaspora community dependent on Jerusalem in calendrical matters, i.e. the proclamation
of the New Moon and the intercalation of a month (cf. M.R.H. 1.4; 2:4).
Letters from "Rabban Gamaliel and the elders" to Jewish communities in
Upper and Lower Galilee, the Upper and Lower South, Babylonia and Medea
give instructions concerning tithing and an intercalated month (T. Sanh.
2.6).[31)] Submission to such instructions coming from Jerusalem was, of
course, not dependent on Roman recognition of the Sanhedrin. This applies
as well to submission to Sanhedrin rulings in a number of matters even in
Judaea: the Romans were scarcely interested in backing Sanhedrin rulings on
tithing, the calendar, and the like.[32)]

Why, then, was the Sanhedrin obeyed? What was the nature of its authority
as far as Jews were concerned? For an answer, we must look at the composition of the Sanhedrin: it was made up of "priests and elders" (Mt. 26:3;
Acts 4:23, etc.). Priests in O.T. times had not only cultic, but also
judiciary and legislative responsibilities (Deut. 17:8-13; 19:17; Ezek.
44:23f., etc.). They are even said to issue "torah" (Ezek. 7:26; Hag. 2:11;

cf. Deut. 33:10). "Elders" of the various towns were responsible for the administration of justice locally (Deut. 19:12; 21:19f.; 22:15-19; 25:7-9; Ruth 4:2-12, etc.). The "elders" of tribes or of the nation as a whole are seen as the people's representatives when divine instructions were to be received (Ex. 3:16-18; 12:21), cultic acts were performed (Lev. 4:15), counsel was sought (1 Kg. 20:7f.; Ezek. 7:26), war was decided upon (1 Sam. 4:3; 2 Sam. 17:4), and kings were chosen (1 Sam. 8:4f.; 2 Sam. 3:17; 5:3; 19:12(11)).

In the Sanhedrin, the "priests and elders" continued to exercise their traditional responsibilities. They decided religious issues and functioned both judicially and legislatively.[33] Suitably, and scripturally, the supreme body dealing with these matters was situated in Jerusalem, "the place which YHWH your God chooses" (Sifre to Deut. 17:8). From the Great Bet Din in Jerusalem, "Torah goes forth to all Israel" (M. Sanh. 11.2; cf. Isa 2:3). Its members were called "elders of Israel" (cf. M. Par. 3.7). This term, and the fact that they numbered 70 (excluding the head of the assembly) reflect the view that the Sanhedrin had as its model the 70 elders who bore the burden of Israel together with Moses (Num. 11:16f.).[34] With the weight of tradition supported by numerous texts of scripture behind it, the Sanhedrin could count on widespread observance of its dictates even independently of any "official" support from the Romans.

2. The Pharisees and the Sanhedrin

Since at least the time of Alexandra, Pharisaic scribes had taken their place with the "priests and elders" on the Sanhedrin, and tried to influence its policies (cf. Ant. 13.408ff.).

They were not alone on the Sanhedrin. Admittedly, M. Sanh. 4.3f. claims that members were drawn from the "disciples of the sages"; and the scholion to Megillat Ta'anit contains a late tradition according to which Simeon b. Shetah managed to replace the Sadducees on the Sanhedrin with sages when the former were unable to answer questions of Torah.[35] This evidence, however, is weak, and conflicts with earlier evidence which indicates that Sadducees too were represented (e.g. Acts 23:6). The high priests, repeatedly named in the N.T. and Josephus as members of the Sanhedrin (indeed, they could scarcely be excluded from the highest religious and judiciary assembly of the Jews in light of their O.T. prerogatives), seem largely to have been Sadducees (cf. Acts 4:1; 5:17; Ant. 20.199). This holds true for the lay nobility as well (cf. Ant. 13.298; 18.17). The Pharisees thus formed part, but only a part, of the assembly.[36]

Nor were the leaders of the Pharisees more than important members of the Sanhedrin.[37] Admittedly, rabbinic tradition appears to affirm that a pair of sages (zugot) were the heads of that assembly, serving as nasi and av bet din. Here it is important to recognize that the support for this tradition is very meagre indeed. Only one text from the Mishnah can be adduced: a subscription [38] to the record of the dispute concerning laying hands on a beast to be sacrificed on a festival day names half the disputants as presidents, half as fathers of the court (M. Hag. 2.2). The tradition gave rise to further speculation, e.g. as to which of the third pair, Judah b. Tabbai and Simeon b. Shetah, was really nasi (T. Hag. 2.8; J. Hag. 2.2). Otherwise the traditions of the various members of the "pairs" almost never assign them the title nasi or av bet din.[39] That the N.T. and Josephus recognize the high priest as head of the Sanhedrin (Mk. 14:53ff. par.; Acts 5:21; 22:30-23:5; Ant. 14.168ff.; 20.199ff.) and see the Pharisaic leaders only as important members (Acts 5:34; Ant. 14.172) is well known;[40] it is also surely the logical state of affairs during a period in which a high priest did exist as cultic and political leader (Ag. Ap. 2.193f.; Ant. 20.251; Acts 23:4f.; Philo, Spec. Laws 3.131-133; M. Hor. 2.1f., etc.).[41] Josephus' statements to this effect can scarcely be attributed to priestly bias on his part,[42] since he was a Pharisee as well as of a priestly family, and exhibited no reluctance in stating that the priests were constrained to follow Pharisaic principles (e.g. Ant. 13.288). Nor is it clear why the N.T. would be biased on that question. Moreover, a satisfactory answer as to why the office of av bet din disappeared after Hillel and Shammai has not been found.[43] The little evidence which does exist for the nasi and av bet din who, as leaders of the Jerusalem Sanhedrin, were drawn from the ranks of the sages is easily accounted for by the suggestion that later historians read back into an earlier period institutions with which they were familiar.[44] A theory for which the evidence is meagre and can be satisfactorily explained in another way, which contradicts clear, more contemporary evidence, and which creates logical difficulties, may well be dispensed with.

These qualifications being made, it can be said that the Pharisees did have an influence on the proceedings of the Sanhedrin. The extent of their influence varied with the times, the legislative skill of Pharisaic leaders, the esteem in which they were held, their relations with the rulers of the land, and so on. During the reigns of Alexandra (War 1.110ff.; Ant. 13. 408ff.) and Agrippa I (M. Bik. 3.4; M. Sot. 7.8; cf. Ant. 19.301, 331), for example, good relations with the rulers seem to have benefited Pharisaic interests. Actually, Josephus (Ant. 18.17; cf. 13.288, 298) as well as various rabbinic traditions (e.g. M. Yom. 1.5; M. Par. 3.7f.; B. Yom. 19b; B. Nid. 33b) indicate that public pressure compelled the Sadducees as a rule to concede to Pharisaic views. These statements do show a measure of exaggeration: the priesthood was far from powerless, and there are also indications within rabbinic tradition that the sages were not always able to enforce their opinions (cf. M. Shek. 1.3f.; M. Ket. 1.5; 13.1f.; M. Eduy. 8.3). Still, pointers to Pharisaic dominance are not all propaganda and later idealization. They were certainly in more favour with the people as a whole than the Sadducees: their numbers included men from all classes of the people, and they enjoyed a reputation for piety and preserving ancestral laws (cf. War 1.110; 2.162, where the Pharisees are called the "leading hairesis"; Ant. 18.12-15); the Sadducees, on the other hand, were drawn primarily from the wealthy classes (cf. Ant. 13.298), and the high priests of their number were discredited both by their appointment by foreigners and by the reputation they acquired for unbecoming conduct.[45] Furthermore, it must be said that, though the Pharisaic capacity to rebuild Judaism after 70 was partly the result of their rivals' loss of men and institutions central to their existence,[46] and partly the result of Pharisaism's adaptability to the changed situation, still, a major factor must have been the esteem and popular support the Pharisees enjoyed even before 70.[47] To what extent they were able to use their public support to enforce their views in the Sanhedrin must remain an open question.

Gamaliel the Elder provides us with a good example of a popular (cf. Acts 5:34), effective Pharisaic legislator in the Sanhedrin. We have already seen that he is said to have sent letters to various Jewish communities outside Judaea giving instructions concerning tithes and an intercalated month. According to M.R.H. 2.5, he ordained that witnesses of the new moon who came on the sabbath to the courtyard in which they were examined might walk 2000 cubits in any direction (previously they had not been allowed to leave the courtyard that day). M. Git. 4.2f. contains three ordinances of Gamaliel regarding divorce documents and a widow's collection of ketubbah (money pledged to her by her husband in the event of his death). Another Mishnah text (Yev. 16.7) contains a story in which Gamaliel is reported to have allowed a woman to remarry on the evidence of a single witness that her husband was dead. These legal traditions of Gamaliel seem to have been shaped at an early period and reliably transmitted.[48]

Rulings of this kind may at times have been made independently by Gamaliel
as he decided on specific cases which were brought to him (e.g. M. Yev.
16.7). At other times, however, they must have been issued by a court,
presumably acting at his initiative. A regulation affecting witnesses of
the new moon before the Bet Din, for example, was presumably approved by
the whole Bet Din. Furthermore, though it is at times unclear whether the
ordinances of Pharisaic sages were issued by the Sanhedrin and thus became
"torah" for all Israel, or whether they were adopted simply by the Pharisees, and applied only in their theory to all Israel, there is, in the
case of Gamaliel, no reason to doubt that at times the former did occur.
He was, we know, a respected member of the Sanhedrin; as such, he was in a
position to influence its decisions.

The Sanhedrin, then, was of great importance for the Pharisees and their
halakhah: partly because, as Jews for whom traditional institutions played
a crucial role, they respected and observed the rulings of the Sanhedrin;
partly because they were at times able to influence these rulings so that
their policies were adopted.

B. A PHARISAIC ASSEMBLY?

1. Convocations of Pharisaic Sages

Pharisaic policies could gain a recognized legitimacy by being adopted by
the Sanhedrin; but that forum, led by the high priest and perhaps numeri-
cally dominated by Sadducees, does not seem a suitable one for the development and formulation of those policies.[49] To the extent that the Pharisees were a recognizable hairesis, guided by certain principles and ad-
hering to certain laws, they must have had their own assemblies in which
issues were discussed and rulings adopted.[50] We have descriptions of parallel assemblies held by the Qumran sect,[51] and certain rabbinic traditions
do seem to indicate that Pharisaic counterparts were held. If, for example,
the evidence of M. Sanh. 4.3f. that members of the "Sanhedrin" were drawn
from the disciples of the sages is not only a reflection of post-70 institutions, it may well apply to such Pharisaic assemblies. Moreover, the ban
(נזוי) to which we find references in the period before 70 (M. Ta'an.
3.8; M. Eduy. 5.6; M. Mid. 2.2) was presumably a Pharisaic affair, imposed
by a Pharisaic assembly:[52] in M. Eduy. 5.6, those who would have made
Akavyah b. Mahalalel "Father of the Court" (i.e. of just such an assembly?)
are the ones who impose the ban on him.

It would be inappropriate to speak of such an assembly at this time as the land's "religious Sanhedrin", partly because the Sanhedrin led by the high priest did deal with religious matters, partly because, in the pluralistic period before 70 A.D., such an exclusively Pharisaic body legislated only in their theory for all Israel. Its limited scope, and the probability that it met only infrequently[53] make it not unnatural that it is not mentioned in the N.T. or by Josephus; nonetheless, it may be presumed to have existed.

Some idea of the proceedings at such a convocation of sages can be gained from rabbinic literature and accounts regarding the practice of the Qumran sect.[54] Problems that had arisen, and matters on which differing views were held, would be discussed. The possibilities of resolving the question by means of exegesis were explored (cf. M. Sanh. 11.2). Relevant material from the already existing corpus of halakhah would be brought up, and testimony borne to the rulings or conduct of a recognized halakhic authority. Arguments based on reason (sevarah) would be heard. Certainly the opinions of the leading sages weighed heavily in the making of a decision,[55] but in theory at least it was a majority vote which determined the halakhah: even the views of "the fathers of the world" did not prevail against the majority (M. Eduy. 1.4f.; cf. 5.7). Support for deciding halakhah according to the majority is traced in the Talmud to a curious reading of Ex. 23:2: "After the majority must thou incline" (B.B.M. 59b). It is not impossible that the rabbinic evidence for a nasi and av bet din in the period before 70 applies to the presiding officers, not of the Sanhedrin, but of such convocations of sages;[56] the suggestion cannot, however, be proposed with more confidence, due to the scantiness of the evidence.

2. The Situation after Hillel and Shammai

The continued existence of such a Pharisaic assembly after the time of Hillel and Shammai is, however, problematical. According to a well-known saying of R. Yose b. Halafta (T. Hag. 2.9), there were at first no disputes in Israel, since matters were settled in the local courts or, if need be, in the Great Bet Din in Jerusalem. However, "when the disciples of Shammai and Hillel multiplied, who had not served (their masters) sufficiently, disputes multiplied in Israel." As a result, there were "two torahs" in Israel. That there were differences of opinion among the Pharisees cannot have been anything new; what seems to be novel in the situation after Hillel and Shammai is that differing views were fostered and transmitted within the two schools with little or no attempt being made to come together and reach a consensus which could serve as party halakhah.

Rabbinic writings evidence a vast corpus of disputes between the schools; admittedly, they are often presented in the form of debates conducted between their representatives, thus implying a common forum for discussion; but, as far as the period before 70 is concerned, the form appears to be largely artificial.[57] Decisions seem seldom to have been reached before the Yavnean period, when the different school traditions were brought together and rulings made (cf. T. Eduy. 1.1). Some evidence of earlier meetings does exist (cf. M. Shab. 1.4; M. Suk. 2.7; B. Men. 41b; Sifre to Num. 15:38), some matters were apparently resolved;[58] but such occasions were the exception rather than the rule.

It is therefore usual to speak of a breakdown in the unity of the Pharisees with Hillel and Shammai, the establishment of separate schools, and the lack of an halakhic centre in the subsequent period.[59] Disciples were free to follow the rulings of their own school, or even, on occasion, the rulings of the rival school (cf. M. Dem. 6.6; T. Suk. 2.3): an indication that matters at issue had not been resolved at an assembly of the different Pharisaic schools and an halakhic ruling binding on all Pharisees published.[60] Not till Yavneh were most issues resolved, occasionally with Bet Hillel adopting Bet Shammai's views (cf. M. Eduy. 1.12-14), but ultimately with Bet Hillel's views prevailing in most cases (cf. J. Sot. 3.4; B. Er. 13b). First when matters were resolved did it become wrong to follow the teaching of the minority view (cf. M. Ber. 1.3).

This view of the state of affairs after Hillel and Shammai and before 70, based largely on the tradition contained in T. Hag. 2.9, is no doubt correct in certain respects, but lacking in nuances. There is no reason to question that the vast corpus of school disputes reflect differences between the Houses of Shammai and Hillel before 70.[61] The result was a measure of freedom as far as individual conduct was concerned. It seems unlikely, however, that Pharisaism during this period was divided into two sharply opposed and easily recognizable camps, championing separate torahs, at times even resorting to force to compel submission to their views (cf. B. Shab. 17a). If matters had developed so, it is strange that the N.T. and Josephus take no notice of them, but continue speaking naively of "the Pharisees", unaware of their opposing camps; strange that they do not mention the two schools at all.[62] Strange, too, that prominent leaders of the Pharisees, like Gamaliel the Elder[63] and Yohanan b. Zakkai,[64] seem to have functioned quite independently of the two schools, with little to indicate that they belonged to either. Indeed, there are references to a House of Gamaliel as well (M. Shek. 3.3; 6.1), and Yohanan, without being associated with either of the two famous schools, had his own circle of disciples (M. Avot 2.8).

It seems likely that Pharisaic scholars in the period before 70 were not divided into two clearly defined camps, but that perhaps a number of different circles flourished simultaneously.[65] Probably none was very large, though the schools of Hillel and Shammai, continuing long after their founders' deaths, may have been larger than others. Certainly in the period after 70 it was their representatives who came to dominate the scene, with the result that, retrospectively, two camps were seen in Jerusalem before its destruction.[66] We may assume that representatives of the various Pharisaic groups did occasionally meet and decide some matters of party halakhah; on such occasions, the Shammaites appear to have been the dominant force.[67] But on the whole, disciples were free to follow the teachings of their masters. Since the Pharisees in point of fact were not yet legislating for "all Israel", the need was probably not felt to achieve unity in all areas.

Chapter IV
The Sages of the Halakhah

Our task in Part One has been to provide a framework for the study of
Jesus' view of scribal authority; this has involved an examination of the
phenomenon by which scribal law was added to scriptural, and treated by
the Pharisees as equally binding. We may now state in summary form the results of this part of our study.

The foundation of Pharisaic law was the Mosaic Torah: God had entered into
a covenant with his people, and given his commandments to Moses on Mt.
Sinai. The age of revelation thus lay, for all intents and purposes, in
the past. God had shown what he required of man: the observance of the
commands of Torah.

The implementation of any corpus of law requires interpreters who can define the precise application of its terms. The implementation of the Mosaic
Torah, which in some respects is little suited to serve as a basis for
statutory law, presented problems of its own: its arrangement is often un-
systematic; legal material is mixed with narrative; some provisions seem to
have been formulated with didactic intent, and lack the precision of statutes; and so on. If biblical law is understood as statute, and the attempt
is made to apply it in practice, then the need for lawyers to interpret it
is inevitable.

Not only did biblical law need to be applied; it also needed to be supplemented. Naturally, there existed throughout Israel's history customs and
standard procedures which found no place in the written law. Further, cases
arose which the Mosaic Torah did not explicitly cover; indeed, at times
its terms had to be updated if they were not to lose their relevance. Such
problems are inherent in the implementation and practice of statutory law.
Complications arise, however, when the law is understood as divine, and
the period of revelation is thought to lie in the past. Yet, if only biblical law is held to be binding law, many areas of life will be left untouched by its statutes, others soon encumbered by provisions no longer
practicable. The Pharisaic alternative was to assign normative status to
regulations derived from other sources than scripture, and to regard the
sages as competent to define, apply, and supplement the divine law.

In a sense, the scholars of the Pharisees thus assumed the prerogatives of the O.T. priests, whose task it had been not only to adjudicate in difficult disputes, but also to interpret and apply divine law. That laymen were able to assume such a role can in part be explained by natural causes: Israel's constitution was fixed in canonical texts, and pious laymen as well as priests made it their task to study it. The respect which the priestly aristocracy might otherwise have commanded was forfeited by their courting of foreign rulers and evident lust for power. Not unnaturally, the pious sages who condemned them soon spoke with an authority of their own. A biblical precedent for non-priestly authority was found in the duties assigned to the lay judge in Deut. 17:9. To these sages, learned in the scriptures and the traditions of the fathers, and respected for their disciplined and pious lives, fell the task of transmitting, interpreting, even formulating the Pharisaic halakhah.

Some of the sages did hold office; to their rulings there was naturally attached the legitimacy of their office. Others were members of the Sanhedrin, and able to influence its policies. Otherwise Pharisaic law had no "official" status. Moreover, there were different groups within Pharisaism at the time of Jesus, with somewhat divergent views and traditions; occasionally they met and resolved some point of dispute.

Pharisaic law was thus a peculiar synthesis of the divine and the human. The law which God had revealed was surrounded by a man-made fence, accompanied by traditions of the fathers, applied and supplemented by sages. Not surprisingly, opponents seized on the human element. Yet, in part because of the sages' claim to be divinely authorized, in part because their intention was only to interpret and apply in a dynamic way the law of God, the Pharisees maintained that their halakhah was divinely approved, and that submission to the will of God meant the study and observance of their law.

This view of the will of God came to play an important role in their assessment of the ministry of Jesus. Confronted by the demands of Pharisaic halakhah, he in turn revealed not only his attitude towards scribal authority, but also something of his view of the will of God.

PART TWO
JESUS' VIEW OF SCRIBAL AUTHORITY
Chapter V
Tithing

The evident purpose of the havurot ("associations") was to enable conscientious Pharisees to put into practice their understanding of the laws of
tithing and ritual purity. The importance of these two subjects for the
Pharisees is reflected as well in the large amount of legal material devoted
to them in the rabbinic traditions about the Pharisees before 70 A.D.[1]
Hence, though the gospel material dealing with tithing is very limited, it
forms a natural starting-point for our investigation.

A. BACKGROUND

For the one who would carefully observe all that scripture commands about
tithing, the definition of his task is no easy matter. We may note briefly
the most important O.T. texts in which tithing regulations are given.

In Lev. 27:30f., the tenth part of the produce of the soil and the fruit of
trees is said to belong to YHWH. How it is to be given over to him is not
specified, though the context perhaps suggests that the priest is to receive
it (cf. 27:1-25). Provision is, however, made for the redemption of the
tenth in these cases, provided one-fifth is added to its value. According
to vv. 32f., a tithe of herds and flocks also belongs to YHWH.

In Num. 18:21-32, the tithes are specifically assigned to the Levites in return for their cultic service. A tithe of corn and new wine is explicitly
mentioned in v. 27(cf. v. 30), though these items are probably only typical
of what is to be offered; animals are not mentioned. From the tithes they
receive, the Levites are to set aside a tenth to be given to Aaron, i.e. to
the priests (v. 28). That which remains may be eaten by the Levites and
their families wherever they choose (v. 31). It may be noted in passing that
these regulations lie behind the tithing observances mentioned in Neh.
10:38(37)f.

In Deut. 14:22-29, quite a different picture is given. A tithe is required
of everything planted in the field in v. 22, though v. 23 mentions specifically a tithe of corn, wine and oil. This latter list became a standard

formula in later accounts of tithing regulations (cf. Neh. 13:5, 12; Judith 11:13; Philo, Virtues, 95, etc.), though, again the items mentioned may have been intended only as typical of what is to be tithed.[2] Herds and flocks are also mentioned in this context, though it is the first-born, not every tenth animal, which is required (v. 23). Here it is not said (as it is in Num. 18) that the tithe is to be given to the Levite who, after separating the tenth to be given to the priest, may eat it with his family; rather, the tither himself is to take what is tithed to Jerusalem and there eat it with his own family (vv. 23, 26). If the journey is too long, the tithe may be turned into money (nothing is said, as it is in Lev. 27:31, of "redeeming" it, or of adding a fifth part) which is then taken to Jerusalem to be spent as the tither chooses. He is, however, told not to forget the Levite (v. 27), and to give the tithe every third year to needy people (including Levites) in the area in which he lives (vv. 28f.; cf. 26:12).

It is of course quite irrelevant for our understanding of the Pharisees to say that the biblical laws reflect practices of different periods, or, indeed, that they were in some respects idealistic from the start.[3] For the Pharisees, the various regulations of Lev., Num., and Deut. were all given by God to Moses, and submission to the will of God meant the careful observance of each of their provisions. From this perspective, the regulations of Num. 18 and Deut. 14 differ too widely to be referred to one and the same tithe. Hence the view arose that a first tithe was to be paid to the Levites in accordance with Num. 18:21-32,[4] a second tithe was either to be consumed by the tither himself in Jerusalem, or redeemed in accordance with the provisions of Deut. 14:24-26; Lev. 27:31 was taken to refer to this latter case, so that an added fifth was required (cf. M. Ma'as. Sh. 4.3; Sifra to Lev. 27:30f.). The view was even held by some that Deut. 14:28f. required a third tithe every third year,[5] but the usual (and the Pharisaic) view was that the "tithe of the poor" replaced the second tithe during the specified years.

The view that different tithes were required was in fact not specifically Pharisaic, but antedated the beginnings of that movement (cf. Tob. 1:6-8; Jub. 32:9ff.[6]). Still, it was fundamental to the growth of Pharisaic halakhah, which then concerned itself with defining what was liable for tithing, details in the process of exchanging money for the second tithe, and so on. With these regulations we need not here concern ourselves.

A significant problem was raised for the Pharisees by the fact that the

people as a whole were not particularly conscientious in their tithing:[7]
not surprisingly, perhaps, since tithes alone would have claimed 20 per cent
of their produce. Certainly the Pharisee could tithe his own produce; but
in purchasing food from others, or in eating food in their homes, he could
scarcely be certain that the prescribed tithes had been paid. What was to
be done with demai, i.e. produce which was not certainly tithed? Scripture
itself does not address the problem, but it was nonetheless a real one for
Pharisaic scruples.

The answer was the creation of the havurot, the "associations" of those who
pledged to tithe their produce in accordance with Pharisaic law. On the one
hand, the member was assured that what he purchased from another member, or
ate as his guest, had been carefully tithed; on the other, the rules of the
"association" spelled out how he was to conduct himself in his contacts
with non-members (the ammei ha-arez).[8] He was, for example, bound in a limited way to tithe what he purchased from a non-member: a part of the first
tithe must be given to a priest (the terumah), and the second tithe must be
observed (cf. M. Dem. 2.2; B. Sot. 48a).[9] Further, though, for reasons of
ritual purity, a full member of a havurah could not be the guest of a non-
member in any case, a partial member was allowed (at least by some) to do
so, but had to separate tithes from what he was given to eat.[10]

The Pharisees thus attempted to give effect to each of the provisions of
the Mosaic laws of tithing. In the process, problems arose which required
further elaboration; such were dealt with by their extrabiblical traditions.
We must now turn to the question what Jesus thought of their efforts.

B. JESUS AND TITHING

1. Of Pharisaic Tithing and Publican Righteousness (Lk. 18:9-14)

Our starting-point is the parable of the Pharisee and the tax collector in
Lk. 18:9-14: a suitable place to begin, both because its authenticity is
not open to serious question,[11] and because it reveals a fundamental aspect
of Jesus' view of the Pharisaic endeavour.

In the parable, a Pharisee and a tax collector enter the temple to pray.
The Pharisee thanks God that he does not live in sin as other men do, and
notes two examples of his piety: he fasts twice a week, and tithes everything he purchases. The tax collector has no such merits to mention. A sinner in his own eyes as well as those of society, he can only cry for mercy.
Jesus gives his verdict: the tax collector is pronounced righteous rather

than the Pharisee.[12] The point of the parable is clear: in Jesus' view, it is the one who recognizes his unworthiness and need of mercy who is righteous before God. Human piety has no claim on divine approval.

Of interest for our purposes is the fact that among the deeds of piety the Pharisee mentions is his tithing of everything he purchases.[13] As we have seen, this was required of the _haverim_. Jesus' view of the measure is not spelled out: neither the fasting nor the tithing is directly criticized. What we do know is that, in Jesus' view, such deeds are not a prerequisite for a right standing before God - the tax collector, who is approved, is certainly not a careful tither - and may even prove a hindrance. For the Pharisees, submission to the yoke of the divine rule required careful tithing, and observance of the halakhah on this point had become a tangible means of distinguishing the pious from the _am ha-arez_. Jesus judges by different criteria.[14]

So much is apparent. But one influential interpretation of the parable sees more, and judges the authenticity of other synoptic sayings on the basis of its understanding of this parable. According to Haenchen,[15] we see in this parable the true nature of Jesus' polemic against the Pharisees. It was not directed against hypocrisy or inconsistency on the part of the Pharisees. On the contrary, the Pharisee of our parable tried earnestly to live in accordance with God's will in every respect; it was his understanding itself that was wrong. The Pharisee thought God could only accept the man who carried out the law in its most minute detail; he did not reckon with a God of love who extends his forgiveness to tax collectors and sinners. This false understanding earnestly pursued, not a false front hypocritically projected, is what Jesus opposed in the Pharisees. The latter type of criticism, found in Mt. 23, cannot go back to Jesus and in fact distorts his views. It is as Pharisaic as the Pharisees themselves. Righteousness is still sought on the basis of human effort, the Pharisees being criticized only because they did not extend their efforts to the purity of the heart as well as that of cups and dishes, or to justice, mercy and fidelity as well as to meticulous tithing.

That Jesus' understanding of the will of God is here shown to differ fundamentally from that of the Pharisees cannot be denied; the difference will be developed further in the course of this study. Whether or not Mt. 23 represents a Pharisaic view of man's relationship to God will also be dealt with below in connection with certain texts from that chapter relevant to our theme. But Haenchen does seem to overinterpret at least one aspect of Lk. 18:9-14. It is true that the Pharisee is not said to be hypocritical or inconsistent in his observance of divine commands; but neither, for that matter, is the opposite claimed. The correct conclusion to be drawn is that this parable does not deal with hypocrisy, not that Jesus' polemic against the Pharisees only reckoned with and criticized earnest, consistent Pharisees. We do not know (as Haenchen seems to presuppose) that the Pharisee of the parable was as concerned about justice, mercy, and fidelity as he was about fasting and tithing. Indeed, the fact that his idea of piety is expressed so ingenuously and exclusively in terms of fasting and tithing may well be thought to prepare us for the further criticism that there are weightier matters to attend to. Such a criticism, raised when the occasion called for it, is at least not incompatible with what is said here. Here we may only conclude, with one early commentator, that no one may "trust in himself that he is righteous"; certainly not on the basis of his adherence to the halakhot of tithing.

2. Of Mint, Dill, and Cummin and Weightier Things (Mt. 23:23 par.)[16]

Pharisaic tithing is also dealt with in Mt. 23:23 par. The O.T. had commanded that all the produce of one's soil be tithed (Lev. 27:30; Deut. 14:22). Rabbinic law formulated a general law (kelal) about tithing in these terms: "whatever is used for food and is watched over (i.e. cultivated on one's property) and grows from the soil is liable to tithes" (M. Ma'as. 1.1). Our text is evidence that the same principle was applied already in the time of Jesus:[17] mint,[18] dill,[19] and cummin[20] were all used as food and thus subject to tithing.[21]

In both Mt. and Lk. (11:42), the saying is one in a series of woes directed against the scribes and Pharisees. Luke's text is probably more original in dividing the woes between the Pharisees and scribes, mentioning only the former here. The polemic is thus more pointed, the charges better suited to the accused.[22] Mt. has combined the two and added the epithet "hypocrites", which he maintains throughout the series (23:13-36).

Probably the Matthaean tradition has also added the phrase "the weightier parts of the law";[23] a distinction between more and less important elements of the law is at least consistent with Matthaean theology.[24] Less likely is the explanation that Lk. omitted the phrase because it was open to misunderstanding in the light of 11:46, where scribes are held responsible for the more burdensome aspects of the law.[25] It is not certain if Matthew's trio "justice, mercy, and fidelity" is more original than Luke's "justice and the love of God". The former is certainly a typical combination of O.T. virtues (cf. Mic. 6:8; Zech. 7:9), but may for that reason be the result of Mt.'s redactional activity.[26] The text of the woe presupposed by Mt. and Lk. can thus be rendered approximately in this fashion: "Woe to you, Pharisees! You tithe mint and dill and cummin, but neglect justice, mercy, and fidelity (or, "justice and the love of God"); these latter must be observed, and the former not neglected."

How is Pharisaic tithing viewed here? It is not directly criticized, though the choice of very minor herbs indeed may well imply that Pharisaic scruples are thought excessive.[27] Clearly tithing is assigned a very subordinate role and does not, in the absence of any concern for "weightier matters", guarantee one's standing before God. Still, in the final part of the saying, its practice, too, is apparently commanded.

But for the final part of the saying, it corresponds closely to Jesus' views as found in the parable of Lk. 18:9-14.[28] True, what is criticized here is a preoccupation with tithing when combined with moral failures, whereas moral failures were not mentioned in the parable; but a similar preoccupation was implied, and the presence or lack of moral virtue was not the point being made. Our text (still leaving out of the picture its conclusion) should not be judged non-authentic because it is "legalistic" or Pharisaic, since Jesus certainly demanded the highest of moral standards - absolute honesty and purity, and active concern for one's fellowman - in other contexts. But the problem remains: could he have said that one must not neglect the minor details of the law?

(i) Some think he did, base their view of Jesus' ethical teaching on this verse (as well as, e.g., Mt. 23:2f.), and conclude that Jesus, like the scribes of his day, taught the careful observance of the ceremonial law, only demanding that moral considerations not be forgotten.[29] But this will not do: the tax collector in the parable was approved without any indication that he had tithed in the past or now intended to begin. In Chapter VI, we will see that Jesus placed little value on the careful observance of the laws dealing with ritual purity. If this text must be understood as saying that careful tithing is a prerequisite of divine approval, it cannot be assigned to Jesus.

(ii) Alternatively, we might regard the first part of the verse as authentic, the conclusion as a later addition.[30] Such a view cannot be ruled out, es-

pecially since the first part of the verse seems to fit Jesus' views so
well, while the latter part suits the careful observance of the Mosaic law
found in at least a part of the Jerusalem church (cf. Acts 15:5; 21:20). But
the saying was a unit already in the source lying behind Mt. and Lk.;[31]
hence the possibilities of interpreting it as a unit should be tested before
dividing it in this way.

(iii) On the lips of Jesus, the verse cannot mean that careful tithing is a
prerequisite of divine approval. Nonetheless, in a polemical context[32] in
which the omission of more important matters was the point of the critique,
it is quite conceivable that such a concession as v. 23c might be made in
order to prevent the objection that tithing, too, was a part of the Mosaic
law. No more here then in Lk. 18:9-14 are the Pharisees criticized because
they tithed. The conclusion to the verse may thus have a place in Jesus'
polemic against the Pharisees without being a statement of his own views
about tithing.

These considerations suggest that the authenticity of the verse cannot be
rejected by the criterion of incompatibility with the views of Jesus. Indeed, the verse seems to fit in well with Jesus' polemic against the Pharisees, the coherence pointing in favour of authenticity. In any case, the
verse plays a very minor role in reconstructing Jesus' view of scribal authority: its polemical formulation means that it cannot be used to indicate
Jesus' endorsement of the tithing regulations. What is said here can only
be used to support the conclusion apparent on other grounds, that Jesus assigned to tithing, despite its scriptural basis, a minor place in the will
of God.

C. CONCLUSIONS

The criticism directed against Pharisaic practice in Mt. 23:23 par., though
quite compatible with Jesus' views, is one with which a pious Pharisee could
well agree: obviously, God had commanded that justice, mercy, and fidelity
be practised as well as careful tithing; and though the latter was more susceptible to the formulation of concrete rules, and though its observance
was thus a more tangible token of obedience to God's commands, the Pharisees were of course aware that moral virtue must be practised as well.

The point is, that the Pharisaic understanding of the will of God required
careful observance of everything God had commanded in scripture; further,
the precepts of scripture were understood as statutes, so that each provi-

sion had to be given practical effect. Of course, in certain respects some
commandments might be considered more important than others: [33)] commandments
might be spoken of as more or less important depending on the severity of the
punishment which scripture assigns their transgression; one precept might
be regarded as weightier than another because more effort is required to
fulfil it; further, since rules had to be formulated as to which commandment superseded another in cases where their demands came in conflict, it
was natural to speak of the commandment which must then be observed as the
more important. Nonetheless, under normal circumstances, the divine origin
of each commandment meant that each commandment had to be obeyed; indeed,
those commands which, by human criteria, might be thought less important became for that very reason a critical indication of one's willingness to submit to the law of God. This point of view finds perfect expression in the
answer given in 4 Macc. 5:19-21 to one who suggested that eating pigs under
compulsion was no serious transgression: "Do not imagine that it would be
a minor sin if we were to eat what is unclean. The transgression of the law,
in matters small or great, is equally serious; for in either case the law
is equally despised."

The evidence of Jesus' views from his references to tithing is slight, and
will need to be corroborated by our further study; but it does suggest that
Jesus showed more freedom in minimizing the importance of careful tithing
than would have been possible had he thought the will of God was fulfilled
by putting into practice scriptural statutes. We dare not conclude too much
at this point, and it must be noted that Jesus does not criticize the observance of rules of tithing as such. But it is at least suggestive that,
at a time when Pharisees stood out from their contemporaries by their serious
efforts to practise each provision of scriptural law, Jesus had no words of
commendation for their efforts, but, on the contrary, painted them in
slightly ridiculous terms (tithing "mint, dill, and cummin"); further, that
he never himself enjoined that his followers observe the laws of tithing,
and even pronounced "righteous" a tax collector who presumably had never
done so and made no promise to begin. The emphasis is rather on moral virtues involving one's fellowman, and the attitude of the heart towards God.

Still, just as Jesus was not alone in insisting on moral virtues, so he was
not alone in requiring a proper attitude of the heart towards God. For the
Pharisees, however, a proper attitude had to come to expression in obedience
to every provision of the divine commands; in Jesus' view, that kind of
obedience might well become a hindrance to a right relationship with God,

60

either because minor commands became a preoccupation which prevented the showing of justice and mercy, or because their observance became too facile a criterion for distinguishing oneself from "sinners", thus obscuring the unworthiness of all before God.

Two further aspects must briefly be noted. First, there is no indication that Jesus made any effort to distinguish scribal law from scriptural in the matter of tithing. The Pharisees are criticized, not for adding to scriptural law, but for omitting its weightier aspects. If we have understood Jesus correctly, the careful definition and application of each provision of scriptural law was for him no urgent matter, since the divine will could not in any case be reduced to formulations of that kind; hence, the need for scribal law would not be felt. But this suggestion, too, requires further corroboration. Second, there is no suggestion that Jesus' relative indifference to the laws of tithing is dependent on a change in their status with the beginning of his ministry, as though careful tithing of mint, dill, and cummin had been required until his day, but, with the dawning of the reign of God, the laws on the subject had been abrogated. At any rate, such a view is not the basis of his critique of Pharisaic practice.

Chapter VI
Ritual Purity

Jesus' attitude towards ritual purity is of particular significance for our study for the following reasons.

(i) In connection with ritual purity, perhaps more clearly than anywhere else, we see that scribes had assumed the task of amplifying and applying O.T. law. In O.T. times, it was clearly the priests' responsibility to define the areas of clean and unclean, and to teach the observance of these distinctions to the people (Lev. 10:10f.; Ezek. 22:26; 44:23; Hag. 2:11-13). In the N.T. period, Pharisees observed distinctions in this area drawn by scribes. Jesus' attitude towards Pharisaic practice must inevitably reflect his attitude towards scribal authority.

(ii) Differing views on ritual purity distinguished the "sects" of first century Palestine.[1] Jesus' attitude towards ritual purity is thus a far more important indicator of his position in the religious life of his day than, for example, the common occurence in the gospel and rabbinic traditions of moral (and quite non-sectarian) principles such as the Golden Rule.

(iii) It is in the context of a dispute about the washing of hands before meals that Jesus, according to both the Markan (7:1-23) and Matthaean (15:1-20) accounts, speaks to the fundamental issue of the validity of scribal halakhah. This passage in particular must be given careful attention.

(iv) Büchler's Der galiläische 'Am-ha'Ares des zweiten Jahrhunderts (1906) has exercised a good deal of influence in discussions of ritual purity by N.T. scholars. More recent research, however, has shown that his views are untenable, and has left us with a quite different picture of the norms and practices of Jews during the period of the Second Temple. The attempt is here made to apply some of the more recent developments to the study of our subject.

A. BACKGROUND

The O.T. purity regulations are to a large extent stated without indications of the thinking behind them. Certain animals are "clean", others are "unclean" (Lev. 11:1ff.; Deut. 14:3ff.); but, though various aids in classi-

fying the animals are supplied (cf. Lev. 11:3, 9-12, 20, etc.), no real motivation for dividing them in this way is given. No explanation is given as
to why, as a result of giving birth, a mother is "unclean" (Lev. 12:2) and
may not enter the sanctuary (Lev. 12:4), nor as to why various skin diseases
require isolation from the community (Lev. 13:46; Num. 5:2-4). Above all,
no explanation is given as to the theory behind certain purificatory rites,
though the procedures to be followed are at times spelled out in great detail. A man "unclean" through contact with a corpse becomes "clean" after
seven days if, on the third and seventh days, he "purifies" himself in water
containing the ashes of an unblemished, unused red heifer which has been
slaughtered outside the "camp", but burnt in the presence of a priest, with
"cedar wood, hyssop and cochineal red" added to the flames (Num. 19:1ff.).
How can such a process purify? We are not told. Reason sufficient is that
it was so "YHWH spoke to Moses and Aaron".

Scholars can of course speculate as to the thinking behind such legislation
on the basis either of the significance they attach to various details of
Israel's ritual, or of parallel phenomena in the cultic life of Israel's
neighbours. Clearly the sphere of the unclean in some sense threatened that
of the clean, and the prescribed rites were intended to remove the threat.[2]
Depending largely on how closely one relates Israel's ritual to that of her
neighbours, Israel's God is seen either as the object or agent of the threat,
the protecting rites either as tantamount to magic or simply as the means
prescribed by a sovereign God for dealing with "impurity".[3] In fact, if we
distinguish popular notions from beliefs better attuned to Israel's faith,
there may well be room for both alternatives within Israel of O.T. times.

Since, however, Jewish law has its basis, not in that which can be shown to
correspond to norms of "reason" (despite the attempts of apologetes like
Philo and the author of 4 Macc. to present it in such a way), but in commands believed to be divinely revealed, the absence of biblical statements
as to the rationale behind the laws of purity was not felt to affect the
validity of those laws. The primary task of the scribes was of course not
to develop a philosophy of ritual purity, but to define and apply the biblical prescriptions on the subject. What God commanded had to be obeyed
whether or not it was understood.

Some of the details of Pharisaic halakhah will be discussed in connection
with the various gospel pericopes to which they relate. Here, however, we
must raise the more general question as to the spheres of life in which, at

the time of Jesus, the laws of purity were held to be applicable.

The commands of scripture itself are somewhat ambiguous on this point.[4] Frequently, in connection with the demand that the spheres of "clean" and "unclean" be kept separate, it is made clear that the purity of God's sanctuary, or of things consecrated to him, is the major concern (cf. Lev. 15:31; Num. 19:13, 20, etc.). Of the "unclean" mother, it is specifically stated that she may not enter the sanctuary (Lev. 12:4). Eating in a state of purity is required only in connection with foods dedicated to God (Lev. 7:19- -21; 22:3ff.). Still, in connection with certain kinds of defilement, the demand for separation from them is stated in general terms (e.g. Lev. 11:1ff.; 13:1ff.). Purification is required from all types of defilement even when no visit to the sanctuary is explicitly in view. Even the Pharisaic (and Essene-Qumran) concern for preserving the purity of ordinary food is not foreign to scripture. We find repeated references to the defilement of (certainly non-cultic) vessels in which food or liquids were kept.[5] Lev. 11:34 speaks specifically of the defilement of (ordinary) food and drink, as do the priests when Haggai questions them as to the state of food touched by one made unclean by a corpse (Hag. 2:13). What we do not find is the explicit requirement that one be in a state of cleanness when eating ordinary food, as was the case with dedicated foods. On the contrary, scripture explicitly allows for the "unclean as well as the clean" to eat unconsecrated foods (Deut. 12:15, 22; 15:22; cf. Lev. 14:46f.). But this is only to be expected. A command that ordinary food must be eaten in a state of purity would leave lepers and mothers of newly born babies without food! Nonetheless, the regulations regarding purifications from defilement make it clear that one was expected, within the bounds of the possible, to be ritually clean. Indeed, the demand for purity is sometimes stated in the most absolute of terms: "I am YHWH your God: you must therefore sanctify yourselves, and you shall be holy, for I am holy" (Lev. 11:44). Hence, there was a biblical base for applying in a general way many of the laws of purity.

That the Pharisees attempted to apply many of these laws in such a way (i.e. not restricting them to priests involved in cultic service and visitors to Jerusalem at the time of religious feasts) is attested by various passages in the synoptic gospels which speak of their concern to preserve the purity of ordinary food. The historical accuracy of such passages was, however, brought in serious question by the works of Büchler, who held that, at the time of the Second Temple, ritual purity was observed by "few priests, and non-priestly scholars only in exceptional cases".[6] In his view, the rules for eating in a state of ritual purity were largely developed in Ushan (mid-second century) times, and were primarily concerned with preserving the purity of the heave-offering eaten by priests.[7] The gospels were thought to reflect in a distorted way conditions of a period later than that of Jesus,[8] or, perhaps, customs in the diaspora which were not yet widespread in Palestine.[9]

The technical nature of the subject, and the imposing nature of Büchler's scholarship, created a formidable problem for N.T. exegesis.[10] Objections to Büchler were of course raised: it was pointed out, for example, that Mark's gospel is at least as much an historical source for the period before 70 as the Talmud;[11] that custom may have preceded ordinance, and that Mark accurately represented the former long before the latter was laid down.[12] But Montefiore felt that scholars raising such objections had not done justice to the weight of Büchler's arguments,[13] and others have been inclined to adopt the view that the gospel accounts cannot be regarded as historically accurate.[14]

Büchler's theory, however, is no longer tenable.[15] It is now generally recognized that ritual purity was a widespread concern in Palestine during the period of the Second Temple. The Sadducees, it is true, seem to have limited the need for purity to the sphere of the temple;[16] and, among the ordinary "people of the land" (ammei ha-arez), many were presumably quite indifferent to the matter. But others, though scarcely rigorous in their observance, did apparently avoid some of the more obvious sources of defilement even in their daily routine; and the Essenes and Pharisees attempted in a consistent way to apply the distinctions of "clean" and "unclean" in all areas of life.

It is clear enough that the ordinary am ha-arez achieved no consistency in his observance of ritual purity: it was partly this which compelled those who wished to preserve the purity of their food to form "associations" (havurot), carefully regulating their contact with outsiders.[17] Still, there were limits which even the average Jew respected.[18] Jewish observance of the dietary laws distinguishing clean and unclean foods was widespread and non-sectarian, in the diaspora as well as in Palestine.[19] It is clear, moreover, that Gentiles were considered unclean,[20] and it was not only Pharisees and Essenes who refused to associate too closely with them (cf. Acts 10:28; 11:3). Furthermore, the accounts Josephus and Philo give of the biblical laws of purity probably reflect to some extent the practice of Jews of their times, thus indicating that certain basic considerations of purity were still widely observed (e.g. Philo, Spec. Laws 3.63, 205-208; Jos. Ag. Ap. 2.202f., 205; Ant. 3.259ff.); and Josephus provides an eloquent testimony to the refusal of Jews to defile themselves with corpse-uncleanness when he reports the problems Herod had in finding inhabitants for Tiberias (built on an old burial site, Ant. 18.36-38). Even efforts to eat one's ordinary food in a state of ritual purity were not confined to sectarian circles. T. Dem. 2.10 indicates that some non-haverim followed the rules of the havurot in private. Most Jews apparently thought it improper to eat with Gentiles (cf. Acts 11:3; Gal. 2:12f.) or notorious sinners (cf. Lk. 19:7): such people may have been thought impure even by the self-respecting am ha-arez. It is even likely that the washing of hands before meals was practised by some non-Pharisees, as Mark, with characteristic exaggeration, indicates (Mk. 7:3).[21)]

It was, however, first within sectarian circles that the observance of ritual purity was strict and consistent. Josephus writes of the concern for purity shown by the Essenes.[22)] Especially significant for our purposes is the apparent fact that they were careful to eat their meals in a state of ritual purity and to preserve the purity of their food. Josephus states explicitly that they purified themselves with cold water before eating (War 2.129), that their food was prepared by priests (Ant. 18.22, obviously to guarantee its purity), that it could be touched only by full members (War 2.139), and that members were under oath not to eat the food of non-members (War 2.143). Similarly, members of the Qumran sect were forbidden to eat or drink anything belonging to non-members (1QS 5.16), and non-members were forbidden to "enter the water (i.e. of purification, cf. CD 10.10-13) in order to touch the purity (i.e. the pure food)[23)] of the holy men" (1QS 5.13). Partaking of the pure food (1QS 6.16f.) and drink (1QS 6.20f.) of the community was not immediately permitted those who decided to join the sect, but was reserved for those at a more advanced stage of initiation. Among disciplinary measures we find the temporary exclusion from the "purity" (i.e. meals) of the community (1QS 6.25; 7.3, etc.; CD 9.21, 23).

The Pharisaic concern for purity is perhaps seen most clearly in the institution of the havurot ("associations"): it was required of a haver that his ordinary food (hullin, as opposed to the dedicated foods eaten by the priests) be kept pure, and that he eat it in a state of purity (T. Dem. 2.2).[24)] As in other areas of Pharisaic practice,[25)] the origin of the fundamental issue is obscure, having apparently been resolved before the period of Shammai and Hillel when traditions with named legislators became some-

what more numerous. Thus the texts containing the points of disagreement between the schools of Hillel and Shammai on the requirements for membership
in a havurah take as their starting-point that hullin is to be eaten in a
state of purity; discussion revolves around such comparatively minor points
as the length of the period of probation before prospective members are accepted (T. Dem. 2.12).[26] But the basic requirement of purity was not in dispute between the schools, and can be assumed to have been established by the
time of Jesus.

This conclusion finds support in other texts as well.[27] The view of Bet
Shammai that olives could only be sold to a full-fledged haver (M. Dem.
6.6) indicates the lengths to which they were prepared to go to preserve
the purity of food. Furthermore, the schools debated whether or not a
perush (i.e. Pharisee) who normally observed the laws of cleanness but was
temporily unclean because of a discharge could, in his state of uncleanness,
eat with an am ha-arez who was similarly unclean: Bet Hillel permitted it,
Bet Shammai did not (T. Shab. 1.15). Clearly the norm was that a clean
perush could not eat with someone in a state of uncleanness. R. Simeon b.
Eleazar aptly remarks: "How far purity spread in Israel! The early (sages)
did not legislate that a clean person must not eat with a menstruous woman,
for men of old did not eat with menstruous women; but they said that a man
unclean because of a discharge must not eat with a woman unclean because of
a discharge since it offers an occasion for sin" (T. Shab. 1.14).[28]

As we have indicated, the origins of the Pharisaic view that ordinary food
must be eaten in a state of ritual purity are obscure. But on the basis of
that view, Pharisaic sages set about the task of defining and legislating
how the purity of food was to be preserved and what rendered it unclean;
when a vessel was clean and when it was not; how the hands were to be purified before eating; and so on. The result in the course of time was the
enormous wealth of detail of the talmudic laws of purity. At what stage of
development the various laws were in the time of Jesus is a question which
must be put to each individual case, and cannot always be answered with cer-
tainty.Still, it is clear that Jesus' attitude towards the matter of ritual
purity in general, and to the Pharisaic halakhot on the subject in particular, is an important indicator of his view of scribal authority.

B. JESUS AND RITUAL PURITY

1. Unclean and Unconcerned

We begin by noting several incidents in the gospels which in fact involved

defilement according to the O.T. purity laws,[29] though the gospels themselves make no mention of the fact. Their silence complicates the assessment of the historical value of the accounts.[30] On the one hand, the apparent disinterest of the gospel tradition (or at least of its final stages)
in ritual purity makes it unlikely that the facts have been purposefully
altered to suit some theological point; on the other hand, the same disinterest prompts the question if the tradition can be relied upon to report
the matters regarding purity with the precision necessary if sound conclusions are to be drawn. In any case, we may note what is said.

According to Lev. 15:19-24, a woman is unclean seven days of the month at
the time of her menstrual flow; anyone who touches her is unclean until
evening; unclean, too, is any bed or seat she uses, and uncleanness is
passed on to the one who touches them. In the verses which follow (25-27),
the same state of uncleanness is said to apply to a woman who experiences a
flow of blood outside of her monthly periods as long as the discharge lasts.
First when seven days have passed after her cure is she clean (v. 28). It
is thus clear that, according to O.T. law, Jesus became ritually unclean
when he came in contact with a woman who had had a flow of blood twelve
years (Mk. 5:25ff. par.). It has been suggested that the woman's knowledge
of this fact contributed to her fear when Jesus asked who touched him.[31]
But there is no indication that Jesus himself was concerned about the defilement.

If we follow the synoptic account, he was in fact on his way to a more serious defilement. According to Mk. 5:38ff. par., he proceeded to enter a house
where a young girl lay dead[32] - thus incurring a defilement which lasted
for seven days (Num. 19:14) - and even took her by the hand, the contact
also bringing a seven-day defilement (Num. 19:11). Again, he seems unper-
turbed, if not unaware.[33]

On another occasion, Jesus is said to have touched a leper[34] in order to
heal him (Mk. 1:41 par.). Since, according to O.T. law, the leper's uncleanness compelled him to "dwell alone outside the camp" (Lev. 13:46; cf.
Num. 5:2f.; 12:14f. etc.), it is clear that Jesus incurred ritual defilement
by such contact. Again, he seems indifferent on that account; but it should
be noted that, according to the evangelists, he then told the healed man to
carry out the Mosaic prescriptions for the purification of lepers.[35]

Finally, according to Mk. 14:3 par., Jesus was "in the house of Simon the
leper" shortly before Passover (cf. 14:1 par.).[36] If we bear in mind that

lepers were commanded to dwell alone because of their uncleanness, it would appear that Jesus incurred defilement on this occasion as well.[37] But it is difficult to believe that a leper could have entertained guests in his house during the period of his uncleanness, considering what we know about the observance of certain basic requirements of purity even among non-Pharisees; we may well suspect that Simon's epithet referred rather to a previous, now cured condition.[38]

We need not pause to weigh the historicity of these accounts. Presumably they are at least typical of Jesus' ministry, but they tell us in any case very little. Incurring defilement in this way did not necessarily involve defiance of Torah, provided that steps were then taken for purification in the cases for which they were prescribed. One might conclude that Jesus was more concerned about healing others than he was about preserving his own ritual purity; this is undoubtedly true, but scarcely a remarkable conclusion, since a reliable part of the tradition informs us that he subordinated the sanctity of the sabbath to the same consideration. Perhaps significant is the fact that he is reported to have told lepers he cured to carry out the Mosaic law of purification, though his reasons for doing so ("for a witness") are not perfectly clear. More we do not know on the basis of these quite incidental references.

2. In the Company of "Sinners"

Here we appear to be on firm historical ground. That Jesus associated, even ate, with notorious "sinners" in a way thought scandalous by his contemporaries can hardly be questioned.[39] To this day Jesus is spoken of in Christian circles as "the friend of sinners"; the epithet was apparently already in use among his contemporaries, for whom it expressed not wonder at his all-embracing love, but contempt for the company he kept (cf. Mt. 11:19 par.).[40] The nature and implications of the scandal he raised may contribute to our understanding of his relations with the Pharisees and his views of ritual purity.

Living among people too lax in their observance of ritual purity to be accounted reliable, the haver had to follow strict guidelines laid down by the sages for contact with outsiders.[41] Specially important was, of course, the question of table fellowship, since the haver was committed to preserving the purity of his food.[42] Apparently practice on this point varied with one's status in the "association".[43] The "reliable" person, who either was not yet, or chose not to be, a full member,[44] was required to be careful

appenheimer

in his tithing, but not to preserve the purity of his food. In the opinion
of R. Judah in M. Dem. 2.2 and of the sages in T. Dem. 2.2 (Meir disagrees),
there was nothing to hinder "reliable" people from accepting the hospitality
of outsiders, nor in practice did they hesitate to do so. But the haver
(full member of the "association") had to observe the regulations concerning
purity as well. He must not accept the hospitality of an outsider;[45] the
latter, it was assumed, had not taken sufficient pains to preserve the purity of his food. Moreover, should the haver receive an outsider (am ha-arez)
as his guest, the latter was not permitted to wear his own (presumably con-
taminated) garment (M. Dem. 2.3).

In the gospels, Jesus is accused of eating with "sinners" (Mk. 2:16 par.;
Lk. 15:2; cf. 19:7). The term is certainly not the equivalent of am ha-arez,
i.e. outsider to the havurah.[46]

(i) Partial members of the havurah at any rate were permitted to eat with
outsiders; thus no one would have been scandalized over the fact that Jesus
did so.

(ii) Jesus himself was not a haver, and was of course free to eat with another am ha-arez; but when he is accused of eating "with sinners", he is
evidently not regarded as such a "sinner" himself.

(iii) The use of the term "sinners" for tax collectors (Lk. 19:7)[47] and
prostitutes (Lk. 7:37, 39), and the standard phrase "tax collectors and
sinners" (e.g. Mk. 2:15f. par.) indicate that the term refers to specially
notorious sinners, or, as Jeremias has shown, to people practising pro-
fessions which all but inevitably led to dishonesty or immorality.[48]

(iv) The charge of associating with such people is, admittedly, often
raised by Pharisees,[49] but seems at times to represent a more general condemnation (cf. Mt. 11:19 par.; Lk. 19:7). The "sinners" were despised by
the self-respecting am ha-arez as well!

It follows, then, that when Jesus is accused of eating with "sinners", the
brunt of the charge is not that he did not observe specially Pharisaic
standards of purity, but that he flaunted the most elementary considerations
of morality as well as of purity:[50] "a discerning son is the one who ob-
serves Torah; a companion of profligates disgraces his father" (Prov. 28:7).

Still, Jesus' practice has significance for his view of Pharisaic purity.
"Sinners" is not the equivalent of "outsiders to the havurah", but refers
to the most notorious members of their ranks. While the risk of impurity

kept the _haver_ from eating with even the most respectable _am ha-arez_, Jesus did not hesitate to eat with the most notorious "sinners". Clearly he expended no efforts to observe scribal regulations on this point.

But that is not all. Jesus did share the view of his contemporaries that such people were sinners; they were the "sick" element of society, in greatest need of a physician (cf. Mk. 2:17a).[51] With such people, the Pharisees had little to do, partly because they were "unclean", but also simply because they were sinners, the wicked who had turned from God and with whom one was not to consort (cf. M. Avot 1.7; note also Ps. 1:1, etc.). For Jesus, they were still, first of all, the objects of divine love. That he directed his message to them indicates that they were included in the divine initiative for the salvation of men. The Reign of God had drawn near to them as well.[52]

In taking his message to the most notorious sinners, Jesus indicated that the matter of ritual purity was at best a very subordinate consideration. We have not as yet seen any evidence that he criticized Pharisaic observance on this point. But the fact that he himself was prepared to disregard scribal prescriptions related to purity in order to reach the lost, and that he placed no demands of ritual purity, biblical or extrabiblical, on the unobservant people to whom he came shows that, for him, obedience to the laws of ritual purity played no decisive role in one's relationship with God. Indeed, just as an unobservant tax collector rather than a Pharisee was pronounced justified in the parable, so, according to another logion, the religious leaders (who presumably observed distinctions between "clean" and "unclean") must give place to tax collectors and prostitutes (who certainly did not) as the latter enter the Kingdom of God (Mt. 21:31). Even had Jesus not directly criticized Pharisaic halakhah, it would be clear that his presuppositions were entirely different.

3. Clean Hands and a Pure Heart (Mk. 7:1-23 par.)[53]

Accounts of the handwashing dispute are to be found in both Mt. 15:1-20 and Mk. 7:1-23. In spite of major differences in the progression and wording of the dispute, Mt. (with the exception of 15:12-14) does seem to be dependent on Mk.,[54] reworking the Markan narrative with an expert redactional hand: besides making numerous stylistic improvements,[55] he arranges the material at his disposal, adding a pointed question here (15:3), a dialogue there (15:12-14), and a summarizing comment at the end (v. 20), thus producing a unified and dramatic account. But the unity is imposed, the drama literarily enhanced. In Mk., the passage hangs together very loosely (note the separate introductory formulas, vv. 6, 9, 14, 18, 20), but does provide a clearer picture of the history of the tradition. In what follows, we will concentrate our attention on the Markan narrative.

Still, one aspect of the Matthaean account must be noted. In Mt. 15:12b-14, we have non-Markan material, though v. 14 has a parallel in Lk. 6:39 and Thomas 34. V. 13, too, has a counterpart in Thomas 40 ("Jesus said: A vine was planted apart from the Father, and it has not become strong; it will be uprooted (and) it will perish"), which, interestingly (but probably coincidentally), follows a logion in which the "Pharisees and the scribes" are the subject. If Jesus did speak of the Pharisees in the words of Mt. 15:13f., we would certainly be justified in drawing some conclusions about his attitude towards the authority of their scribes and the validity of their halakhah: he denies that the scribes are divinely authorized, denies that they lead their followers in paths approved by God. It is not at all improbable that Jesus did speak in this way of the Pharisees;[56] but the context here is secondary, and the Lukan parallel to v. 14 charges no religious group in particular. We can therefore build no argument on these verses.

a. The Accusation (Mk. 7:1-5)

A charge is brought against Jesus by the "Pharisees and certain of the scribes who had come from Jerusalem". A similar group of Jerusalem scribes charges Jesus with exorcising demons through the power of Beelzebul in Mk. 3:22. Neither here nor there are we told that they had come specifically to observe Jesus, though reports of his activities could well have motivated an investigation. The nature of the charge here raised suggests that these scribes were Pharisees: their "traditions" were at stake. It is thus questionable if they had come on an official mission as representatives of the Sanhedrin,[57] of which assembly the Pharisees were only a part. Even so, our text is a witness to the zeal of Pharisaic leaders in attempting to spread their influence and ideas over all Israel.

These "Pharisees and scribes" hold Jesus responsible for the conduct of his disciples (v. 5).[58] The latter (or rather, "some" of them, v. 2) are charged with not conducting themselves in accordance with "the tradition of the elders", but eating bread with "unclean"[59] hands. Two major problems have been raised in connection with this charge. (i) It has been denied that the washing of hands before meals was required during this period even by the Pharisees for non-priests eating ordinary meals. (ii) Since the sequel (vv.

6-13) does not deal with handwashing but exclusively with the validity of
"the tradition of the elders", the accusation is thought either to have been
created secondarily in order to provide a setting for some sayings about
Pharisaic tradition, or to have included only secondarily references to the
tradition by way of preparation for vv. 6-13.[60] These problems will be considered in turn.

(i) That Jesus' disciples could have been criticized for not washing their
hands before eating has been denied, most energetically by Büchler. We have
already noted his view that the rules for eating in a state of purity were
largely from the second century. He was forced to concede that the washing
of hands before eating was introduced earlier, but still insisted that it
was adopted by the schools first in the post-70 period.[61]

But, as we have seen, the haverim of the first century were among those who
attempted to eat their food in a state of purity. Here we need only ask if
handwashing belonged to the practices they observed. A necessary precondi-
tion would seem to be the view that hands were generally suspect of being
unclean,[62] so that they would have to be washed if the purity of food was
to be preserved.[63] Special uncleanness of hands is found at best embry-
onically in scripture (cf. Ex. 30:19, 21; 40:31), but is implicit in certain
texts from the pre-N.T. period which speak of washing the hands before praying or handling the scriptures.[64] Moreover, according to one rabbinic tradition (B. Shab. 14b), Shammai and Hillel declared the hands unclean.[65]
Some scholars have drawn the conclusion that in the time of Jesus handwashing before meals was a recent addition to the halakhah,[66] though, considering the fact that the "innovation" is attributed in another tradition to
Solomon (B. Shab. 14b), we perhaps ought not attempt to date it too closely.
But since Bet Hillel and Bet Shammai are reported to have differed as to
whether or not the handwashing was to precede the "mixing of the cup" (M.
Ber. 8.2; cf. 8.4), we need not doubt that the practice of washing the hands
before eating ordinary meals was observed in the time of Jesus at least by
the adherents of the Pharisaic schools (cf. also M. Mik. 1.5f.; T. Mik.
1.7ff.; John 2:6).

It was not observed by "all" the Jews: Mark exaggerates here (v. 3) in a way
typical for him (cf. 1:5, 33, 39; 6:33); that it is an exaggeration is clear
from the fact that some of Jesus' disciples (Jews all!) did not do so (cf.
also M. Eduy. 5.6). But Pharisees were among those who did. It is even possible that handwashing was a widespread custom before it was adopted as

halakhah by the Pharisaic tradition.[67]

(ii) Strangely, however, the answer Jesus is reported to have given (vv. 6-
-13) contains no reference to the washing of hands. Must we not draw the
conclusion that these verses were not originally intended as an answer to
that charge, and that, consequently, v. 5a is a secondary addition preparing
the way for vv. 6-13?

But here we must remember that the washing of hands before eating was not
derived from scripture; it was recognized, even by the later rabbis, to belong to the "words of the scribes", with scripture offering at best a "support" (B. Er. 21b; B. Hul. 106a). If the disciples did not observe the practice, they were not violating scripture, but precisely the "tradition of
the elders". Adherence to this "tradition" being characteristic of the Pharisees, they were naturally zealous in defending it (cf. M. Sanh. 11.3; M.
Eduy. 5.6; B. Sot. 4b). The blatant violation of their ordinances cast doubt
on the validity of Pharisaic traditions and the authority of their sages: a
challenge they could be expected to take up. If the washing of hands was a
recent addition to the tradition, the Pharisees would have been all the more
eager to see to it that it was taken seriously (cf. B.A.Z. 35a). It is thus
significant that the general question of the authority of the halakhah is
not raised in connection with disputes over the sabbath or divorce, where
it at least had a biblical base, but in connection with handwashing, a regulation recognized by adherents and foes alike as scribal. Thus v. 5a is
quite natural on the lips of Pharisaic scribes, and we need not be surprised
if Jesus, in answering it, concentrates on the validity of the tradition itself.

We need comment only briefly on the explanation in Mk. 7:3f. of Jewish custom. Πυγμῇ has been the subject of a good deal of discussion,[68] but its
meaning is still not certain. As long as the reading was considered unintel-
ligible, it was natural to prefer the less well attested πυκνά,[69] or to see
πυγμῇ as the result of a misunderstanding of an Aramaic term.[70] The text is,
however, capable of satisfactory explanation, either as a Latinism (intelligible for Mark's intended readers) based on pugnus/pugillus, and meaning
"handful" (thus roughly equivalent to the amount of water prescribed in M.
Yad. 1.1),[71] or as a reference to washing by pouring water over "cupped"
hands.[72] Büchler claims that a cleansing by immersion after returning from
the market (v. 4) is not known in rabbinic literature,[73] though Brandt is
probably correct in saying that at least the preconditions for such a view

to be held by a conscientious Jew are found in Torah.[74] Possibly, however,
we should understand either that it was the "hands" or "(things purchased)
at the market" which were to be purified.[75] Regulations concerning the
cleansing of vessels will be considered in connection with Mt. 23:25f. par.

b. The Reply to the Pharisees (Mk. 7:6-13)

According to Mk. 7:6-8, Jesus answers the charge of the Pharisees and scribes
first in general terms with a quotation from Isaiah (29:13): Isaiah's words
are true of these "hypocrites", whose religion is on their lips, not in their
hearts, and whose teachings are the "commandments of men". To the quotation
he adds his own contemporizing midrash: "abandoning the commandment of God,
you hold to the tradition of men" (v. 8). A new introductory formula introduces a new section, in which the same criticism is levelled (vv. 9, 13),
this time supported by a specific example (vv. 10-12).

The progression of the argument, from general charge with scriptural support
to a specific example, is intelligible enough; still, there are reasons for
doubting that Jesus answered the challenge from the scribes in precisely
this way. The new introductory formula in v. 9 suggests immediately that
separate traditions have been combined; similarly, the repetitiousness of
vv. 8 and 9 make it unlikely that they were spoken together on one occasion.
It thus seems probable that either vv. 6-8 or 9-13 are not original in this
context.

Vv. 6-8 are often taken to be secondary; among reasons given for such a
judgment, the following may be mentioned.

(i) Horst notes that the Hebrew text of Isa. 29:13 is directed against a
religion of the lips which does not lead to action, and suggests that the
quotation is not suitable as an answer to v. 5, where Pharisaic religion
comes to expression, not in words without deeds, but in deeds of a wrong
kind.[76] But Jesus could well have met the charge that his disciples did
not wash their hands before eating by accusing his opponents of being hypocrites, concerned far more for such externals as handwashing than for the
attitude of the heart towards God. From this point of view, handwashing is
no less superficial than a religion of the lips. The quotation in fact seems
particularly appropriate.

(ii) The quotation from Isa. 29:13, while not reproducing the LXX, does
follow the Greek version much more closely than it does any known Hebrew
text; hence, it has been argued that Jesus could scarcely have introduced

the quotation here.[77] But, of course, it is possible that he cited a Hebrew form of the text, and that his words have been assimilated towards the LXX.[78] The M.T., too, contains the charge that the religion of "this people" involves the "commandment of men"; hence, it, too, is an adequate base for the argument here. That the quotation is here cited according to the LXX is thus not a decisive argument against its authenticity.

(iii) Isa. 29:10ff. seems to have been used by the early church rather frequently, especially for attacking legalistic religion. We may note Rom. 9:20 (Isa. 29:16); 11:8 (Isa. 29:10); 1 Cor. 1:19 (Isa. 29:14); and Col. 2:22 (Isa. 29:13).[79] This perhaps suggests that the early church may have introduced the quotation here as well, though of course we cannot rule out the possibility that Jesus himself cited a text later used by the church.

These arguments are less than decisive against the authenticity of vv. 6-8 in this context. We will consider the question again after looking at the argument in the verses that follow.

In vv. 9-13, Jesus supports his charge that the Pharisees set aside the commandment of God in favour of their tradition with a specific example. We are to imagine that a son, perhaps in a fit of temper, vows that any benefit his parents might derive from him is korban, i.e. dedicated as a "gift" to the temple.[80] Later, however, either he himself regrets his vow and wants to be released from it, or his parents seek to have it nullified. But the position of the Pharisees is that the vow cannot be broken: "You no longer permit him to do anything for his father or mother" (v. 12). Jesus sees here an example of Pharisaic tradition going against the word of God which commands a son to honour his parents; possibly he even sees the vow as a case of addressing parents contemptuously (if the quotation in v. 10b, from Ex. 21:17, is not meant simply to emphasize the importance Torah places on a son's proper attitude towards his parents). Such a vow is scarcely to be upheld.

The answer given in these verses is often denied to be the words of Jesus because it purportedly shows a great ignorance of the Pharisaic position with regard to vows. Here Pharisaic tradition is said to make the breaking of such a vow impossible, whereas "the annulling, not the maintenance, of vows, was the work of tradition".[81] In fact, M. Ned. 9.1 is cited to prove that the sages ruled that, when honour to one's parents is at stake, a vow may be dissolved. The problem demands that we pause in our discussion of Mk. 7, and consider the Pharisaic halakhah related to vows.

According to biblical law, a vow was to be adhered to strictly (Num. 30:3
(2); Deut. 23:22(21); cf. Eccl. 5:3(4)f. In the story of Jephthah (Judges
11:30ff.), we have a particularly grim example of the extremes to which
that view could lead; but it is only one of a number of passages reflecting
what must have been a common enough occurence: a man "pays" to God what he
vowed in a time of distress (cf. 1 Sam. 1:11, 28; 2 Sam. 15:7f.; Jon. 2:10
(9), etc.).

In the Mishnah, the strictness of the biblical position has been consider-
ably relaxed. Rules outlining the circumstances under which releases may be
granted are supplied: "The sages have declared that four kinds of vows are
not binding: vows of incitement, vows of exaggeration, vows made unwittingly,
and vows of constraint" (M. Ned. 3.1). In view of the strictness of the O.T.
position, it is not surprising that the releases from vows allowed by sages
are said to "hover in the air with nothing (in scripture) to support them"
(M. Hag. 1.8). But the movement in this direction was gradual. In M. Naz.
5.4, we do have an early[82] example in which a sage (Nahum the Mede) releases certain Nazirites from a vow, but it is from the immediate post-70
period. Many old halakhot are based on the understanding that a vow could
not be dissolved.[83] Interestingly enough, one such text is M. Ned. 5.6,
and the vow in question (from the consequences of which an attempt is made
to escape by way of legal fiction) is one which forbade a parent to derive
any benefit from a son: a close parallel to our text.

With this in mind, we may look more closely at M. Ned. 9.1.

> R. Eliezer says, "They may open the way for a man (to retract his vow)
> because of the honour due to his father and mother." But the sages
> forbid it. R. Zadok said, "Instead of opening the way for him because
> of the honour due to his father and mother, they should open the way
> for him because of the honour due to God; (but) were that the case,
> there could be no vows." The sages agreed with R. Eliezer that, in a
> matter between a son and his father and mother, they may open the way
> for him because of the honour due to his father and mother.

Eliezer and Zadok both envisage the release from vows which they suggest can
be considered vows made in error. In the case Eliezer mentions, a son could
be released from his vow if he could say that he would not have made it had
he known that his parents would have been despised for bringing up a son so
casual in his vows;[84] in Zadok's, a man is released if he could say he
would not have vowed had he known that the one who vows is evil in God's
eyes. It should, however, be noted that this text appears to attribute the
releasing of a vow similar to the one in Mk. 7:11f. to R. Eliezer, i.e. to

a period half a century or so after the time of Jesus.[85] In fact, the text says first that the sages were opposed, and it seems to be only later sages, taking cognizance of the views of both R. Eliezer and R. Zadok, who side with R. Eliezer.[86] Thus, Neusner concludes that Eliezer's view is innovative: "the antecedent law certainly held one may not release vows by reference to the honor of parents."[87]

Mk. 7:9-13 does, then, reflect the position of the early, stricter Pharisees,[88] even if later tradition moved towards the view of Jesus on this question. We need not suppose that the early scribes encouraged or delighted in a case like the one in our text; but, in the early period, the dominant view seems to have been that such a vow must be kept.

There are thus no grounds for denying the authenticity of vv. 9-13 because they misrepresent the halakhah. Nor, indeed, is what is said here inconsistent with the teaching of Jesus elsewhere.[89] If there were those who felt that the laws regarding vows must be applied strictly and formally, even though they were aware that this could lead to abuses and human suffering,[90] it is but to be expected that Jesus would disregard such formal considerations in the same way as he did, for example, in connection with the sabbath.[91] There seems, then, to be no sufficient reason for denying the substantial authenticity of vv. 9-13,[92] and the coherence of what is said here with what we know of Jesus seems to point decisively in favour of authenticity.

Significant for our purposes is the fact that Jesus here clearly distinguished between Torah and the scribal tradition:[93] "Moses said... but you say..." The former represents the "command" (v. 9) or "word" (v. 13) of God, the latter the tradition of Jesus' opponents. Just as Jesus set his own word against what had been said to those of old (Mt. 5:22, 28, etc.), so the tradition of the Pharisees clearly went beyond what Moses had said: ὑμεῖς δὲ λέγετε (v. 11). But not only did it go beyond; according to Jesus, in this case at least it went against the will of God as revealed in Torah: the latter was "set aside" (v. 9), "rendered null and void" (v. 13) by the Pharisaic tradition. Clearly the "words of the scribes" have no binding force for Jesus.[94]

This suggests that Jesus, like the Sadducees, distinguished scribal law from scriptural, and held that only the latter was binding. Still, his position must not be too hastily identified with that of the Sadducees. The Sadducees, like the Pharisees, regarded scriptural laws as statutes, rejecting only the amplifications which Pharisaic tradition made to the statutes of scripture. Yet we have seen in the matter of tithing that Jesus placed little value in the careful fulfilment of biblical statutes; the will of God was defined in other terms. Here, too, though the divine will is found in what "Moses said", i.e. in scripture, it is not really conceived in a statutory way. Had it been so, the case in question would not have been as obvious as, for Jesus, it apparently was.

In point of fact, scripture commands, not only that parents be honoured, but also that vows be kept. For the Pharisees at least, the case put by Jesus involved a conflict between two biblical laws. With their view of bib- lical law as statute, such a dilemma could only be resolved (as, in the course of time, it was) by further legislation on the part of scribes (e.g. M. Ned. 3.1; 9.4) and the lavish use of legal fiction which, while upholding in principle the inviolability of vows, found in practice a way of dissol- ving or circumventing them (cf. M. Ned. 4.7f.; 5.6). Humane considerations could thus operate while at the same time the letter of the law on vows was upheld.[95] Such casuistry is the inevitable result of a formal view of the authority of scripture which requires every law in the biblical text to be honoured, if necessary by a fiction.

Jesus, like the sages of a later day, thought the selfish vow of a son should not be upheld, but evidently felt no need to introduce the legal fic- tion of a "vow of error" to dissolve it. That scripture demands the fulfil- ment of vows is not even mentioned to be dismissed. Though Jesus found the will of God expressed in scripture (Ex. 20:12; 21:17), he seems no more in this case than in the matter of tithing to have understood the divine will in a statutory way. One's course of action is not determined by the subtle exegesis and casuistic application of scriptural precepts, carefully weigh- ing the relative claims of conflicting commands. It is derived rather from that part of the word of God which expresses what a heart rightly related to God and other men must do in the given situation. That the selfish in- terests of men are formally expressed in a vow does not transform their pur- suit into the will of God. God demands, not the formal observance of stat- utes, but a heart in tune with his will. The biblical command which gives expression to that demand is called "the word of God"; that which stands in its way can only be ordinances of men.

Hence, though in a given instance Jesus may have attacked the traditions of the scribes for conflicting with the word of God in terms reminiscent of

the Sadducaic critique, the motivation behind his polemic was apparently a
different one: it lay, not in a distinction between statutes which are scriptural and those which are only scribal, but in an impatience with a statutory codification of the divine will which obscured the demands God makes
on the heart.

We may now return to the question whether vv. 6–8 or vv. 9–13 represent Jesus'
answer to the charge in v. 5. Against vv. 9–13 it might be argued that handwashing (v. 5) does not involve the "setting aside" of a divine command in
favour of the tradition, which appears to be the thrust of the argument in
vv. 9–13.[96] But the point of the answer need only be that a tradition which
could do so in one case has no binding force in another. In favour of the
supposition that vv. 9–13 were from the beginning transmitted together with
the charge in v. 5 is the fact that the former speak of "your tradition"
(vv. 9, 13) in a way which seems to presuppose an earlier, more explicit
reference to the "tradition of the elders" (v. 5). When we add to this the
considerations (in themselves, not decisive) mentioned above for seeing vv.
6–8 as secondary here, it seems best to assume that vv. 9–13 represent
Jesus' actual answer.[97] It is of course possible that he faced a similar
charge on more than one occasion, and that separate answers have here been
combined. But it is perhaps more likely that he answered as in 7:9–13; to
this vv. 6–8 were added, either from church polemic, or from an attack
Jesus himself made against the Pharisees for hypocrisy, v. 8 being shaped
to adapt the quotation to its present context.

c. A Paradox Spoken to the Crowd (Mk. 7:14f.)

The scene in Mk. continues with a summons to the crowd (v. 14a), a demand
for careful attention (v. 14b), and a mashal in which it is stated that
nothing external is capable of defiling a person by entering him, whereas
that which comes from within can. We will first consider (i) the genuineness
of the mashal before taking up (ii) its setting and (iii) significance.

(i) V. 15 is widely (though not universally) regarded as an authentic
logion.[98] Perhaps the reason most often given in recent literature for this
view is that the verse meets the "criterion of dissimilarity": it can neither be derived from Judaism nor ascribed to the early church.[99] Interestingly enough, the same principle has recently been invoked for denying the
verse's authenticity: Berger argues that the position stated here does not
at all go beyond what was possible in the Judaism of that period, but is in
fact close to, and derived from, the views of Hellenistic Judaism.[100]

Hübner has replied by again affirming the uniqueness and, consequently, authenticity of our text;[101] in fact (as we suggested in the Introduction), this criterion is of very limited value in affirming or denying the authenticity of the words of an historical figure.[102] Other criteria must be sought. The following considerations based on the criteria developed in the Introduction are suggested; their cumulative witness at least would seem to be decisive.

In content, the mashal is at least consistent with what we know about Jesus (criterion of coherence).[103] He must have held some such view as the one here expressed; otherwise he could not have been so indifferent to considerations of ritual purity as we have seen him to be. Consistent, too, with his teaching is the concentration on what is within a man, tracing the root of all evil to "what is inside", i.e. to the disposition of the heart. Montefiore remarks aptly of our text, "There is no reason whatever why he should not have said it, and much reason why he should."[104]

In form, the mashal is typical of what we know about the teaching of Jesus (criterion of style). This is scarcely conclusive in itself - others could have imitated the same form - but it is telling nonetheless. Here we have a mashal of one who was known to teach with meshalim,[105] in the form of antithetic parallelism which characterizes the words of Jesus in all the gospel sources.[106]

Moreover, both the form and content of the mashal are such as to guarantee that, if any of Jesus' words were ever preserved by his disciples, these would have been (criterion of pregnant speech). Meshalim were formulated so as to be easy to remember,[107] and this certainly applies to our text: it is concise, rhythmic, includes a play on words,[108] and is formulated (surely purposefully) in a paradoxical way which invites, even demands, that the words be remembered, reflected upon, and applied.[109] Moreover, the startling nature of what Jesus here says with all its implications make it almost incredible that neither he nor his disciples would have taken the trouble to see to it that it was remembered.

Finally, it should be noted that we do in fact have evidence that the verse was recalled, commented upon, and applied in the halakhic disputes of the early church.[110] Whether or not we understand all of vv. 18-23 as such an application, it seems clear that v. 19c ("declaring all food clean") does draw an halakhic conclusion.[111] Paul, too, was "persuaded in the Lord Jesus that nothing is unclean of itself" (Rom. 14:14). It seems more reasonable to assume that he who claimed to be an apostle of Jesus Christ, who felt himself to be "under the law of Christ" (1 Cor. 9:21; cf. Gal. 6:2), who does cite the words of Jesus in other halakhic contexts (1 Cor. 7:10f.; 9:14), and who seems to emphasize the connection between this conviction and the historic person of his Lord[112] is here referring to the _mashal_ in our text than to think that he came independently[113] to the same revolutionary conclusion.

The problem remains that, if Jesus is the source of the _mashal_ in v. 15, it is difficult to understand the controversies in the early church related to table fellowship with Gentiles (Acts 11:3; Gal. 2:11ff.) and the eating of meat offered to idols (1 Cor. 8).[114] Jesus here appears to do away with considerations of ritual purity; how could the church have hesitated in the matter? But the church's reaction is perhaps not so strange. Jesus' statement is made in general terms; it may very well have been made in connection with some such controversy as the one mentioned in vv. 1-5. It is thus not surprising that the church did not universally see its implications in widely different circumstances, or draw the same conclusions as to what those implications should be, especially since Jesus himself seems to have generally confined his mission to the Jews (cf. Mt. 10:6; 15:24), and the eating of meat offered to idols was problematical for reasons other than ritual purity - reasons which made even Paul hesitate on the question (cf. 1 Cor. 10:14ff.). Even reservations on the part of certain Christians about eating food unclean by the standards of Leviticus (cf. Acts 10:14) are not quite incomprehensible. That Jesus' statement would in time lead to the doing away of such distinctions was perhaps inevitable. But even if we grant that such a development was in line with his conscious intention, we must admit that there is no record of his explicitly attacking or openly violating the O.T. laws as to which foods could be eaten. He may have thought the point of relatively little importance - not even Paul was prepared to press it (cf. Rom. 14); and Jesus does seem to have confined his attacks on the piety which concentrated on the formal observance of the law to the abuses to which such a view led (cf. Mt. 6:16-18; 23:23 par., etc.). What we have here is a general statement, the implications of which seem clear to us, as, indeed, they did for Mark (7:19c) and Paul (Rom. 14:14), but, in the absence of any specific application to the laws of Lev. 11, may not have been immediately so clear for the whole church.

(ii) Mark places the _mashal_ in connection with the handwashing dispute. Whether or not it was first stated then is of minor importance; its general character means that it has implications ranging far beyond that limited question. It is in fact as logical a setting as any, though any dispute concerned with ritual purity could have occasioned it.[115] It is less likely that it was given to the disciples in connection with their commissioning, indicating that they might feel free to eat whatever they were offered (cf. Lk. 10:7f; Thomas 14). If the connection with vv. 1-13 is secondary, it would have been brought about by the question common to both passages: what really defiles a man?[116]

(iii) Whether or not v. 15 is connected with the preceding, it has important consequences for our subject.

After saying that the mashal implicitly goes against the O.T. food laws, it is perhaps labouring the obvious to say that it also goes against Pharisaic halakhah on the subject of ritual purity. But the point is not without significance. The careful application of the laws of purity, together with those of tithing, seems in this period to have been characteristic of the Pharisees. Jesus' statement places him outside the boundaries of that movement, rejecting one of its major concerns.[117]

Moreover, Jesus' presuppositions here are different from those of the sages of the halakhah. We cannot be sure if Jesus really intended to do away with the O.T. laws of ritual purity. Probably he did not. Semitic idiom does permit, in the emphasis of one aspect of a matter, its opposite to be denied categorically, even though the denial, taken by itself, goes further than the speaker's intentions.[118] This may well apply to Mk. 7:15a; the sense would then be, "A man is not so much defiled by that which enters him from outside as he is by that which comes from within." Further, we must be on our guard against using a statement polemical in nature and paradoxical in expression to reconstruct anything like a systematic theology.[119] Nonetheless, while, for the Pharisees, the divine origin and statutory nature of scriptural law meant that every provision had to be applied and observed, and none was more binding than another, Jesus certainly treated this area of O.T. law with what, from the Pharisaic point of view, could only be regarded as indifference: he apparently made no effort to apply it, but concentrated rather on matters more decisive for "purity" before God.

Not only his understanding of scriptural commands differed from that of the Pharisees, but also his statement of the will of God. He supplied no exhaustive guidelines as to proper behaviour. Unlike the world of externals - of pots and pans and unclean hands - the disposition of the heart is scarcely accessible to the definitions of halakhah; yet it is in the realm of the heart, in what "comes from within", that God's will is ultimately obeyed or broken. Hence, the "rule" which Jesus stated here with regard to true purity is left open, paradoxical, capable of providing guidance but lacking the precise applications of halakhah. Halakhic rules are neither the prerequisite, nor their observance the guarantee, of a heart right before God.

Finally, we should note that there is no suggestion on the part of Jesus that he intended to enunciate a new principle, institute a new law, or consciously revoke an old one. He was concerned only with defining the true nature of impurity. A man is defiled rather by what comes from within than by external things. Nothing suggests that anything else was true in the past.

d. An Explanation Given to the Disciples (7:17-23)

The explanation given to the disciples is almost universally judged to be secondary. Some of the reasons for this judgment seem quite insufficient. We may consider the matter briefly in the light of the criteria for non-authenticity suggested in the Introduction.

It might be thought that the whole section, following an important logion in v. 15, represents the church's reflection over, and application of, the words of Jesus (criterion of derivative speech). Certainly this appears to be true of v. 19c, which syntactically as well as logically represents a parenthesis in the argument. It may well be true of the list in vv. 21f. as well, since such lists are characteristic of the catechetical teaching of the church (a variant of the criterion of style).[120] Furthermore, v. 18a is so typical of Mark (cf. 4:13; 6:52; 8:17, etc.) that we may well attribute it to him.

On the other hand, it is not self-evident[121] that gospel material presented as private instruction for the disciples can automatically be taken to be the creation of the church. It seems reasonable to assume that already the disciples of Jesus would have wanted his somewhat paradoxical, but clearly important, statement more fully explained. Nor is it obvious that the interpretation is incompatible with Jesus' words, unduly rationalizing, even vulgarizing his statement.[122] It identifies the centre of true purity and impurity as the heart; what does not reach the heart cannot defile; what comes from the heart does. This seems consonant with the teaching of Jesus.

We cannot be certain; it is not likely that the explanation of a mashal would be preserved as exactly as the mashal itself in any case. But we must at least allow for the possibility that these verses contain, not only the reflections of the early church and its adaptations of the words of Jesus, but also the substance of the Master's own explanation.

4. On Cleansing Vessels Inside and Out (Mt. 23:25f. par.)

Finally, we must examine one of the most difficult logia in the gospel tradition, that concerning the cleansing of vessels in Mt. 23:25f. par. Lk. 11:39-41 (cf. also Thomas 89). Certainty in its interpretation cannot be attained, and it is fortunate that Jesus' view of purity can be reconstructed from clearer texts. Yet what we are able to learn from this text is quite consistent with that view, and confirms our understanding of it.

a. The Original Logion

Despite considerable differences in the Matthaean and Lukan versions, it is clear that the same logion lies at the root of both. In Mt. it is the fifth of seven "woes" (23:13-36) directed against the scribes and Pharisees; in Lk. it is not a "woe", but precedes a series of six "woes" divided between the Pharisees (11:42-44) and scribes (vv. 46-52).[123] The wording is not particularly close in the two versions, and may at times show different translations (possibly even mistranslations) of an Aramaic text. It is clear that our saying was very early a part of the Palestinian tradition.[124]

In Mt., the saying is quite intelligible - unfortunatly, in more than one way. The "scribes and Pharisees" are said to cleanse the outside of cups and dishes, the insides of which (the subject of γέμουσιν must be the vessels) are "full of extortion and intemperance". They are told to cleanse first the inside in order that the outside also may be clean. One possibility is that the vessels "full of extortion and intemperance" represent the scribes and Pharisees themselves, and the reference to cleansing specially the inside of the vessel, while conforming to one view of scribal law, is only a metaphor suggesting that if the heart is clean, externals will automatically be clean.[125] Alternatively, it may be that the vessels are said to contain what has been gained by[126] extortion and greed; the command then would be to see to it that the contents are honestly gained, and then the vessel may be considered clean.[127]

In Lk., matters are still less clear. It is certain that the Pharisees themselves are said to be full of extortion and evil (v. 39). But v. 40 is capable of quite different renderings: "Did not he (God) who made the outside (i.e. material things, or perhaps the human body) make the inside (i.e. the heart of men) as well (i.e. ought one not to be at least as concerned for the purity of the latter as for that of the former)?" or (less probably), "He who has dealt with (i.e. cleansed) the outside has not (thereby) dealt with (i.e. cleansed) the inside."[128] Furthermore, the reference to alms in v. 41 is in this context jarring, to say the least.

If we are to come to some understanding of what the underlying statement meant, we must compare the two forms, deciding at critical points which is more likely to represent the original.

(i) In both gospels, there are introductory words placing the logion in its context. Matthew's "Woe to you, scribes and Pharisees, hypocrites!" adapts the saying to his series of woes, but is probably not an original part of our logion.[129] Lk. introduces it as the answer to a certain Pharisee who had invited Jesus for a meal, but was perplexed by the fact that he did not wash (presumably his hands, as in Mk. 7) before eating. This is a possible enough setting, but is likely only a frame supplied by Lk.[130]

(ii) In both Mt. and Lk., the point is made that Pharisees (in Mt. "Pharisees and scribes", as throughout the series of "woes", but the reference to "scribes" is probably secondary here[131]) cleanse the outside of a cup (τὸ ἔξωθεν τοῦ ποτηρίου) and dish (here Mt. and Lk. exhibit a translation variant?); at this point it is clear that both accounts have a common root.

(iii) This concern for externals is then contrasted with the state inside, which is full of "extortion" (ἁρπαγή, both Mt. and Lk.) and "incontinence" (Mt. ἀκρασία) or "evil" (Lk. πονηρία). Three possibilities for the meaning of the original suggest themselves.

First, the vessels may be said to contain what has been gained by wicked means. This is a possible reading of Mt.; if original, Lk. has misunderstood or altered it by adding ὑμῶν, thus applying the saying to the Pharisees themselves.

Second, the vessels, used as a metaphor for the Pharisees themselves, may be said to be full of wickedness. This is perhaps a somewhat violent metaphor, but a possible reading of Mt. If original, Lk. would have understood it correctly and, by adding ὑμῶν, destroyed the metaphor but made the intention clear.

Third, the Pharisees themselves may be said, without metaphor, to be full of wickedness; so Lk. Mt. misunderstood (perhaps supplying the wrong subject for an Aramaic participle[132]), thinking the vessels themselves (literally or metaphorically) were meant.

The third alternative is unlikely: why would it be explicitly said that the Pharisees clean the outside of the vessel (so both Mt. and Lk.) if a contrast with the state of its inside (literally or metaphorically) were not forthcoming?[133] The first alternative, though quite possibly Matthew's understanding of the saying, is probably also to be rejected as the meaning of the original. If Lk. 11:40 belonged to the original (cf. also Thomas 89), this understanding is impossible. Moreover, the conclusion of the saying, which seems to have been preserved best in Mt., is slightly more awkward by this interpretation: τὸ ἐντός must then refer to the contents of the cup, gained by robbery and greed; but the inside of the cup itself, as a metaphor for the human heart, would seem a more suitable object for "cleansing" than such dishonest gain. The second alternative seems best to account for the differences in the form of the saying, and provides good sense. We suggest the saying claimed that the vessels (= the Pharisees) are full of evil, and Lk. made the implied reference to the hearts of the Pharisees more apparent.

(iv) The opponents are then addressed, in Lk. as "Fools!", in Mt. as "Blind Pharisee!" (cf. vv. 16, 24; also 15:14), curiously in the singular. If not the result of an error in transmission, the singular may indicate that the saying originally had a different context and has been imperfectly adapted to the "woes".

(v) Lk. alone has the problematical v. 40. The meaning is probably that, since God created the heart of man as well as material things, its purity, too, should be a subject of concern. It may be that Mt. ohitted it, finding it perplexing or unsuitable in the context as he understood it.[134]

(vi) The common reference to the "inside" makes it clear that we are still dealing with two versions of one saying. Mt. is certainly more appropriate, and probably original: the inside of the vessel is to be cleansed. Lk. can scarcely be original, though we may leave open the question whether the reference to alms is based on a mistranslation[135] or simply represents the introduction of a favourite Lukan theme (the proper use of money; cf. Lk. 12:13ff.; 16:1ff., 19ff., etc.).[136]

(vii) Here again it is clear that the two texts have a common root: the result of the action prescribed in (vi) is that the whole cup (so Mt.; Lk. "everything") will be clean.

What may we conclude? Despite the uncertainties brought about by imperfect transmission and redactional activity, there is here evidence that, among the early traditions of sayings of Jesus, there was one in which he criticized the Pharisees for cleansing the outside of vessels but not being so concerned about the inside, by which he undoubtedly meant the human heart. Before we raise the question if the saying can go back to Jesus, we must look briefly at Pharisaic practice on this point.

b. Pharisaic Practice

Already in the O.T. we find references to the defilement of everyday vessels as well as prescriptions for their cleansing where this was possible (Lev. 11:32ff.; 15:12; Num. 19:15, 18). When, for example, a dead animal designated unclean among those "crawling on the ground" fell into any vessel, the vessel became unclean. If it was earthenware, it must be broken; otherwise it must be immersed in water, then left until evening when it became clean (Lev. 11:32f.). It is thus not surprising that, among the Pharisaic practices related to purity, we find the cleansing of vessels (cf. Mk. 7:4; Mt. 23:25f. par.); their concern for the matter is confirmed by rabbinic tradition, in which certain texts mentioning legal discussions or decisions apparently from the period before 70 (e.g. Sifra to Lev. 11:33; M. Mik. 5.6) or shortly afterwards (e.g. M. Kel. 14.7; 17.1, etc.) assume that everyday utensils, when defiled, must be purified, and discuss only details of their defilement or purification.[137]

Among such details may be mentioned the distinction which was drawn between the inside and outside of a vessel, perhaps on the basis of the reference to a vessel's "inside" in Lev. 11:33.[138] This distinction was established long before R. Tarfon and R. Akiva, at approximately the beginning of the second century, spoke of still a third part of the vessel, that by which it is held (M. Kel. 25.7); in fact, the division between outer and inner is assumed in a testimony given before Gamaliel the Elder in Sifra to Lev. 11:33, as well as in a debate between the Houses of Shammai and Hillel mentioned in J. Ber. 8.2. And, as we have seen, it is implied by the original saying lying behind Mt. 23:25f. par., since cleansing the outside of vessels is specifically mentioned in both Mt. and Lk., and Mt. seems to preserve the original saying with his "First cleanse the inside of the cup."

The distinction drawn by the Pharisaic scribes between the inside and outside of a vessel has not only possible biblical support in Lev. 11:33, but also definite practical advantages: it makes it possible for one part of

the vessel to remain clean even if the other part becomes unclean.[139] Thus,
if the outside of a vessel becomes unclean, its inside (and what it contains)
is not necessarily affected (cf. M. Kel. 25.6). In the debate of J. Ber.
8.2,[140] the view of Bet Hillel is that the uncleanness of the outside of a
vessel is without significance; hence, even hands which have not yet been
washed may touch the outside of a cup; should moisture (which usually com-
municates uncleanness) come in contact with the hands, run off via the outer
part of the vessel to another part (i.e. the inside, or the part by which it
is held), no uncleanness from the outer part is communicated to that other
part. According to Bet Shammai, however, the outside of a vessel can have
significance for the uncleanness of another part in this case: moisture
which comes in contact with unclean hands and runs off via the outer part
to another part of the vessel does contaminate it. Thus the hands must be
washed before coming in contact with a cup.

The usual view that the Shammaites were dominant in the pre-70 period seems
to be confirmed by Mt. 23:25f. par.: if the Houses were already divided on
this question in the way reflected in J. Ber. 8.2, then the statement that
the Pharisees "cleanse the outside of the vessel" may refer specifically
to Shammaite practice, since they alone would devote special attention to
the outside of a vessel.[141]

To such people, concerned about the cleanness of the outside of a vessel,
our logion speaks metaphorically: cleanse the inside of the vessel, and the
outside will be clean of itself. This, interpreted literally of a vessel,[142]
corresponds roughly to the position of the Hillelites: the cleanness of the
inside of a vessel is important, that of the outside is indifferent. But
in fact neither side of the halakhic discussion is affirmed or denied. The
point here is moral: if the heart is clean, all else will be clean as well.

c. The Question of Authenticity

Can the saying behind Mt. 23:25f. par. be assigned to Jesus?

Certainly it is consistent with what we have seen of his assessment of Pharisaic ritual elsewhere: while not condemning such observances directly, he
assigned them little significance for one's relationship with God. The
cleanness of the "inside" itself guarantees the cleanness of the "outside".
No distinction is drawn between scriptural and scribal regulations related
to the cleansing of vessels; the matter itself is treated with indifference.
In this respect, the original setting for our saying is more likely to be
found in the ministry of Jesus than in the early Palestinian church, many

of whose members were "zealous for the law" (Acts 21:20; cf. Gal. 2:12f.).
Consistent, too, with the teaching of Jesus is the insistence that what
really matters is the condition of the heart (cf. Mk. 7:15).

On the other hand, the reference to "extortion and intemperance (or "evil")"
which is said to fill the vessels (i.e. the Pharisees) is somewhat jarring:
if meant as a blanket condemnation, it does not seem warranted by what we
know about the Pharisees. Such a charge is of course problematical whether
we assign the saying to Jesus or to the early church; but perhaps it can
best be explained as a retort prompted by some specific occasion during the
life of Jesus, its sting being directed towards the particular Pharisees
encountered.

Finally, the authenticity of the saying ought not to be denied because it
is found "legalistic", even Pharisaic.[143] Not only does it demand that purity of the heart match the external purity Pharisees strive for, a senti-
ment with which a pious Pharisee would certainly agree; it also appears to
say that the purity of the heart alone matters, it being determinative for
the purity of the outside ("so that the outside may be clean as well"). And
this a Pharisee could scarcely accept. If the purity of the heart alone
matters, one's standing before God may be quite independent of one's observance of the laws of ritual purity, be they scriptural or scribal.

The probability, then, is that an authentic logion is at the root of Mt.
23:25f.[144] In any case, it provides confirmation for our reconstruction
of Jesus' view of purity, coming as it does either from Jesus himself or
from an early follower who had grasped his view of the matter.

C. CONCLUSIONS

It seems apparent that Jesus was not a Pharisee,[145] and that he did not recognize scribal authority as binding. Characteristic of the Pharisees of
this period was an earnest effort to practise the biblical laws of tithing
and ritual purity as they were defined and developed by their halakhic tradition. But Jesus offended Pharisaic sensitivities by eating with those
with whom Pharisees (and the self-respecting am ha-arez) refused to eat. On
one occasion he sharply distinguished the scribal tradition from the words
of scripture in order to condemn the former. On another he apparently expressed the view that Pharisaic attempts to purify vessels had no value. In
general, Pharisees could not but have been appalled by what they considered
to be his indifference towards parts of the law of God.

We can, however, go further: not only must Jesus be placed outside the bounds
of the Pharisaic movement of his time because of repeated displays of indifference towards details of Pharisaic law, indeed, violations of their
laws and polemic directed against them; it seems clear that he conceived the
will of God and the nature of biblical law in a different fashion. What appeared to be true in the case of tithing has been confirmed in the matter of
ritual purity: whereas Pharisaic halakhah found the will of God in the divinely ordained statutes of scripture, all of which had to be carefully
obeyed, Jesus' shows an apparent indifference towards certain aspects of
scriptural law. It is not sufficient to say that he, like the Sadducees, rejected scribal additions to scriptural law; with the exception of the polemic connected with the handwashing dispute, he made no attempt to distinguish the two. His repeated statements that purity is an inner, not external, matter make the observance of scriptural rules of ritual purity for
their own sake as religiously indifferent as was, for the Sadducees, the observance of scribal halakhah. Hence, his attacks against the tradition are
not motivated by the view that it is extrabiblical and thus lacking in authority, but by a fundamentally different conception of the will of God.

Jesus did not define the will of God in terms of the careful fulfilment of
scripture's statutes; for him, the attitude of the heart was critical. It
was (we may repeat) important for the Pharisees, too, but they felt bound
to observe every provision of scriptural law. Jesus' assessment of their
practices in the field of ritual purity shows an awareness of the same two
dangers we noted in connection with tithing: that the punctilious observance
of such concrete commands as those regarding tithing and ritual purity may
easily become a preoccupation overshadowing the demands placed on the heart,
which are less susceptible to halakhic definition; further, that the observance of such commands may become too facile a criterion for distinguishing
the pious from their "sinful" neighbours. The categories of _haver_ and _am
ha-arez_, apparently necessary for the careful observance of biblical commands, can only have contributed to this latter danger. Jesus, who found
the will of God not in statutes but in a heart in tune with the divine purposes, avoided these dangers, but inevitably offended the proponents of
halakhah in the process.

Chapter VII
Sabbath

Perhaps nowhere do we see more clearly the essential characteristics of the
Pharisaic halakhah, and the fundamental differences of Jesus' approach,
than in connection with the sabbath. Here, on the one hand, the Pharisaic
halakhah on a number of points can be related both to its scriptural base
and to non-Pharisaic sectarian practice in an illuminating fashion; on the
other hand, whatever problems may remain about details of the gospel narratives, the main features of Jesus' conflicts with the Pharisees over the
sabbath law are generally agreed upon. We begin our study with a look at
the sabbath halakhah.

A. BACKGROUND

The basis of the sabbath halakhah is, of course, to be found in scripture.
A number of texts insist that no "work" be done on the seventh day (e.g.
Ex. 20:10; 31:14f.; 35:2). But if such a prohibition was to have statutory
force, it required further definition and precision; the forbidden activities had to be spelled out. Already in Jubilees we have short lists of
this kind (2:29f.; 50:6ff.).[1] The so-called "Damascus Document" of the
Qumran sect provides an example of a more substantial sabbath code (CD
10.14-11.18). In the course of time, rabbinic schools would draw up still
more comprehensive lists.[2]

Some activities were explicitly forbidden by Torah: lighting a fire was one
(Ex. 35:3). Naturally, the biblical prohibition was observed by non-Pharisaic as well as Pharisaic groups (cf. Jos. War 2.147); typically, Pharisaic
schools discussed how the prohibition could be observed with a minimum of
hardship. Thus ways were found for keeping food warm without actually lighting a fire on the sabbath: stoves (the permissible types were defined) could
be preheated but kept warm om the sabbath (regulations regarding fuels were
added) so that hot water (and cooked food; but the latter was debated) could
be set on them (only the Hillelites allowed that which had been warmed to
be removed from the stove and set back again) (M. Shab. 3.1f.). Moreover,
the Pharisaic schools discussed the circumstances under which it was permitted to cover warm food so that it would retain its heat (M. Bez. 2.6; cf.
M. Shab. 4.1f.).

Ex. 16:29 forbids the Israelite to leave "his place" on the seventh day. A prohibition of travel might also be derived from Isa. 58:13 ("If you keep back your foot from the sabbath... if you honour it by refraining from making your journeyings..."). Again, the biblical basis of the prohibition assured its widespread observance. Jubilees forbids going on a journey (50:12) without defining the matter more closely. In Josephus we note that Jews in military action refused to march on the sabbath (Ant. 13.252; 14.226). Still, if the prohibition was to have statutory force, a definition of what constituted a forbidden journey was necessary. The idea of a fixed distance from the edge of one's city (so one's "place" in Ex. 16:29 was interpreted) within which one was permitted to move about on the sabbath was adopted early.[3] It was accepted at Qumran, where, however, the usual distance of 2000 cubits (apparently derived from the 2000 cubits of pasture-land which Num. 35:5 attaches to each town; cf. M. Sot. 5.3) was allowed only if one was giving pasture to an animal; otherwise 1000 cubits was the limit.[4] Archaeological finds reveal that the distance of 2000 cubits from the city wall of Gezer was marked off by boundary stones probably from the time of Herod.[5] Acts 1:12 speaks of a "sabbath day's journey" which amounted to approximately 2000 cubits.[6] Moreover, Gamaliel ordained that witnesses who had come to Jerusalem to report on the appearance of the new moon might be allowed the privilege of the city's inhabitants, namely, to walk 2000 cubits in any direction (M.R.H. 2.5).[7] It is clear from his ordinance and from the further development of Pharisaic-rabbinic halakhah that the idea of a sabbath day's journey was a basic part of the Pharisaic sabbath code. In the course of time, the sages would add further definitions and introduce legal fictions, permitting even that distance to be exceeded (M. Er. 5.1ff.; 8.1f.).[8]

According to Jer. 17:21f., God commanded that no burden be carried on the sabbath, that nothing be brought through the gate of Jerusalem nor taken out of one's house. Josephus tells us that the Essenes were more rigorous in this regard than other Jews, and would not move any vessel on the sabbath (War 2.147). This is, indeed, stricter than the standards we find even in Jubilees and the Damascus Document, but may be a somewhat misleading ab-breviation of the regulations in those texts. Josephus tells us as well that Jews as a rule refused to carry arms on the sabbath (Life 161; Ag. Ap. 1.209; Ant. 14.226). Not surprisingly, "Jews" object in John's gospel when a healed man carries his bed on the sabbath (5.8ff.).[9]

Apparently at an early period, the command that burdens not be borne out

of one's house on the sabbath (Jer. 17:22) gave rise to a distinction between one's private domain and the public domain, and the rule was formulated that nothing was to be borne from one domain to another, though it
was permissible to bear at least some vessels within the confines of one's
private domain. The distinction is perhaps implied already in Jubilees,
which forbids that a man take up "any burden to carry it out of his tent or
out of his house" (50:8; cf. 2:30). It is at any rate clear in CD 11.7-9:
"Let no man take out (on the sabbath) anything from the house outside, or
from outside into a house. Even if he be in a booth (for Tabernacles), let
him not take anything out of it or bring anything into it."

The distinction was not, then, a peculiarly Pharisaic one, and probably antedated the beginnings of the Pharisaic movement. But it was clearly essential
to the further development of Pharisaic-rabbinic halakhah.[10) The Mishnaic
tractates Shabbat and Eruvin show how distinctions were drawn between ornaments which could be worn when "going out" (i.e. into the public domain)
and burdens which could not be carried (M. Shab. 5.1-6.10); moreover, they
show how unusual ways of carrying and the sharing of burdens were allowed
so that the letter of the law could be observed while its effects were circumvented (M. Shab. 10.2ff.). Above all, they show how, already in the pre-
70 period,[11) the principle of "amalgamations" (eruvin) was adopted, by
which various private "domains" in a single courtyard could be combined
into one large private "domain" within which vessels could be borne.

Another important matter discussed already in the pre-70 period was the
various circumstances which took precedence over the sabbath and permitted
exceptions to its laws. Again, scripture itself provided a base. All parties
accepted the principle that the service of the temple took precedence over
the sabbath,[12) for which the scriptural warrant is clear (Num. 28:9f.; 1
Chr. 23:31, etc.). According to a famous story, Hillel argued that the passover sacrifice takes precedence over the sabbath, and claimed that his
teachers taught the same (T. Pes. 4.13f.). Scripture taught that circumcision was to be performed on the eighth day (Lev. 12:3); there can be no
doubt that it was allowed by Pharisees and non-Pharisees alike when the
eighth day fell on a sabbath.[13) Furthermore, witnesses to the new moon were
permitted to exceed the sabbath limits to bring word to the court in Jerusalem (M.R.H. 1.4).[14)

According to 1 Macc. 2:29ff., the decision was reached by Mattathias and
his friends after a catastrophe in which 1000 Jews were slaughtered without

defending themselves on the sabbath, that they would offer resistance if attacked on the sabbath. This seems afterwards to have been the policy of Jewish forces.[15] It has been suggested that the principle, well-known from rabbinic sources, that the sabbath may be disregarded where human life is in danger (M. Yom. 8.6; Mek. to Ex. 31:13) dates from the period of the Maccabees.[16]

This brings us to a question of some importance for our study: did the Pharisees permit healing on the sabbath? It can scarcely be doubted that the principle "wherever there is doubt whether life is in danger, this over-rides the sabbath" would have been applied by the Pharisees. But in cases where life was not in danger, the matter is not so clear. According to M. Shab. 6.10, it was a subject of debate at the time of Meir if various "means of healing" (a locust's egg, a jackal's tooth, a nail used in a crucifixion) could be carried on the sabbath; the only objection raised is that the cus-tom of wearing such items is pagan. In any case, their "curative" powers were not dependent on any act of healing which was performed on the sabbath. On the other hand, M. Shab. 14.3f.[17] prohibits taking certain medicines on the sabbath, allowing only such as, while having medicinal value, can be re-garded as food as well. Thus the act of taking medicine to be healed is for-bidden on the sabbath (cf. also M. Shab. 22.6; M. Eduy. 2.5). The same basic principle is seen in the fact that an exception was made allowing medicine to be taken when life was in danger. Even if the latter phrase was later given a most liberal interpretation (M. Yom. 8.6; B. Yom. 84a-85b), it is clear that, as a general rule, medicine was not to be taken on the sabbath when life was not in danger.

Similarly, an exception was made which allowed plaster to be replaced on a wound in the temple on the sabbath, and a priest to cover a wounded finger with reed-grass in the temple (M. Er. 10.13f.). Clearly the general rule prohibited such activities. Furthermore, we know that Bet Shammai opposed praying for (T. Shab. 16.22) and visiting (B. Shab. 12a) the sick on the sabbath, apparently because such actitivity was out of character with the sabbath as a day of joy. None of these cases is an exact parallel to Jesus' healings, and it may be doubted that the halakhah was formulated in speci-fic terms which covered his activities.[18] But it seems reasonable to assume that Pharisees would oppose such action where life was not in danger;[19] and this, of course, corresponds with what we find in the gospels.

A number of further details might be mentioned, but the general character of the Pharisaic sabbath halakhah has been sufficiently shown. It was based on scripture, though the view that the laws of scripture were statutes whose terms were to be interpreted and applied, and the methodological rigour which characterized the discussion of the Pharisaic schools,[20] led to a plethora of rules out of all proportion to the scriptural base. Typically, the extrabiblical character of many regulations was recognized (cf. M. Hag. 1.8), legislators were at times identified (e.g. M.R.H. 2.5), the schools held their characteristic views, and apparently met on occasion for the taking of votes (cf. M. Shab. 1.4). Here as elsewhere Pharisaic halakhah represents a synthesis of human and divine law.

That being said, the lenient tendency of Pharisaic halakhah in comparison with that of other groups must be noted. As we have seen, the Pharisees went much further than other groups in making the sabbath laws practicable and humane.[21] Furthermore, however complicated their halakhah may appear to us, there is no reason to doubt that faithful Pharisees found the sabbath a day to be honoured and celebrated with joy, not a burden impossible to be borne.[22]

B. JESUS AND THE SABBATH

Before we turn to the narratives of Jesus' conflicts with the Pharisees over the sabbath, the limitation of their scope should be pointed out. With one exception (Mk. 2:23-28 par.), they concern healing on the sabbath. Moreover, we do know that Jesus frequented the synagogue on the sabbath and often took part in the synagogue service (Mk. 1:21 par., 39 par.; 3:1 par.; 6:2 par., etc.). There is thus no reason to believe that Jesus actively and systematically opposed sabbath regulations, be their origin scriptural or scribal, for their own sake. On the contrary, the lack of evidence for conflicts on other matters should probably be interpreted as indicating that his conduct was not found exceptionable.[23] But cases of opposition did arise; their nature, and the nature of Jesus' defence, tell us much about his approach to the biblical command and its scribal interpretation.

1. Sabbath Reaping (Mk. 2:23-28 par.)

Though this pericope has been the subject of intensive study,[24] a consensus has not been reached as to the history of the tradition. The following points, however, are generally agreed upon.

(i) The pericope is composite. The new introductory formula in v. 27 indicates either that this verse (and perhaps v. 28) have been added to what precedes,[25] or that vv. 25f. have been inserted between vv. 23f. and 27 (f.?), which at one stage of the tradition were together.[26]

(ii) Vv. 27 and 28 involve a <u>non sequitur</u> as they now stand. Either they represent a juxtaposition of two stages of the tradition with quite different meanings,[27] or the words "man" in v. 27 and "son of man" in v. 28 were originally synonymous, both rendering the same Aramaic phrase בר אנש.[28] In the latter case, both referred at one time either to "man" in general (the usual view), or to the Son of Man (so Manson, understanding the Son of Man as the community of disciples).[29]

(iii) V. 27 is an authentic logion of Jesus. On this point, though we must note some dissenting voices,[30] there seems to be a growing consensus.[31] Certainly the verse is consistent with what we know about Jesus, since he did heal on the sabbath, and seems to have regarded such healings, not as violations of the sabbath command, but as expressions of the sabbath's true meaning (cf. 3:4 par.).

The charge brought against the disciples of Jesus by the Pharisees in these verses is that they violate the sabbath by picking ears of corn (vv. 23f.).[32] This constituted reaping,[33] the prohibition of which has a biblical base (cf. Ex. 16:25f.; 34:21) and was certainly widely accepted (cf. Philo, Moses 2.22). Now it seems unlikely that vv. 25f., in which an answer to the charge is given, existed at any stage of the tradition independently of vv. 23f.[34] Not only are hunger (v. 25) and eating (v. 26) mentioned to correspond to what may be assumed from vv. 23f.,[35] but the words ποιεῖν (v. 25) and οὐκ ἔξεστιν (v. 26) take up the charge in v. 24. Furthermore, the answer stresses "those with him (i.e. with David)", whose partaking is not mentioned in 1 Sam. 21:2(1)ff., but is necessary for the parallel with v. 23. Thus, whether vv. 25f. originally belonged with vv. 23f. or were added to provide a further answer to the charge, they can only have been transmitted together with what precedes.

Vv. 25f. appear to be an halakhic argument justifying the conduct of the disciples. At times the argument is even said to be on a level with the legalistic discussions of the Pharisees,[36] and scarcely in line with Jesus' attitude towards the sabbath. On the other hand, it has often been pointed out that, as an halakhic argument, it is scarcely convincing:[37] it draws support, not from a scriptural precept, but from a narrative; further, from a narrative dealing, not with the violation of the sabbath, but with the eating of consecrated bread. Perhaps the question ought to be raised if vv. 25f. were even meant to serve as an halakhic argument.

The rabbis do mention David's evident violation of Lev. 24:9 in eating the consecrated bread; still, when they do so, they always introduce considerations which might legitimize his action and bring it in line with the halakhah:[38] David's violation of Torah thus became only an apparent one; in fact he behaved quite "lawfully". Since, in Mk. 2:25, it is related that David was "in need and hungry", it is often assumed that this was meant to serve as just such a legitimizing factor; but, though the words are clearly intended to motivate David's action, the claim is not made here that they constitute the legal grounds for justifying it. Nor, indeed, is the point made in connection with the disciples that they, too, being "in need", are within their legal rights in picking the ears of corn; there is no indication that their need was particularly great.[39] It is thus misleading to see the verses as an halakhic argument making the point that the sabbath laws are subordinate to the demands of human need in a kind of casuistic hierarchy,[40] and insisting that the disciples, like David, only did what is lawful. On the contrary, satisfaction is taken and an argument built on the very fact that David's action was unlawful: he ate "what is unlawful to eat" (v. 26). His action is not brought in line with Torah, but cited as a biblical example where the letter of Torah is broken. No Pharisaic argument, this!

Nor ought vv. 25f. to be read christologically. Matthew (12:5f.) inserts here another argument which is clearly christological:[41] the priests serving in the temple "violate" the sabbath without incurring guilt; it is implied that the disciples serving Jesus may also "violate" the sabbath and remain innocent, since "a greater than the temple is here", i.e. the Messiah.[42] But no such comparison is drawn here between David and Jesus; nor should one be assumed, since neither here nor in the rabbinic discussions of the incident is it suggested that David's office entitled him to behave as he did.[43] The argument is rather that David's action, though contrary to the letter of the law, is countenanced by scripture; it thus cannot be the intention of the divine lawgiver that the terms of Torah be interpreted rigidly and every deviation from such an interpretation condemned.[44] We may well ascribe the argument to Jesus, representing as it does the creative application in a new setting of the same inner logic which we have seen expressed in other authentic materials (criterion of coherence): a statutory understanding of scripture, which finds the divine will in the application of each provision of scripture's precepts, is rejected.[45] Jesus defends his disciples, not by showing that their action corresponds to a correct understanding of the halakhah, but by attacking the halakhic understanding of the divine will shown by those who rebuked them.

That this accurately represents the views of Jesus is proven by v. 27, which is best understood as a mashal formulated by Jesus in a memorable way, and summarizing his understanding of the sabbath. Its placing after the dispute in vv. 23-26 is indeed appropriate,[46)] though it would fit equally well in connection with one of the healing controversies. A positive attitude towards the sabbath is shown: the sabbath has been ordained by God (this is the implication of the "divine passive" ἐγένετο, "was made"), and that for the good of men. Thus the divine origin of the sabbath command is not disputed, but rather one way of interpreting it. Man was not made for the sabbath. This, in the context of Jesus' controversies with the Pharisees, must mean that God's intentions are not met by treating the sabbath command as a legal statute, defining in minutest detail what constitutes permitted and forbidden activities, and subjecting human behaviour to the resultant rules. For the Pharisees, what is primarily at stake in a given situation is whether or not man will obey what God has commanded. Jesus, however, sees the divine intention in the sabbath command, not as demanding obedience for its own sake, but as providing for the physical needs of men. Hence, the sabbath command is applied, not by the casuistic definition of each provision of a legal statute, but by considering how, in a given situation, men's needs may be met.

The fact that sayings similar to Mk. 2:27 are found in rabbinic writings (e.g. Mek. to Ex. 31:13) does not disprove the distinction we have drawn. It does show that the Pharisaic-rabbinic tradition was not insensitive to human need; that it did, in extreme cases, allow the sabbath command to be overriden. But the fundamental difference remains. For the Pharisees, even such a concession had to be formulated as a rule of halakhah, and behaviour patterned after the rule. Thus, for the rabbis, the words "Man is not given over to the sabbath" are used, not to justify violations of the halakhah, but to justify the halakhic principle that human life takes precedence over the sabbath laws. The case where human life is in danger thus finds satisfactory solution within the sphere of halakhah. The latter takes on a humane character, but man is still its subject. And the will of God is still seen as human submission to divine statutes. On the lips of Jesus, the words "Man was not made for the sabbath" affirm that the primary purpose of the command was the securing, not of human submission, but of human well-being. To subject man to a code of law based on the casuistic application of the command is to distort and defeat the divine purpose.

Conceivably, v. 28 may originally have restated the principle of v. 27: "Man is lord of the sabbath!" It is perhaps more likely that the verse was added within the Christian community as a conclusion to the section, affirming the right of its Lord to reinterpret the laws of the sabbath.[47]

2. Sabbath Healings

The controversies aroused by Jesus' healings on the sabbath belong to the bedrock of the gospel tradition.[48] It is apparent, to judge by the explicit statements of the gospel narratives (e.g. Mk. 3:1 par.) and by the opposition with which the healings met, that he acted on behalf of those suffering from chronic conditions which by no means threatened their lives. The Pharisees were prepared to allow the sabbath laws to be overriden in cases where life was in danger; they were appalled by the sabbath healings of Jesus. A detailed study of the various narratives[49] is not here required; of interest for our purposes are the various ways in which Jesus defended his actions.

In Mk. 3:1-6 par., Jesus heals a man with a withered hand, to the consternation of the Pharisees. In Mk. (3:4) and Lk. (6:9) he anticipates their reaction with an argument which is usually taken to be authentic[50] and is certainly consistent with what we have seen about Jesus' views of the halakhah. He formulates a question in terms familiar from Pharisaic legal discussion: "Is it permitted on the sabbath...?" The frame suggests a discussion of halakhah; the content, however, does not concern the application of the sabbath halakhah, but raises a moral question about the very propriety of that halakhah. The Pharisees apparently opposed healing on the sabbath where there was no immediate danger to life; the "lawful" thing to do in such a case was not to heal till the sabbath was over.[51] But Jesus draws a parallel between, on the one hand, healing, "doing good", and "restoring life", and, on the other, leaving such a man to suffer, "doing evil", and "destroying life",[52] and asks, "Is doing good (i.e. healing) the lawful thing to do on the sabbath, or doing evil (i.e. not healing)?" When the matter is put in this way, the halakhah is seen as condemning what is good and approving what is evil; it cannot possibly be in accord with God's will.[53] Jesus' words may even imply that there is a special appropriateness in healing on the sabbath, presumably because (as in 2:27) the sabbath was made for the well-being of man. Here we have but another example in which, for Jesus, the will of God is determined, not by reference to a code of regulations, be they scriptural or scribal, but by penetrating to the divine purpose.

Matthew preserves but a fragment of this argument (12:12b). Instead he offers another argument, taken from the tradition, around which Luke, too, has built a narrative (14:5, in 14:1-6). In Matthew's version (12:11-12a), Jesus asks if his hearers would neglect to draw up one of their sheep[54] from a pit into which it had fallen, even if it meant doing so on the sabbath; and "how much more valuable is a man than a sheep!" As in Mk. 2:25f. par.; 3:4 par., the argument here has a frame reminiscent of halakhic discussions: the case where an animal fell into a pit on the sabbath was in fact discussed by the rabbis (cf. T. Shab. 14.3). Still, closer examination reveals that the thinking here too is on a different plane. A sophisticated halakhic argument could be made of Mt. 12:11-12a if a common practice (drawing up sheep on the sabbath) were cited as a custom (minhag) having the force of law, which could then serve (kal vahomer) as a precedent for healing. And, to be sure, Matthew's version is somewhat more strictly argued than the Lukan parallel: it is made explicit that the consideration in Mt. 12:11 ought all the more to be applied where human well-being is at stake (12:12). Nonetheless, no more in Mt. than in Lk. is Jesus arguing the legality of the case.[55] The example of the sheep is not cited as a legal precedent, as though, since halakhic experts had decided that it was lawful to draw up the sheep (in fact, the opposite seems to have been the case; cf. T. Shab. 14.3), they ought also to permit healing a human being. The appeal is rather to actual practice, in which common sense and compassion rather than rules of halakhah must often have determined behaviour.[56] Jesus' intention is thus not to provide a sophisticated argument which will satisfy scribal objections, but to appeal to basic instincts of humanity, to challenge his hearers to take a position in the matter ("Which of you...?"), and so to silence and shame those who raise legalistic niceties in the face of human need.

Similarly, in Lk. 14:5, Jesus does not ask whether it is lawful to draw up a son (or ass?) or ox[57] who had fallen into a well,[58] but how, in practice, his hearers (among whom were certainly non-Pharisees) would behave. Whether we adopt Matthew's or Luke's form of the saying as the more original, the argument is clear: behaviour in certain cases is, commonly and rightly, not determined by reference to a casuistic law, but by a perception of need and feelings of compassion; should not such feelings be allowed to operate where human suffering is the issue?

In Lk. 13:15f.,[59) the common practice[60) of untying an ox or donkey and taking it out for water forms the basis of an argument that, like Mt. 12: 11-12a par., leaves the bounds of legal discussion and becomes an appeal for compassion: should not a daughter of Abraham also be "released" from the bonds of Satan on the sabbath?

Thus, in each of these cases (Mt. 12:11-12a par. Lk. 14:5; Lk. 13:15f.), Jesus defends his sabbath healings, not with legal arguments bringing them in line with Pharisaic or any other halakhah, but with appeals to compassion as a criterion for sabbath behaviour transcending casuistic regulations. It is a defence quite in line with his principles elsewhere; there is no reason to question its basic authenticity.[61)

C. CONCLUSIONS

We cannot speak of a systematic opposition on the part of Jesus to the sabbath halakhah for its own sake. The issues on which he opposed it were limited; further, there is no indication that his opposition was based on a distinction between regulations scribal in origin and those more directly traceable to scripture. It was rather a difference in his understanding of the divine will that led to conflict with the Pharisees.

The simple explanation that Jesus showed greater concern for the needs of men is insufficient. Certainly his approach to the sabbath command permitted him to go much further than Pharisaic halakhah in what we may call a humanitarian direction. But, as a comparison with the regulations of other groups has shown, the Pharisaic halakhah itself was, relatively speaking, a humane one. The essential difference is another. The Pharisees treated the scriptural commands as binding statutes, to be interpreted for practice by the competent authorities. Certainly practical and humanitarian considerations coloured their exegesis of scripture and supplementary legislation; but behaviour was still to be determined by the resulting system of casuistic regulations. Jesus for his part not only opposed specific regulations in cases where they prevented the meeting of human needs, but showed in general a non-halakhic approach to sabbath observance. His opposition never took expression in specific regulations proposed as alternatives to Pharisaic ones. When pressed as to the legality of his behaviour, he countered by undermining on moral rather than legal grounds the understanding of his opponents. And, in a mashal summarizing his views on the sabbath, he indicated that subjecting man to a casuistic system defeats the purpose of the sabbath. In his view, not casuistry, but compassion; not rules developed on the basis of scripture's letter, but an awareness of the purposes of scripture's Author, determines what in a given situation is the will of God.

It should be noted once more that there is no suggestion that Jesus intended to bring a new law for the sabbath, or that his coming marked the end of the old one. His words are concerned only with a true understanding of what God intended with the sabbath command.

Chapter VIII
Oaths

In Matthew's gospel, Jesus deals with the subject of oaths on two occasions: once giving personal instructions on the matter (5:33-37), and once attacking the casuistry of the scribal halakhah (23:16-22). A study of his views in these passages in the light of Pharisaic halakhah may well shed light on our theme.

A. BACKGROUND

An oath attests the truth of a statement of fact or intention by means of a conditional curse, operative if the facts are falsely represented or the declared intention not carried out. A primitive view sees the curse as an entity in itself, formed by the power of the spoken word;[1] it is perhaps "placed into" another being or object named in the oath, ready to strike the one who swears falsely.[2] A specially solemn oath may invoke a god as depository of the curse; such an oath is more fearful, but, by this view, not different in kind from an oath by stones, trees, water, or parents.[3] The god is still the medium, not the agent, of the curse; he, too, is subject to its laws.[4]

Within the framework of a more developed religious society such as ancient Israel, the deity is usually invoked in a more direct way.[5] It may be stated explicitly that he is to punish the defaulter: "May God (or "the gods") do this to me and more besides, if..." (1 Kg. 2:23; 20:10, etc.). Here God is clearly invoked as the agent of the curse. Alternatively, he may be invoked as a witness to the truth of one's statement.[6] A conditional curse is still involved, since God as witness will certainly punish the maker of a false oath. Paul makes this clear when he writes, "I call God to witness upon my soul..." (2 Cor. 1:23; cf. 11:31). Finally, one may swear simply "by God", "by the life of God",[7] or, indeed, by anything held sacred (a temple, altar, sacrifice, etc.).[8] Here one's relationship with the deity is put at stake, to be forfeited should the oath prove false.[9]

The common element in each of these cases is the conditional curse, of which God is no longer merely the medium, but the agent. Still, he is made subject to the oath: the demand is placed upon him that he act in such and such a way if certain conditions arise. In this sense, his sovereignty is always impinged upon by an oath.[10]

Oaths are an accepted part of O.T. religion; but certain stipulations are made. Israel must swear by YHWH alone (Deut. 6:13; 10:20): to swear by any other god would involve apostasy (Ex. 23:13; Josh. 23:7; Jer. 5:7; 12:16; Amos 8:14). Moreover, one must not swear falsely, lying either as to the facts or as to one's intentions (Lev. 19:12): to do so would be to mock God's power or will to punish sin. But a serious oath in the name of YHWH is always the mark of his faithful servants (1 Kg. 17:1; 2 Kg. 2:2, etc.), and will one day mark his universal rule (Isa. 19:18; 65:16; Jer. 12:16).

At the time of Jesus, the divine name YHWH was carefully avoided in ordinary speech to ensure that it was not taken "in vain";[11] hence, various substitutes (כנויין) were employed in oaths.[12] Popular usage included oaths by anything thought sacred or specially precious. But the matter did not stop there: rabbinic literature witnesses to the widespread use of the most capricious oaths to attest even trivial statements.[13]

Certainly there were those who opposed the proliferation of oaths.[14] Ben Sirach discouraged their use, saying that the one who "swears and takes the name (of God) continually" will not be free from sin (23:9ff.). According to Josephus (War 2.139), oaths were involved in becoming a full member of the Essene sect, and this appears to have been true at Qumran (1QS 5.8); but further oaths were apparently prohibited (War 2.135; 1QS 6.27(?)).[15] And many of the rabbis emphasized the evils of swearing.[16]

Still, the rabbis were confronted with a de facto situation in which oaths of every kind were being used. If the precepts of Torah, which permit oaths in the name of YHWH but require that that name not be taken in vain, were to be observed, it might well be asked which oaths could be used and which could not. Furthermore, if answers to that question could be supplied, perhaps some of the excesses of popular practice could be checked. Here was a task for the scribes![17]

Rabbinic literature attests to the energy they expended on the problem, and the subtle distinctions they introduced. The Palestinian halakhah on the subject seems to have been defined as follows.[18] If the speaker used the word שבועה ("oath", i.e. "I swear...") or one of the accepted substitutes for שבועה (M. Ned. 1.2) when he swore, his oath was considered valid (M. Ned. 2.2f.). Alternatively, if a name regarded as a substitute for the divine name (e.g. "By the Merciful and Gracious One", or "by him who is patient and great in kindness", M. Shevu. 4.13), the oath was also valid.

Oaths taken by other objects, however, were not.

It should be noted that vows at times overlap with oaths, and that the terminology is not always kept distinct.[19] Theoretically, the difference is clear enough: an oath attests the truth of a statement by means of a conditional curse; with a vow, something is either to be reserved for sacred use or at least treated by those named in the vow as though it were so reserved. Still, a person's intentions may be solemnly affirmed by means of either an oath or a vow. Already in the O.T. the terms are combined in such cases (Num. 30:3(2); Ps. 132:2). And, in fact, only the formula used distinguishes the two: "May anything belonging to you which I might eat be korban" is a vow; "By my oath! I will not eat anything belonging to you!" expresses the same resolution in the form of an oath. It is thus not surprising if, in popular speech, where exact formulas were not always observed, terms for oaths and vows were sometimes used interchangeably.[20] The matter is complicated further by the fact that certain terms can be used either to swear by or to designate a vowed object. Thus, if something was designated "(as) a korban", a vow was being made; but oaths were also taken by "the korban",[21] creating some ambiguous situations which could be interpreted either way.[22] Moreover, a vow can of course be strengthened by an oath (e.g. "Konam be any benefit (by the God of Israel) my wife might have of me...", B. Ned. 22b).

We cannot be certain on the basis of the rabbinic texts alone which oaths and vows the scribes of Jesus' day would have regarded as valid. But the texts we will be examining in Matthew indicate something of the plethora of oath-terms in use, and of the casuistic distinctions already being drawn between them by the scribes. We must now consider Jesus' view of the matter.

B. JESUS AND OATHS

1. The Fourth Antithesis (Mt. 5:33-37)

The fourth antithesis of the Sermon on the Mount contrasts Jesus' teaching with that of the O.T. regarding oaths. The latter is not cited directly, but a summary is given (Mt. 5:33). We have seen above that the distinction between oaths and vows was not always observed; here, too, the terminology is mixed. Mt. 5:33 alludes to O.T. texts which speak of vows in order to make the point that oaths must be observed (cf. CD 16.6ff.): "Again, you have heard that it was said to men of old, 'You must not swear falsely, but must keep your oaths to the Lord!'" The first part of the citation corre-

sponds to Lev. 19:12: God's name is not to be invoked in oaths if the statement to be sworn is false or the intentions declared are not going to be
carried out. The latter part of the citation is close to O.T. texts which
require that one fulfil (LXX ἀποδίδοναι)one's vows to the Lord (Ps. 50:14;
cf. 22:26(25); 61:9(8); 65:2(1), etc.); but here ὅρκους, "oaths" takes the
place of the usual εὐχάς, "vows". As we have seen, the confusion is common,
and need not indicate that Mt. 5:33b has been secondarily inserted into our
passage.[23] Oaths are not distinguished from vows in the case where they
overlap, i.e. a statement of one's intentions. Thus, the O.T. teaching on
oaths is summarized by saying that what is sworn to the Lord must be made
good.

What is here stated is O.T., not scribal law: oaths are permitted, but must
be performed. Scribal law, with an eye to Ex. 20:7, defined further what
constituted a valid oath. For Jesus, however, the O.T. precepts permitting
oaths do not adequately represent the will of God: "But I say to you, Do
not swear at all!" Four examples of common oaths follow and, in connection
with them, one reason for not swearing (vv. 34b-36); then, in connection
with the admonition that a simple "yes" or "no" should be enough, a second
reason for not swearing is mentioned (v. 37).

It is not said that the four examples are oaths which the scribes would
approve. If the Palestinian halakhah as outlined above was observed in its
essentials at this time, then presumably scribes would have approved an
oath "by heaven", if "heaven" was understood as a substitute for the divine
name. God was thus invoked, though the formal avoidance of his name protect-
ed its sacredness. But here it is argued that the formal avoidance means
nothing: the one who swears by heaven still swears by God's throne; earth,
God's footstool, must not be invoked;[24] Jerusalem is the city of his choosing (cf. Ps. 48:3(2)); even one's own head is subject to changes God alone
can bring.[25] Thus all oaths, not just those which mention the divine name,
infringe on divine prerogatives; therefore all oaths are to be avoided.

Furthermore, one's simple "yes" or "no" ought to be enough (v. 37).[26] The
very fact that oaths are required to specially attest the truth of some
statements indicates that not all we say is true. Thus, oaths are a product
of the evil state of affairs in which we live[27] and should be avoided.

At first sight, the treatment of O.T. law in these verses appears quite different from Jesus' views as we have hitherto seen them. From a Pharisaic
point of view, Jesus was not sufficiently strict in the matters of tithing,

ritual purity, and sabbath observance; here, on the other hand, his demands
go far beyond anything which can be derived from scriptural precepts or
reasonably demanded of men. But, in fact, the same inner logic which came
to expression in the other subjects we have treated takes on a striking new
form in these verses. Here, too, we have a rejection of the view that the
precepts of scripture are to be interpreted as statutes whose terms are
binding on subsequent practice, an adequate expression of the will of God.[28]
In other matters, the careful fulfilment of each provision of scriptural
law was not seen as the prerequisite of a heart in tune with the divine purposes; hence, what from the Pharisaic point of view must be called a measure of laxity was permitted. Here, however, the terms of the biblical precept fall short of the radical demands by which such a heart must be governed;[29] hence, a stricter standard is set. Oaths may have biblical support.
Nonetheless, they represent, first, an infringement of the divine sovereignty,
even where the divine name is formally avoided: Jesus brooks none of that
formal observance of the law to which the view of scriptural precept as
statute inevitably led; and oaths represent, second, a limitation on the demand for absolute truthfulness by making it more important to tell the truth
on one occasion (i.e. when confirmed by an oath) than on another. A prohibition of oaths is thus fully consistent with what we know about Jesus, and
we may well ascribe such a prohibition to him (criterion of coherence).

This does not, however, mean that everything in Mt. 5:33-37 must go back to
Jesus. We have already argued that the mixing of the terminology of oaths
and vows in v. 33 does not prove that that verse (or part of it) is secondary; but it is of course possible that the verse has been added to adapt
the authentic teaching which follows to the antithetic pattern of 5:21-48.[30]
Moreover, if, as is likely, James 5:12 is a version of the same saying, then
Jesus may simply have mentioned "heaven" and "earth" as common oath forms
to be avoided because one is to be truthful at all times; in that case, the
particular explanations and further examples given in vv. 34-36 would have
been added later.[31] We will return to this question below.

2. The Third "Woe" (Mt. 23:16-22)

In the third of the seven "woes" directed against the "scribes and Pharisees" in Mt. 23:13-36, Jesus attacks the scribal halakhah on the subject of
oaths (vv. 16-22). Probably these verses were not an original part of the
"woes": there is no parallel in the Lukan "woes" (11:42-52); even in Mt.,
the standard phrase, "Woe to you, scribes and Pharisees, hypocrites!" which

introduces each of the other "woes" is missing.[32] It is clear enough that Jesus here attacks scribes who had taken it upon themselves to adapt and expand with casuistic definitions a matter of biblical law. The context suggests that these scribes were Pharisees; but since vv. 16-22 probably had a separate history, an argument from context cannot be decisive. In fact, the subject matter - oaths by the temple, its gold, the altar and its offerings - would have been of special interest for Sadducaic scribes, the temple priesthood being largely Sadducaic (cf. Acts 5:17; Jos. Ant. 20.199).[33] Still, we do know that Pharisaic scribes had their own views of the procedures which should be followed in the temple (cf. Jos. Ant. 18.15; B. Yom. 19b, etc.); that the schools of Hillel and Shammai did discuss oaths and vows; and that the halakhah on this subject preserved in rabbinic sources shows points of contact with that of these verses. Hence we are probably correct in concluding that here, too, Jesus' disagreement is with the "scribes of the Pharisees".

The position of the scribes, according to vv. 16 and 18, is that an oath taken by the temple or altar[34] is not binding, whereas one taken by the gold of the temple (i.e. that of temple ornaments, or the treasury) or a gift on the altar is considered valid. This particular distinction is not found in rabbinic literature.[35] Saul Lieberman has, however, suggested a case where just such a distinction as is drawn in Mt. 23:16, 18 corresponds to the Palestinian halakhah as it can be defined from rabbinic sources.[36] His explanation well illustrates the subtleties of scribal halakhah.

According to Lieberman, the rabbis, in determining whether or not an oath or vow was binding, were concerned both with the oath- or vow-term that was used, and with the oath- or vow-formula. The oath-term, as we have already seen, could be a substitute for the divine name, or the simple word שבועה ("oath"), but not other holy objects such as the altar, temple, or korban (cf. M. Ned. 2.1f.; M. Shevu. 4.13). Acceptable vow-terms usually contained the preposition כ, "as", e.g. "(May what I eat of yours be) as the altar." Without the "as", terms like "altar" and "temple" were considered vague and not acceptable (cf. M. Ned. 1.3). An exception, however, was made for the word korban: since it is the usual term in a dedication, more leeway was allowed with its use, and either "as a korban" or simply "korban" was considered an acceptable vow-term (cf. J. Ned. 1.4).

Similarly, there were clearly recognizable and acceptable formulas for oaths (usually the simple expression...ש, which can be rendered "that"; i.e. "I

swear that...", M. Shevu. 3.1ff.) and vows (e.g. "Konam be that which I
(שאני, i.e. any benefit which I) might have from you...", M. Ned. 8.7). A
vow using such a distinct vow-formula was usually recognized as legitimate;
even in cases where the vow-term in itself was a vague one, a distinct formula was a sufficient indication that a vow was intended.[37] In cases, however, where an ambiguous formula (i.e. one which could be used in either an
oath or a vow) was used, the pledge was held to be binding only if the oath-
or vow-term it used was an acceptable one.

The result of these distinctions is that a pledge in question would usually
be held binding (i) as an oath, if it contained a valid oath-term; or (ii)
as a vow, if it contained either a valid vow-term or a valid vow-formula.

We may now consider the following three statements, each containing the formula שאני which the rabbis considered ambiguous,[38] but which was certainly in common use.

(i) קרבן שאיני אוכל לך , lit. "Korban, that I shall not eat anything
of yours!"

(ii) היכל שאיני אוכל לך , lit. "Temple, that I shall not eat anything
of yours!"

(iii) מזבח שאיני אוכל לך , lit. "Altar, that I shall not eat anything
of yours!"

It is clear that (ii) and (iii) cannot by these rules be regarded as binding.
They cannot be binding oaths, since neither "temple" nor "altar" are acceptable oath-terms: they are holy objects, but not substitutes for the divine
name; nor are they acceptable vows since, without the preposition כ, "as",
neither "temple" nor "altar" is an acceptable vow-term, and the formula
שאני is ambiguous. In the first case, however, though korban is not an
acceptable oath-term, it is acceptable as a vow-term, since it is the usual
term for a dedication and does not need the preposition כ. Thus (i) constitutes a valid vow. If, then, we regard the "gold of the temple" of Mt. 23:16,
and the "gift on the altar" of v. 18 as equivalents of korban - certainly
a reasonable proposition -[39] then we must conclude that statements using
an ambiguous formula were considered binding if sworn by the gold of the
temple or the gift on the altar, but not binding if sworn by the temple or
the altar themselves. So argues Lieberman.

Whether or not this particular distinction forms the background to our text,
it is clear that Mt. 23:16-22 is no caricature[40] of scribal halakhah, and

need not misrepresent it.[41] The subtle distinctions which the scribes
brought to the task of defining what constituted a valid oath or vow could
well result, by these or other means,[42] in just such an anomaly as that
spoken of in Mt. 23:16, 18.

According to vv. 17 and 19, Jesus pointed out the anomaly involved: how
could a pledge sworn by a sacred object be considered valid while one taken
by the object which imparted its sanctity is not considered valid? The principle involved in the objection, that the temple and the altar are the
sources of the offerings' sanctity, was one which the scribes certainly recognized (cf. M. Zev. 9.1, 7). On their own principles, they must have found
such a case an anomaly and unsatisfactory.

It is conceivable that Jesus was content to attack scribal casuistry in this
way, pointing out the curious results to which it led. Bultmann finds vv.
16-19 a strong and fully adequate rejection of such casuistry, while vv.
20-22 constitute pedantic and secondary material.[43] But vv. 16-19 contain
no fundamental criticism of the developing halakhah; the object of the
attack is simply an anomaly to which it had led. Certainly an occasion may
well have arisen in which Jesus saw fit to attack such an anomaly without
stating fully his views on oaths. But when the verses which follow expand
the attack into a fundamental critique on current oath practices, and that
in a way quite consistent with what we have seen in Mt. 5:33-37, it seems
unnecessary and unfortunate to limit the authentic material to vv. 16-19.

V. 20 makes explicit what one might have assumed from the previous verse,
namely, that, for purposes of oaths, the altar cannot be separated from
that which is on it. Yet the verse is not a pedantic repetition of v. 19,
but a pivotal turn in the argument: in the same way, an oath by the temple
cannot be separated from one by the God who inhabits it (v. 21). There are
thus no "greater" or "lesser" oaths, none more binding than others. Every
oath is an oath "by God". Formal distinctions are thus done away and, with
them, the basis of a casuistry of oaths. Admittedly, the next step – that
all oaths encroach on divine prerogatives and should be prohibited – is not
taken here. It is no great leap.

The argument is complete with v. 21. V. 22 rejects further any distinction
between an oath "by heaven" and one "by God". An oath "by heaven" has not
been mentioned or prepared for in what precedes. There are thus formal
grounds for suggesting that the verse is secondary here, added on the basis
of Mt. 5:34;[44] or, naturally, Jesus himself may have continued his attack

by doing away with another popular distinction.

If the view is correct that at least Mt. 23:16-21 represent an attack by Jesus on the casuistry of swearing, it is worth raising again the question of authenticity with regard to the explanations in 5:34-36. No certain answer can be given. We must be content to say that the arguments of these verses in chapter 5 are at least quite consistent with Jesus' words in Mt. 23: distinctions between oaths are done away; every oath invokes God. Whether Jesus himself, or the tradition on the basis of such words as those found in 23:16ff., is the source of those explanations in chapter 5 may be left an open question.

C. CONCLUSIONS

The scribes began, in the matter of oaths as with other subjects, with two things given: the unalterable words of Torah, and the almost equally un-alterable ways of men. Their task was to formulate laws which, while doing justice to the terms of scriptural law, might serve as practicable guidelines for the conduct of men. They accomplished it by introducing formal and casu-istic distinctions: by permitting the use of substitutes, to protect the sanctity of the divine name; by approving certain formulas and rejecting others, to limit the irrelevant ones in common use. In this way a workable (if complicated) code was established on the authority of the scribes.

For Jesus, the will of God was not found in the careful application of scriptural statutes. Oaths, though permitted in the O.T., are a sign of human sinfulness and cannot be in line with the divine will. Further, Jesus feels no need to introduce formal distinctions which preserve the letter of the biblical text while making its demands practicable for men; nor does he recognize the distinctions drawn by the scribes. All oaths are oaths by God. Whatever formal differences they may show cannot alter that basic fact.

In the matters of tithing, ritual purity, and sabbath observance, Jesus appeared to be concerned rather with a true understanding of the divine will than with introducing a new law or, indeed, abrogating an old. This is probably the case in the matter of oaths as well, though the antithetic form of Mt. 5:33-37 might be thought to suggest the contrary. It is of course not certain that the prohibition of oaths was originally stated in that form; in any case, "You have heard..." is best understood as introducing, not a law hitherto valid but now being replaced, but a command which, when interpreted literally and treated as a statute, leads to an inadequate understanding of the divine will. The proper understanding is then introduced by the words, "But I say to you..."

If this is correct, then it is a misunderstanding of Jesus' intent to treat his words as a new statute, the very wording of which is meant to be binding on subsequent practice: as though the will of God involved the literal fulfilment of a new legal code! Here as elsewhere in the teaching of Jesus, the demands of God are seen as radical, only to be fulfilled by a heart in tune with his purposes. Since certain types of conduct, though falling short of those demands, were seen as entirely permissible by those who understood O.T. law as statute, Jesus inculcated his understanding of the divine will by rejecting them categorically. But it is typical that he did not pause to point out how his words were to be applied in specific situations that might arise: whether or not, for example, oaths might be permitted in a court of law. It was thus not his intention to supply a set of rules which cover all situations, the careful observance of which might guarantee that a man does what is right before God; in fact, the observance of any set of rules may serve to blind its adherents to the fact that all is not as it should be, that God demands more. A heart submissive to the rule of God, a heart which draws back in horror from every infringement of the divine sovereignty and every suggestion of deceit, is alone capable of pleasing God. It is a heart of this kind, not the fulfilment of a new statute, which Jesus here required.

Chapter IX
Divorce

A. BACKGROUND

The rabbis' treatment of divorce parallels closely their treatment of oaths.
In both cases, we must distinguish between haggadah and halakhah, i.e. between exhortation and law. Unmotivated divorce, like thoughtless swearing,
was an evil whose dire consequences were doubtless the subject of many a
sermon (cf. B. Git. 90b);[1] but law recognized that divorce, like oaths, was
in some cases necessary, in others inevitable, and contented itself with
trying to eliminate certain excesses.[2]

Still, the Pharisaic halakhah in this matter was not determined solely by
the realization that divorce was an inevitable evil. Divorce was also part
of the Mosaic law. In fact, both the haggadic and the halakhic treatment of
divorce have their parallels in scripture.[3] Wisdom literature contains com-
mendations of conjugal fidelity (Prov. 5:15ff.);[4] in a prophetic text, divorce is apparently pronounced hateful (Mal. 2:14-16);[5] but the legal material assumes the legitimacy of divorce and deals with special cases. Thus
a man may not remarry the woman he has divorced if she has been married to
another in the meantime (Deut. 24:1-4; cf. Jer. 3:1); a priest may not marry
a divorced woman (Lev. 21:7, 14; cf. Ezek. 44:22). Further, in two cases divorce is explicitly prohibited: for the man who has falsely accused his wife
of not being a virgin at the time of their marriage (Deut. 22:13-19), and
for the one who has been forced to marry a girl he has raped (Deut. 22:28f.).
These legal texts all assume that divorce is normally a legitimate option.

That husband and wife are not treated as equal partners in marriage is clearly seen in the biblical discussion of divorce. Initiating a divorce is a
man's prerogative (cf. Deut. 24:1, 3; Isa. 50:1; Jer. 3:1, 8); with the exception of the two cases mentioned above, no limitations were placed on his
freedom to do so. A wife, however, cannot initiate a divorce; she is spoken
of in the passive voice as a "divorced" (גרושה , lit. "driven away", Lev.
21:7, 14; 22:13; Ezek. 44:22) or "dismissed" (שלחה , Isa. 50:1) woman.
Still, if she is to be sent away, her husband must make out a writ of divorce entitling her to enter a new marriage (Deut. 24:1f.; cf. Isa. 50:1;
Jer. 3:8). Presumably such a document is intended to cancel a written marriage contract, though the latter is not specifically mentioned in the O.T.[6]

Thus the Pharisaic halakhah, in allowing but regulating divorce, is not
simply abandoning impossible ideals for the realities of life; here, as in
other areas, it has as its base the laws of Torah and builds on that foundation a casuistic corpus of law. It is impossible to say exactly how extensive that corpus was at the time of Jesus. Nonetheless we may cite a few
features which appear to have applied already in the pre-70 period, and
which illustrate once more the now familiar character of Pharisaic law.

The schools of Shammai and Hillel are said to have debated what constituted
legitimate grounds for divorce.[7] For an answer to the problem, they turned
to the "statute" on divorce in scripture: the differing interpretations of
the schools reflect differing interpretations of Deut. 24:1 (cf. Sifre to
Deut. 24:1). There divorce because of a "matter of indecency (?)" (ערות
דבר , where the exact force of ערות is uncertain[8]) is mentioned. For
the Shammaites, the operative word was "indecency": a woman could only be
divorced for shameful behaviour of some kind; unfaithfulness was one possibility, though there were others as well.[9] For the Hillelites, the word
"matter" was crucial. Since it is very general, a husband might divorce his
wife for any reason at all: "even if she spoiled a dish for him" (M. Git.
9.10). This interpretation has given rise to many comments on the moral laxity of the Hillelites. In all fairness, it should be pointed out that the
statement is part of an exegetical debate. To illustrate that the word
"matter" (דבר) in Deut. 24:1 excluded nothing, the most trivial examples
were given. In any case, we cannot speak of an established rule as to the
legitimate grounds for divorce; the matter was still debated by the schools.

The biblical view that a man may divorce his wife, but not the wife her husband, continued to be Jewish custom in our period (cf. Jos. Ant. 15.259),
and is taken for granted in Pharisaic halakhah (cf. M. Yev. 14.1). It led,
for example, to the state of affairs in which a wife's reasons for seeking
a divorce against her husband's will were recognized as legitimate, but the
divorce was not granted until the man had been forced, if need be by physical means, to agree to it (M. Arak. 5.6).[10] Still, the halakhah does show
that efforts were made to limit by means of legislation a husband's arbi-
trary treatment of his wife. Two examples may here be noted.

(i) According to M. Git. 4.2, Gamaliel ordained that a man who has given
his wife a bill of divorce cannot cancel the bill before a different court
at which she is not represented.[11] Obviously, if the husband's freedom was
not limited in this respect, a divorced woman's plans could be brutally in-

terrupted without her knowledge by her former husband's change of heart.

(ii) Another measure was designed to make a man think twice before even di-
vorcing his wife (cf. B. Yev. 89a; B. Ket. 11a).[12] The prospective bride-
groom was forced to pledge in the marriage contract (ketubbah[13]) that his
wife would receive a certain sum of money in the event of divorce or his
death. The history of this measure is difficult to trace. It is often assigned to Simeon b. Shetah on the basis of B. Shab. 14b, but the cryptic
statement there is probably only an abbreviation of the tradition in T. Ket.
12.1 and B. Ket. 82b,[14] where it is assumed that ketubbah was an older institution. Further, M. Ket. 1.5 suggests that the Sadducees, too, accepted
the institution of the ketubbah, and had their own ideas as to the amount
to be pledged. Hence we are not dealing with a specifically Pharisaic institution. Nonetheless, it is clear that it was adopted as a part of the
Pharisaic halakhah, and that details of its application were debated in the
Pharisaic schools (cf. M. Yev. 4.3; M. Sot. 4.2; M. Eduy. 1.12).

One other aspect of the Pharisaic halakhah should be noted. Biblical law demands that a woman guilty of adultery be put to death with her paramour
(Lev. 20:10; Deut. 22:22); this extreme punishment, however, was apparently
not enforced at the time of Jesus.[15] It is typical of the Pharisaic position that they maintained the fiction of a death penalty for adultery in
accordance with scripture (M. Sanh. 7.4; 11.1), but avoided it in practice
by demanding that certain requirements be met before the penalty could be
enforced: the guilty parties must have been observed in the act of their sin
by two witnesses subsequent to their being warned by the witnesses (cf.
Sifre to Num. 5:28; also B. Sanh. 41a).[16] Still, even if a woman guilty of
adultery was not put to death, her lot was an unenviable one: her husband
was compelled to divorce her, she forfeited the money pledged to her in case
of divorce, and she was forbidden to marry her paramour (M. Sot. 5.1; 6.1ff.;
Sifre to Num. 5:28).[17]

In conclusion, we may note briefly the position of the Qumran texts with regard to divorce. One ambiguous text has been the subject of much debate.[18]
CD 4.19ff. accuses the "builders of the wall" of "unchastity" (זנות) in
that they "take two wives in their lifetime (בחייהם), whereas the principle of creation is, 'Male and female created he them', and those who entered the ark 'entered the ark in twos'". The suffix on "lifetime" is masculine in form, which suggests that the sectarians were opposed to any second marriage for a man, whether the first had been terminated by death or divorce. Many have suggested, however, that the masculine suffix may have a

feminine antecedent (here "wives"), and that the text means that a man is not to marry a second wife while his first wife is still alive; this would appear to involve a prohibition of polygamy on the one hand, and divorce and remarriage on the other. But some of those who understand the suffix as referring to "wives" think polygamy alone was the target of the attack.

It is difficult to avoid the conclusion that both polygamy and divorce followed by remarriage are prohibited: certainly if the suffix is interpreted as masculine, but also if it is interpreted as feminine. If a man may not marry a second wife while his first wife is still living, then divorce and remarriage is not an option open to him. Further, the Temple Scroll (57. 17-19) seems to support this conclusion.[19] There it is said that the king may not take a second wife, for the first "alone shall be with him all the days of her life. But if she dies, he shall marry another." If this text may be used in the interpretation of CD 4.19ff., it is evident that Jesus was not alone in condemning divorce.

B. JESUS AND DIVORCE

1. Adultery Because of Divorce (Mk. 10:11f. par.)

Behind the reference to Mk. 10:11f. par. as our first witness for Jesus' attitude towards divorce lies the view that Mk. 10:11f. par. Mt. 19:9 and Mt. 5:31f. par. Lk. 16:18 represent a saying of Jesus existing in two separate traditional forms, and further adapted to meed the needs of different Christian communities. This we will now attempt to demonstrate.

It seems clear that Mt. 19:9 and Mk. 10:11 are parallel versions of the same tradition. Admittedly, the exception μὴ ἐπὶ πορνείᾳ is not to be found in Mk.; this, however, does not signify a separate form of the tradition, but an adaptation of the tradition to the needs of the Matthaean community, as will be suggested below. Mt. may well have omitted the difficult ἐπ᾽αὐτήν by which Mk. indicates that the one who divorces[20] his wife and marries another woman commits adultery "against her (i.e. his first wife[21])". Otherwise the wording is identical. Mk. 10:12 is best understood as an adaptation of the rule in Mk. 10:11 par. to the Greco-Roman world, in which a woman could divorce her husband.[22] Since the conditions presupposed in the verse are improbable for Palestine at the time of Jesus[23] (he must be supposed to refer to Gentile practice[24] or to the particular case of Herodias and Herod Antipas[25]) but present in the milieu for which the gospel was intended, the verse may with some probability be considered secondary (criterion of altered milieu). The fact that, in Mark's gospel,

vv, 10-12 are attached loosely to the preceding debate in the form of private instruction given afterwards to the disciples is an indication that the
saying in v. 11 was originally transmitted separately.[26]

At first sight, Mt. 5:31f. and Lk. 16:18 do not at all appear parallel. If,
however, we assume that Mt. has adapted the saying behind Lk. 16:18 to the
antithetic form of 5:21-48,[27] and, as in 19:9, has added an exceptive
clause for the case of πορνεία, the parallel becomes apparent. Some differences remain. The variations between Mt. 5:32b and Lk. 16:18b are not substantial and need not detain us; in both cases, the man who marries a divorced woman is said to be guilty of adultery. More significant is the fact
that, whereas in Lk., the man who divorces his wife is said to be guilty of
adultery when he marries another woman, in Mt. his remarriage is not mentioned, but he is held responsible for the adultery of his former wife
("causes her to commit adultery"), i.e. when she remarries. The difference
in the two forms should not be exaggerated, as though Mt. condemns divorce
in itself, Lk. only divorce and remarriage.[28] The simplest explanation is
that Jesus thought divorce in itself a violation of the will of God, but,
since the term "adultery" (μοιχεία) implies extramarital intercourse, applied it first to the case where the divorced person draws the natural consequence of the divorce and enters a new marriage.[29] That Jesus could speak
of intercourse between a man who has been divorced and remarried and his
lawful wife as adultery indicates clearly that he found the dissolution of
the first marriage unacceptable.

If this correctly reflects his thinking, then Lk. 16:18a may well reflect
his actual words. Mt. 5:32a preserves their substance (the one who divorces
his wife is condemned), but refuses to use the word "adultery" for a case
which a Palestinian Jewish reader could not recognize as such.[30] In the
view of such a reader, a husband committed adultery only when he had intercourse with a woman married or betrothed to another; a wife committed adultery when she had intercourse with anyone other than her husband. The formulation in Mt. 5:32a preserves both this distinction and Jesus' condemnation of divorce:[31] "adultery" is committed by the divorced woman when she
remarries, but the husband who divorced her is held responsible.

In this context we may briefly mention what seems the most likely explanation of the "exceptive clause", here as in Mt. 19:9.[32] We have already seen
that the Mishnah reflects the view that a husband whose wife was guilty of
adultery was compelled to divorce her. Probably the exceptive clauses in Mt.

take this view into account and point out that the husband who divorces a
wife already guilty of adultery[33] cannot be held responsible for the adultery incurred when she remarries. Mt. is thus not restating the words of
Jesus in statutory form and allowing for an exception in which divorce and
remarriage are legally permissible, but merely pointing out that the moral
condemnation of the man who divorces his wife cannot apply in this particular case.[34]

It appears, then, that Mt. 5:31f. and Lk. 16:18 are two forms of the same
tradition, though in Mt. it has been adapted to the context of the antitheses and the needs of his community. It seems unlikely that Mk. knew the
tradition in this form; still, the similarity between Mk. 10:11 and Mt.
5:32a par. Lk. 16:18a suggests that the same saying may lie behind the two
forms of the tradition. Whether the form with $\pi\tilde{\alpha}\varsigma$ and the participle (Mt.
and Lk.) or the conditional relative clause (Mk. 10:11 par. Mt. 19:9) is
more original cannot be determined. The substance of the saying is the same
in either case. Nor can it be decided with certainty whether or not Mt.
5:32b par. Lk. 16:18b belonged to the original saying. All that can be said
is that it represents a further extension of the view that intercourse in a
second marriage is tantamount to adultery regardless of the fact that the
first has been legally terminated by divorce.

It should be noted that the saying in both versions is rather casuistic than
apodictic in form: the hearer is not addressed directly and warned what not
to do, but a concrete case is posited and the consequences ("guilty of adultery") drawn. Admittedly, we expect of casuistic law a statement of the
sanctions to be enforced; but even the casuistic law of the Mishnah contains
many provisions in which the only consequence mentioned is the innocence or
guilt (often the cleanness or uncleanness) of the party involved. Hence,
formally, our saying must also be classified as casuistic.

The synoptic gospels thus reflect, in different ways, a casuistically formulated logion in which the view is stated that sexual relations in a second
marriage, when the first has been terminated by divorce, are no different
than sexual relations outside of marriage: the same judgment of adultery is
passed upon both. Nothing suggests that legal sanctions ought to be applied,
that the adultery ought to be considered a crime and punished by man. In
that respect, the logion, though casuistic in form, is not meant as a statute whose wording is to be binding on any court of law. Nor, indeed, was it
interpreted as a statute by the evangelists, who showed great freedom in re-

stating the terms of the logion so that its import would be grasped by their readers.[35] But the label of "adultery" for intercourse in a second marriage clearly implies that divorce violates the will of God.

Apparently the saying was known to Paul, though his periphrastic rendition does not permit a reconstruction of the exact form in which he knew it. He too regards it as a saying of the "Lord", the starting-point of any discussion on divorce (1 Cor. 7:10ff.). We are thus dealing with a saying apparently original in its use of the word "adultery" (criterion of dissimilarity); a saying known to Paul, to Mark, and to a source drawn upon by Matthew and Luke, held to be authoritative by them all, and applied to different situations arising within the early church[36] (criterion of pregnant speech); further, a saying which is not bound by a statutory understanding of the O.T. law of divorce, and is thus parallel to Jesus' views in the other matters we have considered (criterion of coherence). We may safely attribute it to Jesus.[37]

2. Divorce and the Creator's Design (Mk. 10:2-9 par.)

Jesus' views on divorce are also to be found in a debate contained in both Mk. 10:2-9 and Mt. 19:3-9. In spite of considerable differences, the two passages are probably not independent of each other.[38] This is shown, not only by the similarity of the Greek wording, but also by the fact that both gospels continue along parallel lines, dealing in turn with divorce, children, and riches (Mk. 10:2-31 par. Mt. 19:3-30). Either a common source, or the dependence of one evangelist on the other, is to be assumed.[39]

Contrary to the majority view for the relation between the gospels as a whole, Matthaean priority has often been argued for this pericope: partly because the form of the question in Mt. 19:3 is thought to be much more probable than that in Mk. 10:2 (the Pharisees did not in fact question the legitimacy of divorce), partly because the argument seems to progress in a much more logical, credible way in Mt. than it does in Mk. The first consideration, however, is not a weighty one. It now seems clear that the sect of Qumran rejected divorce, so that Jesus could well have been asked for his view on a contemporary debate;[40] in any case, his own views were undoubtedly expressed on more than one occasion, and it would only be natural if he were asked to restate them in the light of the classic divorce text in Deuteronomy.[41] In fact, both Mt. (19:3) and Mk. (10:2) speak of the question as a "trap". The term is suitable enough in Mk., where the introductory question invites a response contrary to the usual understanding of

Moses' law; but it is quite unsuitable in Mt., where Jesus is simply asked to state his views on a subject debated by the Pharisaic schools.[42] It seems best to assume that Mt. chose to follow Mk. in speaking of a Pharisaic attempt to "trap" Jesus (a common Pharisaic activity in Mt. too!), but altered the words of the initial question either to reflect the school debate or to prepare for the exception which (as we have seen) he was to introduce in 19:9.[43]

It is true that certain logical distinctions are better preserved in Mt. than in Mk., and that at places the argument progresses more smoothly in Mt. Given, however, that the accounts are not independent of each other, it is easier to assume that Mt. has improved the Markan account than that Mk. has spoiled Matthew's![44] We have already dealt with a similar case in Mk. 7: 1-23 par. Just as Mt. there did away with separate introductions, removing in the process the evidence that originally isolated traditions had been combined, so here he introduces the substance of the Markan postscript (10:10-12) into the body of the debate (Mt. 19:9). Other changes, too, have been pointed out which are typical of Matthaean redaction.[45] Hence, though Mt. is much more consistent in distinguishing between the "concession" in Deut. 24:1 (contrast Mk. 10:5) and the absolute will of God as it is found in Genesis, we must attribute this to his learned revision of Mk.[46]

It should be noted that the presence of the Pharisees in the debate in Mk. depends on an uncertain reading in v. 2. It is very possible that the verb ἐπηρώτων should be read as an impersonal plural: "People asked him..." If so, it is easy to understand how a reference to the Pharisees, Jesus' traditional opponents in debate, was introduced in Mt. and the textual tradition in Mk. No distortion was involved, since the position of Jesus' interlocutors here does at least correspond to that of the Pharisees: divorce was permitted on the basis of the Mosaic law.

If we leave open the question whether or not Mt., with his careful distinction between "command" and "concession", better represents the views of Jesus, we can nonetheless draw two conclusions from the debate which apply whichever account we follow: (i) though Deut. 24:1 allows for divorce, it is here maintained that that does not represent God's absolute will, but an arrangement necessitated by the hardness of human hearts; (ii) God's absolute will may be deduced from Gen. 1:27 and 2:24; it precludes the possibility of divorce.

(i) The Pharisees, who characteristically understood the O.T. commands as statutes, could not but conclude that the references to divorce in such legal texts as Deut. 24:1 meant that it was a legitimate option. Here, as in other matters we have considered, Jesus does not interpret the wording of the O.T. text as a statute adequately expressing the will of God, but derives the latter on the basis of other considerations. This particular case, however, is of special interest. Whereas elsewhere we have no record as to how he accounted for specific O.T. regulations which, at least in the Pharisaic view, prescribed (or proscribed) certain actions, here he does account for the text in Deut.: it was an arrangement "for (i.e. "with a view to", or even "because of"[47]) the hardness of your hearts". The heart of man refused to submit to the will of God. Though this necessitated the introduction of limited measures to prevent further abuse, those limited measures are not to be confused with the (absolute) will of God. This being said, Jesus shows no interest in further defining the wording of the rules by which human society is governed, but turns immediately to the absolute will of God, which those preoccupied with defining statutory law may easily forget.[48]

If this interpretation is correct, Jesus does not so much abrogate the Mosaic prescription as relativize its claim to state the will of God. His criticism is not directed against Moses: the Mosaic legislation is not ascribed to Moses' own hardheartedness, and the will of God is still deduced from the books of Moses. It is the Pharisaic understanding of the divine will, which contented itself with applying biblical precepts instead of penetrating to the divine purpose, that comes under attack. Against such an understanding, he offers his own.

(ii) God's will is expressed in his act of creation:[49] "From the beginning of creation he made them male and female." Hence human sexuality has its origins in the divine purpose. And "for this reason" (the words, though a part of the quotation from Gen. 2:24, must here refer to the divine purpose in creating the two sexes) man and woman are to unite and form "one flesh", i.e. one new being.[50] Their union thus corresponds to the divine will; consequently, the dissolution of that union must violate that will: "That, then, which God has united, man must not divide."[51]

Here, too, it should not be thought that Jesus is introducing a new law. He is not suggesting that marriage without divorce represented the divine will from the creation of man until Moses, that divorce was in line with God's will from Moses until the present, and that he is now abrogating the Mosaic order and restoring that of creation. The divine will has remained constant.

Whenever measures are introduced which allow for divorce, whatever their limited legitimacy may be, it must still be recognized that divorce stands under the judgment of God, an expression of a heart hardened against his will.

We are, of course, not dealing with a transcript of an actual debate in which Jesus took part. There is, however, no reason to doubt that such a debate took place: if Jesus opposed divorce, it was almost inevitable that someone would ask him how his views could be made compatible with Deut. 24:1. Further, there is no reason to doubt that the substance of what Jesus is reported to have said here corresponds to his handling of the question.[52] The same views we have seen to be those of Jesus in other contexts find here a fresh expression (criterion of coherence): scripture is not statute; the will of God may be sought in what scripture reveals of his purposes; divorce is opposed to that will.

C. CONCLUSIONS

In the case of divorce, as in other matters we have studied, the differences between Jesus and the Pharisees can in part be explained by different views of the O.T. law in question. Even though there may have been Pharisees who thought divorce as a rule deplorable, they neither could nor did prohibit it altogether. After all, divorce was a part of the Mosaic law, and the terms of that law were felt to be binding on subsequent practice. Hence the legal experts of the Pharisees defined the scope of the biblical provisions and developed a casuistic corpus of law on this foundation. Since the Mosaic law was divinely revealed, and the scribes were its divinely authorized interpreters, submission to the will of God lay in the careful and cheerful observance of the halakhah.

For Jesus, too, the Mosaic law was divinely revealed; but here, as in other matters, he did not interpret its provisions as statutes, nor submission to them as conformity to the will of God. The law, by taking human sinfulness into account, may contain measures which do not correspond to the absolute will of God. The one who takes advantage of such limited measures in scripture stands under God's judgment in spite of the fact that Torah apparently permits his behaviour. Sin is thus defined not so much as the transgression of a prescriptive text, but as the falling short of the absolute will of God.

As far as scribal measures are concerned, Jesus does not here comment on them directly; still, inasmuch as the scribes were concerned with the appli-

cation of the divorce laws, he could at best regard their efforts, not as
defining the will of God, but as limiting the effects of a deed diametrical-
ly opposed to his will. An action complying with the halakhah may be sin in
God's eyes. Jesus' differences with the Pharisees were primarily based, not
on a rejection of their additions to biblical law, but on divergent understandings of the will of God.

So much is clear enough. For many, however, the fact that Jesus himself
appears to state the will of God in a casuistic rule (Mk. 10:11 par.) is
distressing: does he merely replace an inadequate statute with an adequate
one? Elsewhere, it seems, not obedience to ordinances but actions springing
from a heart in tune with the divine purpose were the mark of true piety.
How, then, can Jesus here state God's will in casuistic form?

The problem is not greatly alleviated by pointing out that Jesus is not
identifying the law of God with a statute binding on human courts. Certainly
he does not suggest that divorce should be punished by man. Divorce and remarriage are labelled "adultery", a wrong subject to the judgment of God in
spite of the fact that human (indeed, the Mosaic) laws are not infringed.[53]
But the problem remains: even if we grant that the casuistically stated
rule prohibiting divorce is not meant to be applied in human courts, how can
it be imagined that the will of God can be summarized in such a rule?

But, in fact, Jesus is not here inconsistent. It is not the case that he
elsewhere requires only a heart in tune with the divine intention but here
requires, in addition, submission to a casuistically formulated rule; it is
simply that certain activities are in themselves so utterly opposed to the
divine intention that it is impossible for one whose heart is sensitive to
it to engage in them. Divorce is not alone in that category. It is possible
for Jesus to say (almost casuistically!), "If you do not forgive men, neither
will your Father forgive your transgressions" (Mt. 6:15): not because forgiveness is seen as a commandment and the will of God is that man submit to
commandments, but simply because a refusal to forgive is incompatible with
a heart warm to the character and purposes of God. Similarly, Jesus can command that his disciples love their enemies (Mt. 5:44), that they not accu-
mulate treasure on earth (Mt. 6:19), that they not worry about the future
(Mt. 6:25): not because God's will is fulfilled by submitting to commandments (the Pharisaic view), but because any other course of action is impossible if the heart is right with God.[54] The same applies to divorce.
God's will in creation is clear: a man and his wife are "one flesh", and are

so to remain. And Jesus' prohibition of divorce is not to be understood as a statute demanding submission for its own sake, but as the definition of an area of potential human activity impossible for the one who rightly understands God's will and obeys it radically.

The basic difference between Jesus' view of the will of God and that of the Pharisees is well illustrated by the debate in Mk. 10:2-9 par. It has often been pointed out that, whereas Jesus is concerned exclusively with the purposes of God, his interlocutors in the debate wonder what is permitted to man. This is correct, but is capable of more than one interpretation. It can mean that the question put to him comes from hearts unsubmissive to God's will, seeking as much leeway as possible for human lust without incurring the divine wrath. Less cynically, however, the question can be the expression of a sincere desire to obey the will of God accompanied by the belief that that will is expressed in statutes whose precise scope must be defined. The latter position, which represents Pharisaism at its best, need not lead to a superficial or mechanical obedience. The Pharisees were well aware that obedience must come from the heart; but the will of God which they tried to obey from the heart was expressed in statutes. Jesus' answer springs from a different understanding of that will. He abandons immediately the question of what an O.T. "statute" may be construed to permit or proscribe and proceeds to illuminate the divine intention. What, for him, is wrong with divorce is not that it transgresses an O.T. statute, for the O.T. contains no explicit proscription of divorce. Divorce is wrong because it is the expression of a heart hardened against the Creator's design.

It follows, then, that if Jesus prohibits divorce in Mk. 10:11 par., his words must not be interpreted as a statute, conformity to which means the fulfilment of the divine will, the transgression of which means sin. As in the case of oaths, Jesus' understanding of the will of God comes to expression in a concrete prohibition because certain activities which fall short of the radical demands of God were nonetheless approved by those who understood O.T. law as statute. But it must not be thought that, by merely conforming to the wording of the prohibitions, by merely avoiding oaths or the formal act of divorce, one has fulfilled the will of God. If certain areas of potential human activity are impossible for one whose heart is submissive to the will of God, it is nonetheless the attitude of the heart, not the mere avoidance of those activities, which is Jesus' concern.

125

Chapter X
Jesus and the Sages of the Halakhah

To this point we have considered a number of cases in which Jesus came into
conflict with the Pharisees, not so much because he consistently and categorically rejected the validity of extrabiblical law as because his view
of biblical law and the will of God in general differed from theirs. Before
we conclude our study, however, we must briefly consider a few texts which
seem to indicate a more positive attitude towards scribal authority.

A number of scholars[1] have pointed out that Jesus is often reported to have
observed customs which the Pharisees had apparently adopted as halakhah,
but which cannot be traced directly to scripture. The sabbath found him together with the pious in the synagogues of Galilee (Mk. 1:21; 3:1 par.,
etc.), and he is even said to have participated in the synagogue service
(cf. Lk. 4:16ff.); yet such a service, though widely attested as a first
century practice,[2] has no real basis in O.T. law. The same is true of his
habit of pronouncing a blessing before "breaking bread" at mealtimes (cf.
Mk. 6:41 par.; 8:6 par., etc.). If we are correct in seeing the Last Supper
as a Passover meal, then the gospels witness to Jesus' observance of a number of details of the Passover rite (seder), at least some of which were
traditional, not biblical.[3] He is said to have paid the temple tax (Mt.
17:24-27) which, despite the precedent provided by Ex. 30:11-16, was really
a postbiblical development supported by the Pharisees.[4]

We need not pause to assess the historical value of these references, for
they tell us very little. At best they indicate (if proof was needed) that
Jesus did not break radically with all things Jewish, nor, indeed, with
every custom lacking support in scripture. But such incidental references
fall far short of proving a deliberate affirmation of Pharisaic tradition
or scribal authority.

Another text, however, appears to provide such a proof. At the beginning of
a long polemic against the "scribes and Pharisees" in Mt. 23, Jesus apparently acknowledges their legitimate role as interpreters of the law of Moses
and teachers of the people[5] at the same time as he denounces their behaviour: "The scribes and Pharisees sit on the seat of Moses. Practise and observe, then, everything they tell you, but do not go by what they do; for
they do not live up to what they say." (Mt. 23:2f.) Can Jesus have spoken

these words?

It must be admitted that they do not meet any of the criteria for authenticity which we have used in our study. Indeed, it is very difficult to reconcile what is said here about the authority of scribal teaching with the examples we have seen in which Jesus himself violated and denounced the regulations of the scribes. Further, it is difficult to believe that he could acknowledge the authority of teachers whose behaviour he found reprehensible: did he not insist that they be judged "by their fruits" (cf. Mt. 7:16-20; 12:33-35)?

Do these verses, then, meet a criterion of non-authenticity, so that we may regard them as primary evidence, not for the views of Jesus, but for those of some element in the early church? Certainly they appear incompatible with Jesus' teaching; and certainly we can document a tendency within the Jerusalem community of early Christians to observe Jewish law carefully. That such Christians would have attacked Pharisaic conduct as harshly as does Mt. 23:3 may be thought doubtful, but on the whole the verses do seem to correspond somewhat better with views they may be thought to have held than with those of Jesus. We cannot, however, be certain. The possibility remains that the contradiction between Mt. 23:2f. and what we have seen elsewhere of the views of Jesus may be formal rather than essential. Mt. 23:2 is not a policy statement on scribal authority, but the introduction of a polemic against Pharisaic conduct. In such a context, it may rather have the character of a concession granted for the sake of argument than an objective assessment of the legitimacy of scribal teaching. In this sense there is, of course, nothing to prevent these verses being spoken by Jesus.

The question of authenticity must be left open. Still, two points appear certain. First, these verses confirm the conclusion that Jesus did not categorically and systematically reject the authority of the scribes;[6] otherwise Mt. 23:2f., authentic or secondary, would scarcely have found a place in the tradition. Second, these verses cannot form the basis on which to reconstruct Jesus' views of scribal authority. They may be secondary; if authentic, they were spoken in a polemical context; they cannot be used to refute the carefully documented and fairly consistent picture which has emerged from a study of Jesus' conflicts with the Pharisees.

We may now draw conclusions from our study.

The difficulties inherent in the use of the gospels as historical sources must be recognized and taken into account. Carefully defined criteria for separating materials which may be used as evidence for the views of Jesus from those which witness a development within the early church would seem to be a prerequisite for any historical study; yet, in the nature of the case, such criteria are at best indications, not proofs, of authenticity or non-authenticity, and the subjective element in their application must be acknowledged. Nonetheless, our subject seems well suited for historical study; there is in fact widespread agreement as to the basic historicity of much of the relevant material. Despite the subjective nature of many judgments and the uncertainty that remains in many details, our main conclusions have been based on perhaps the most reliable elements of the gospel tradition and confirmed by the fresh form they have taken in each new context we have considered. With some justice they may claim a place with what we know about Jesus of Nazareth.

He was not a Pharisee. Points of similarity may of course be found. But the Pharisees of his period distinguished themselves from their neighbours by at least the careful observance of rules of tithing and ritual purity. Jesus treated these areas of Pharisaic concern with indifference, did not conform to their rulings or feel bound by the authority of their scribes; indeed, his understanding of the demands of God was fundamentally different. This much, then, seems historically certain: Jesus was not a Pharisee.

Our task has been to define Jesus' position on a contemporary issue which, according to Josephus, separated the Pharisees from the Sadducees: how did he view the extrabiblical traditions of the former? That he did not recognize their authority as binding should now be clear; still, his position must not be identified with that of the Sadducees. They rejected the binding character of regulations not found in scripture for the very reason that they were extrabiblical. Something similar is perhaps suggested by Jesus' distinction between human traditions and divine commands in Mk. 7:6-13 par.; yet he apparently made no effort to distinguish systematically scribal regulations from scriptural, and it is evident that his differences with the Pharisees were rooted in opposing views, not as to the status of extrabiblical law, but as to the nature of biblical law and its relation to the will of God. The Pharisees understood the regulations of scripture as statutes, applied and supplemented them by their tradition, and found the fulfilment of the will of God in the cheerful, wholehearted observance of the halakhah. That Jesus did not view scripture or the will of God in this way has been demonstrated in three different types of situation, and may also be regarded as a part of what we know about his teaching.

(i) The violation of a statute is, by definition, unlawful. This basic fact is completely unaffected by the relative importance of the statute in question. When God's commands are seen as statutes, none can be thought more binding than another. Seen from this point of view, Jesus showed an unacceptable indiffence towards the divine commands of tithing and ritual purity. If he assigned little weight to the fulfilment of certain provisions of biblical law,[7] then he did not understand that law as statute.

(ii) The very wording of a statute is binding. Hence, when moral and practical considerations demand a course of action contrary to that dictated by the letter of the law, a crisis arises for the one who understands that law as statute. When, moreover, the law in question is held to be divinely revealed, it cannot simply be set aside. The Pharisees, who were far from insensitive to the demands of equity but were bound to respect the letter of the law, were compelled to introduce further legislation and resort to legal fiction in order to resolve such conflicts: the formal authority of the divine law was upheld while the needs of the situation were met. Where such an escape did not present itself, the divine law was of course to be complied with. That Jesus was not bound by a statutory understanding of the law is apparent from the fact that crises of this kind did not arise for him. He experienced no conflict between the demands of Torah on the one hand and contact with the unclean, or sabbath "reaping" and healing on the other. He was not troubled to uphold the formal validity of a vow which could not be in accord with the divine will (Mk. 7:9-13 par.). And, just as he felt no need to uphold the letter of the law in a formal way, so he refused to recognize the formal distinctions of the scribes: all oaths were oaths "by God", whether they mentioned the divine name or avoided it with a substitute.

(iii) The category of actions which morality condemns but law allows is a large one. The use of oaths and the institution of divorce may be deplorable, but were a part of reality and, indeed, of scriptural law, and Pharisaic halakhah could only legislate further on that basis. Jesus, who believed that oaths and divorce were opposed to the divine will, and who was not bound by a statutory understanding of O.T. law, condemned them categorically.

In the nature of the case, this negative conclusion - that Jesus did not share a statutory understanding of the commands of God - can be stated with more certainty than any positive conclusions as to how he did understand them. Our task has led us to consider those passages in which he rejected the Pharisaic view, whereas many of the passages in which he inculcated his own are outside the scope of this study. Nonetheless, the following suggestions may be made, to be confirmed or disproven by study of the larger subject.

(i) The fact that Jesus did not regard O.T. law as statute makes it difficult to believe that he thought the will of God was now expressed in new statutes which he himself was to proclaim. And, indeed, we have found no indication that he intended to abrogate the Mosaic law in order to replace it with laws of his own. His concern was with the true understanding of the will of God; that will had always remained the same, though it had been obscured by the hardness of human hearts. Even when he did go beyond O.T. law in explicitly condemning oaths and divorce, there is no suggestion that oaths and divorce were wrong first when he had prohibited them: rather they were wrong and had always been wrong because of what they revealed about the human heart.

(ii) Thus, in Jesus' view, the will of God is fulfilled not by compliance with a legal code (the Pharisaic view, though it must be remembered that compliance was to come from the heart), but by a heart whose attitude is right. Of course there are areas of possible human activity incompatible with a proper attitude of the heart, and these may be proscribed. But it is the heart's attitude, not the mere avoidance of what has been proscribed, that is at issue.

(iii) When Jesus did find the will of God in scripture, it was not by carefully applying the provisions of its legal clauses, but by penetrating to what, in his view, was the purpose of its Author. A heart in tune with that purpose is alone seen as capable of fulfilling the divine will. Furthermore, though no distinction is drawn between ritual or ceremonial law on the one hand, and moral law on the other, it is striking how the laws of tithing, ritual purity, and sabbath observance are subordinated to the demands of mercy, fidelity, and absolute truthfulness: the former are of course laws which may be formally complied with regardless of the attitude of the heart, but scarcely the latter.

(iv) All of this suggests that the commandments to love God and to love one's neighbour are indeed a suitable summary of the moral teaching of Jesus. They can only be fulfilled by a heart in tune with the divine purposes; they are not susceptible to the definitions of statutory law; yet that which is proscribed by Jesus is indeed incompatible with a heart given in love to

God and other men (cf. Rom. 13:8-10!). Rules of tithing, ritual purity, and sabbath observance lose their place as the necessary ingredients of human piety. The facile distinction between "sinners" and "righteous" based on the observance of these latter commands is done away; so, too, the danger of omitting the "weightier matters of the law" because of a preoccupation with the details of its every phrase. The fulfilment of the law is love.

It is probably correct to say that, from the point of view of the Pharisees, this difference in the understanding of God's law was the crucial factor in their reaction to Jesus' ministry. One who disobeyed the divine law could not be a divine messenger (cf. John 9:16); and Jesus' actions and teaching did not conform to their understanding of the law.

On the other hand, the centre of Jesus' ministry was not his understanding of the law of God, but the message of a divine intervention in the history of God's people: the Reign of God was upon them! That this, and not his view of the law, was the focus of his attention is clear from his relations with "sinners" as well as with scribes. Jesus' message for "sinners" was not that a true understanding of God's law showed them to be either more or less sinful than the Pharisees made them out to be; sinners they were, but God's salvation had come near to them as well! As for the scribes, though different understandings of the will of God were bound to result in conflicts, he did not systematically attack their law. There are even texts which indicate that, but for the abuses to which their understanding led, he would not have rebuked them (cf. Mt. 23:23 par., 25f. par.). From his point of view, the most important factor in his relations with the scribes was their rejection of the message of the Reign of God (cf. Mt. 21:31f.).

Nonetheless, the message would not have taken the form it did had he understood the will of God in any other way. As long as the divine will is thought to be expressed in statutes the observance of which is both visible and possible, categories of "sinners" and "righteous" will be raised, and reason will be found for not associating with those who make no effort to carry out what God has commanded. When, however, the will of God is understood radically; when pains taken to tithe every herb, purify every vessel, and avoid every suggestion of "work" on the sabbath are given little value; when, indeed, such faithfulness to the word of God is seen as opposed to the will of God, in that weightier things are too easily forgotten, and the label of "righteous" is too lightly assumed; and when, instead, the claims of God are placed on the human heart, where the delimitations of halakhah do not apply and obedience can neither be measured nor imagined complete, then distinctions between "sinners" and "righteous" give place to the patent need of every man for the mercy of God.

Jesus' view of divine forgiveness was thus of a piece with his view of divine law. All needed to repent; to all, the gates of the kingdom were thrown open. Some, accustomed to the role of sinners and their exclusion from the numbers of the pious, seized gratefully the chance to enter in. For others, however, the undiscriminating nature of the message proved offensive. God commanded statutes; they had kept them. Clinging to their claim to be righteous, they refused to enter a kingdom where such merits had no place, where "sinners" and "righteous" sat together at a table spread by God. But such, in Jesus' view, is the kingdom of heaven.

Notes

INTRODUCTION

1) We cannot pause here to suggest nuances in the Sadducaic position; see Gerhardsson, Memory, 23f.; Lauterbach, Essays, 23ff., 113ff.; Le Moyne, Sadducéens 369-379.

2) See e.g. Beilner, Christus; Finkel, Pharisees; Merkel, Jesus; note also Baumbach, Jesus.

3) See e.g. Banks, Jesus; Branscomb, Jesus; Hubaut, Jésus; Schoeps, Jesus.

4) Such a contrast in fact leads to a distorted view of the Pharisees; against the view represented by Rössler, Gesetz, see Davies, Origins, 19-30; Nissen, Gesetz, 241-277; Sanders, Paul 48f., 423f.; Smith, Sect, 360.

5) Note that even the Pharisaic provenance of the Psalms of Solomon, long regarded as certain, is now seen to be highly questionable; cf. O'Dell, Background, 241-257.

6) Cf. Käsemann, Problem, 205 ff. The criterion is critically discussed by Hooker, Christology, 480-487; see also Dunn, Utterances, 197f.

7) Cf. Gerhardsson, Anfänge, 48-52; R.O.P. Taylor, Groundwork, 46ff.

8) Cf. Jeremias, Theologie I, 19-45.

9) Again, Hooker's article (Christology, 480-487) provides a helpful discussion of this criterion.

10) Cf. Gerhardsson, Anfänge, 50ff.; Schürmann, Untersuchungen, 39-65; R.O.P. Taylor, Groundwork, 46-53.

11) Cf. Fitzmyer, Languages, 507-518.

12) The point is made repeatedly in the articles collected by Cross and Talmon, Qumran.

13) Cf. Gerhardsson, Anfänge, 51.

14) Cf. Schmid, Markus, 165ff.

CHAPTER I - THE PHARISEES AND THEIR LAW

1) Note that when Josephus first mentions the Pharisees in his history of the Jews, they are already an organized group (Ant. 13.171; cf. War 1.110).

2) Jos. Life 10, 12, 191, 197, etc.; Acts 15:5; 26:5.

3) Cf. Bauer-Arndt-Gingrich 23; also Schlier, haireomai, 180f.

4) Cf. Bikerman, Chaîne, 44-54; Smith, Judaism, 79-81.

5) Cf. Bikerman, Chaîne, 49f.; Schlier, haireomai, 180.

6) Smith (Sect, 347-360) finds it characteristic of the sects of first century Palestine that they "(bound) themselves together by entering into a covenant to maintain their peculiar practices" (356). Different sectarian practices were based on different legal interpretations (359f.).

7) For characteristic Pharisaic beliefs, see Jos. War 2.162f.; Ant. 18.12-15; Acts 23:8.

8) On the relation between the Hebrew and Greek terms, see Meyer, Tradition, 12f.

9) For a concise treatment of the disputes, see Bowker, Jesus, 53-76; also A. Guttmann, Judaism, 136-161.

10) Cf. Rivkin, Pharisees, 234-238.

11) For the haverim, see especially Meyer, Tradition, 23-33; Neusner, Fellowship, 125-142; Oppenheimer, 'Am Ha-Aretz, 118-169. The havurah is compared with the Qumran community by Rabin, Studies, 1-36; cf. also Jeremias, Jerusalem, 259-262; Lieberman, Discipline, 199-206.

12) Cf. especially Neusner, Fellowship, 129-135; Rabin, Studies, 1-21.

13) Cf. Schürer, Geschichte II, 470f. n. 57.

14) Cf. Bowman, Gospel, 338f.; Sanders, Paul, 154ff.

15) Cf. Neusner, Traditions I, 376.
16) Ibid., 386.
17) Ibid., 298.
18) Ibid., 158f.
19) Neusner, Traditions III, 291-294.
20) Cf. Bowker, Jesus, 53-76.
21) Alon, Jews, 18-47.
22) Cf. Meyer, 'Am ha-'Ares, 184.
23) The regulations for the haverim are specially significant for us in that it is now generally agreed that the institution of the havurah dates back at least to the beginning of the first century of our era; cf. Burgsmüller, 'am ha-'ares, 97ff.; Meyer, 'Am ha-'Ares, 184f.; Neusner, Fellowship, 127; Oppenheimer, 'Am Ha-Aretz, 142f.; Rabin, Studies, 1-21, etc. As arguments pointing in this direction we may note: (i) the schools of Hillel and Shammai debated the requirements for membership in a havurah; (ii) there is a close correspondence in terms of organization and, in some cases, even regulations, between the havurah and the Qumran community; (iii) the regulations of the havurah and the N.T. picture of the Pharisees complement and illuminate each other.
24) We may compare what Belkin (Philo, 29) writes of Philo: "Judging by Philo's discussion of the law in De Specialibus Legibus and many other treatises, one can find no evidence to support the supposition that Philo knew of any distinction between the written law and the oral traditions."
25) Cf. Schlatter, Josefus, 205f.
26) Cf. Gerhardsson, Ethos, 27f.; Schlatter, Josefus, 205.
27) Cf. Jeremias, Theologie I, 198. Quite possibly disputes such as the one recorded in Mk. 7:1-13 between Christians and defenders of these traditions stimulated the formulation of the dogma of the Sinaitic origin of the Oral Torah. Suggestive in this regard is the fact that, when the necessity of the two Torahs is explained, it is said that the Oral Torah would be necessary to keep Israel distinct from the Gentiles, who would take the written law from them (cf. the references in Moore, Judaism III, 74f. n. 17).
28) Cf. Carmignac, Eléments, 215-221; Meyer, Tradition, 58-66.
29) Cf. Meyer, Tradition, 60.
30) Cf. Bacher, Tradition, 22-24; Chajes, Guide, 1-16; Urbach, Sages I, 286-314.
31) Cf. Urbach, Sages II, 815 n. 19.
32) Cf. Neusner, Traditions I, 343.
33) Cf. Gerhardsson, Memory, 19-29.
34) Ibid., 160-163; Weingreen, Bible, 78ff. This formulation takes into account the evidence for notes which may have been kept as aids for the memory, but which could not be introduced as authoritative evidence for the tradition.
35) Cf. Baumgarten, Law, 13.
36) Cf. Bacher, Tradition, 9ff.
37) For a detailed treatment of the various uses of the word "halakhah" in rabbinic literature, see M. Guttmann, Einleitung, 11-30. Cf. also Daube, Testament, 97f.; Falk, Introduction, 11.
38) Pharisaic influence will be discussed in Chapters II and III. Note that Sanders (Paul, 156 n. 52, 425 f.) distinguishes a "sect" from a "party" by suggesting that, while a "party" believes its programme to be right and wishes others to submit to it, it does not regard all dissenters as cut off from the divine covenant; the latter is characteristic of "sects". In this sense, too, it is probably correct to say that the Pharisees were not sectarians (cf. Sanders, Paul, 155-157).
39) The distinctions between casuistic and apodictic law applied by Alt to O.T. law (Ursprünge, 278-332) need some redefinition, but are still useful. See Andrew's remarks in Stamm and Andrew, Commandments, 45f., 67, and

Gerstenberger, Wesen, 23-28. Gerstenberger's definitions are adopted in the discussion which follows.
40) The definition is adapted from Jackson, Essays, 16.
41) Cf. Banks, Jesus, 39ff.
42) Cf. Alt, Ursprünge, 322ff.
43) Cf. especially Weinfeld, Deuteronomy, 3, 157, 167f., etc.
44) Cf. Jackson, Essays, 1-63, especially 27-29.
45) Ibid., 29; cf. Starfelt, Studier, 34-37.
46) Cf. Elon, Takkanot, 713.
47) Cf. Sanders, Paul, 76ff.
48) For the following, cf. especially Cohen, Law I, 31-57.
49) Cf. Starfelt, Studier, 35.
50) Cf. Cohen, Law I, 50f., 54.
51) On legal fiction in Pharisaic-rabbinic law, see Cohen, Judaism, 15f.; Falk, Introduction, 21-23; Zeitlin, Halaka, 29-31; Zucrow, Adjustment, 75-100. For Hillel's prosbul as an example of legal fiction, see Falk, Introduction, 22; A. Guttmann, Judaism, 71f.
52) Cohn, Secularization, 88.
53) Cf. Zeitlin, Halaka, 27f.
54) Cf. Falk, Introduction, 23-26. The legislative activity of the sages is usually divided into takkanot and gezerot; the former are taken to be positive ordinances, the latter prohibitory in nature. But the sources do not always preserve this distinction. Cf. Albeck, Einführung, 35f. n. 68; Elon, Takkanot, 714.
55) Cf. Chajes, Guide, 118-130; Falk, Introduction, 15-18; Zeitlin, Halaka, 26f.
56) At times it is even said that greater stringency applies to the "words of the scribes" than to those of Torah (M. Sanh. 11.3; B. Er. 21b); this was presumably because the former were more likely to be neglected than the latter; cf. B.R.H. 19a; Urbach, Sages I, 353ff. In point of fact, rabbinic sources do speak of a difference in the application of rabbinic and scriptural law: doubtful cases must be resolved leniently in the former case, stringently in the latter (B. Beẓ. 3b).
57) Cf. Cohn, Secularization, 78f.
58) Note that such exegesis was at first resisted; cf. Ishmael's famous objection to Akiva, "Torah uses the language of men" (Sifre to Num. 15:31; B. Ber. 31b, etc.). Perhaps the sages who objected feared that their distinctive view of extrabiblical tradition and the authority of the sages would be compromised if biblical support was sought for all measures. Moreover, the attempt to base a traditional law on a text of scripture was not always successful: at times it was admitted that a scripture verse only "supported" or "alluded to" a given law, but did not prove it; cf. M. Shab. 8.7; 9.4; M. Sanh. 8.2; and note Lk. 20:37.
59) Cf. Herford, Pharisees, 107-123.
60) Cf. Büchler, Studies, 36-118; Urbach, Sages I, 400-419.
61) Cf. Sanders, Paul, 111ff.; Zeitlin, Halaka, 2.
62) Cf. Herford, Pharisees, 53ff.; Nissen, Tora, 250ff.; Urbach, Sages I, 286ff.
63) Cf. Sanders, Paul, 1-238; note also Odeberg, Fariseism, 32ff.
64) Cf. Falk, Introduction, 29-31; Urbach, Sages I, 330ff.
65) Cf. Büchler, Studies, 122-130, 140-150; Nissen, Tora, 255f.
66) Cf. Falk, Introduction, 32-34; Greene, Prerogatives, 152-176.
67) Cf. Maher, Yoke, 98-102; Urbach, Sages I, 390ff.

CHAPTER II - "THE SCRIBES OF THE PHARISEES"

1) Urbach (Talm.Sage, 117; cf. Derasha, 172f.; Sages I, 568f.) maintains a distinction between the scribe and the sage in Sir. 38:24-39:11, classing

the scribe with the farmers and craftsmen (38:25-34) who play a necessary role in the life of a city, but who do not serve as councillors or judges. The sage, by way of contrast, gives himself to wisdom and serves among great men (39:1-11). But this appears to misinterpret the passage. The scribe of 38:24 is the same as the wise man of 39:1-11. Both are alike in occupying themselves with wisdom rather than with business affairs; both attain wisdom. In these respects the scribe/sage is contrasted with craftsmen. Cf. Meyer, Tradition, 41f.

2) Moore (Judaism I, 57) speaks of the "guild of scholars (Scribes)". Cf. also Gerhardsson, Tradition, 21.

3) Neusner, Eliezer II, 304.

4) Cf. Schürer, Geschichte II, 380f; and note Jos. Ant. 18.16.

5) Légasse (Scribes, 498f.) rightly sees that the NT γραμματεύς is often a "doctor" of the law. He regards it as unlikely, however, that this can be the meaning in passages where a scribe is seen as mixing with the crowd, posing questions, or even seeking to follow Jesus. Since the "scribes" here certainly are not mere copyists either, he adopts a third meaning of the Hebrew word soferim, namely, "elementary schoolteachers", as the meaning in these cases (499-502). But nothing in the texts points to this meaning; and even if the "scribes" in these passages hardly sound like "doctors" of the law, they could well have been among those who had studied with the masters and so were known as men of learning.

6) Cf. Jeremias, grammateus, 741; Schlatter, Josefus, 200 n. 1.

7) For the textual activity of the early scribes, see Daube, Methods, 241 n. 7; Finkel, Pharisees, 22-37; Gerhardsson, Memory, 43-55; Lieberman, Hellenism, 20-37.

8) Note B. Sot. 15a. Cf. Bacher, Terminologie I, 134 n. 4; Bowker, Jesus, 22.

9) Urbach (Derasha, 166-182) discusses this view; see also Lauterbach, Essays, 27-32 and 163-256.

10) See Gilat, Soferim, 79-81; Urbach, Derasha, 166-182.

11) Cf. Urbach, Class-Status, 38f.

12) Urbach, Sages I, 569; Talm.Sage, 117f.

13) Cf. especially Budd, Instruction, 1-14.

14) Cf. Meyer, Tradition, 22f.; and note Neusner, Traditions I, 64.

15) Cf. especially Leivestad, Dogma, 288-299.

16) Cf. Vermes, Jesus, 93.

17) Cf. Urbach, Sages I, 573 on Simeon b. Shetah and Onias the Circle-maker.

18) Cf. Bamberger, Revelations, 97-113.

19) Cf. Urbach, Halacha, 1-27.

20) Cf. Leivestad, Dogma, 290.

21) For the Sadducees as the defenders of priestly authority against the lay-scholars, see Lauterbach, Essays, 23-48.

22) For the sorry story, see Bruce, History, 56-68.

23) Cf. Cohn, Secularization, 77; Daube, Methods, 242; Finkelstein, Pharisees I, 264; Urbach, Sages I, 593 and Talm. Sage, 128. Note also Jos. Ant. 20.264.

24) Cohon, Authority, 614. See also Lauterbach, Essays, 102f., where it is suggested that Ex. 19:6, in which all Israel is named a "kingdom of priests", may have been used to support lay authority.

25) Cf. Urbach, Talm. Sage, 121.

26) Cf. Schürer, Geschichte II, 386f.

27) Ibid., 242.

28) E.g. Yohanan the High Priest, cf. M. Ma'as. Sh. 5.15. Note also the two judges of civil law in M. Ket. 13.1-9, who are not claimed as sages, but whose rulings are discussed and approved or disapproved by the sages.

29) For the master-disciple relationship in rabbinic Judaism and its background, see Rengstorf, manthano, 434-443.

30) Cf. the four types of disciples in M. Avot 5.12: "swift to hear and swift to lose"; "slow to hear and slow to lose", etc.; and note the praise

Eliezer b. Hyrcanus received from his teacher for being "a plastered cistern which loses not a drop" (M. Avot 2.8).
31) Cf. Gerhardsson, Memory, 181-189.
32) For exceptions, see T. Suk. 2.3.
33) Mantel, Ordination, 328.
34) Ibid., 328.
35) Ibid., 340f.
36) Ibid., 344.
37) Ibid., 344.
38) E.g. Daube, Testament, 208; Lohse, Ordination, 29; Newman, Semikhah, 13f.
39) Mantel, Ordination, 329, 336, etc.
40) Ibid., 329.
41) Ibid., 341; cf. also 325, 329.
42) Ibid., 329.
43) For a discussion of the development indicated in this text, see Alon, Jews, 401ff.
44) See Bacher, Geschichte, 122-127. According to Bacher, the term for ordination changed in Palestine (but not in Babylonia) from סמיכה to מנויי when the laying on of hands was no longer part of the ceremony. For the distinction between סמיכה and סמיכות in J. Sanh. 1.2, see Lohse, Ordination, 28f.
45) Mantel, Ordination, 330 n. 37.
46) For the following, see, in addition to the works of Lohse, Mantel and Newman already cited: Daube, Exousia, 45-59; Ehrhardt, Ordination, 125-138; Ferguson, Ordination, 13-19; Strack-Billerbeck II, 647-661. Hruby, Notion, 30-56 provides a summary of Newman's book.
47) See Lohse, Ordination, 31f., and especially Newman, Semikhah, 11f.; also A. Guttmann, Judaism, 34-38.
48) Newman, Semikhah, 10.
49) See the debate on the subject between Shanks (Title, 337-345; Origins, 152-157) and Zeitlin (Reply, 345-349; Title, 158-160).
50) Dalman, Worte, 273.
51) Cf. Ehrhardt, Ordination, 131; Ferguson, Ordination, 17; Lohse, Ordination, 50-52.
52) Cf. B. Sanh. 13b. Lohse, Ordination, 51 n.6 lists Mishnah passages in which the word has apparently the same meaning.
53) The case is strengthened if we accept Daube's suggestion (Testament, 244-246; adopted by Jeremias, presbuterion, 127-132) that 1 Tim. 4:14 reflects the Hebrew phrase סמיכת זקנים, "the leaning on of hands on persons in order to make elders, Rabbis, of them". We cannot, however, regard a possible understanding of a phrase in the Pastorals as proof for an institution in the time of Jesus.
54) Lohse, Ordination, 30.
55) Cf. Safrai, Self-Government, 391.
56) Ehrhardt, Ordination, 125-138.
57) Sifre to Num. 11:16f., while speaking generally of the institution of the "70 elders", does not discuss the formal act of authorization by which one joined their number.
58) Mantel, Ordination, 343f.
59) Mantel sees a parallel in a student's expounding before his teacher; but the high priest who is not a sage is no parallel to a teacher who was.
60) Daube, Exousia, 56; cf. also Testament, 217-223.
61) Against Daube, see Légasse, Scribes, 500f.
62) Daube rightly points out (Testament, 217f.) that it does not have this meaning in Jesus' reply.
63) Cf. Daube, Testament, 220-223.
64) E.g. Lohse, Ordination, 34; Mantel, Ordination, 340f.; Safrai, Self-Government, 391. Note, however, that Ehrhardt (Ordination, 125-138) and

Ferguson (Ordination, 13-19) argue against rabbinic ordination as a background to Christian practice.

65) Jeremias, Jerusalem, 235 n. 9.
66) So Daube, Testament, 239; Lohse, Ordination, 73.
67) Cf. Daube, Testament, 239: "We are expressly told that Paul and Barnabas belonged to that group of prophets and teachers. They were not students to be promoted. They were equals - indeed, leading figures - to be detailed for an exceptional task."
68) Lohse, Ordination, 74-79.
69) Cf. Ehrhardt, Ordination, 135.
70) Lohse, Ordination, 77; see also Daube, Testament, 238f.
71) Lohse, Ordination, 77.
72) Ibid., 79.
73) Ibid., 79. The latter two contrasts are significant if we accept the evidence of J. Sanh. 1.2 that at first teachers ordained their own students.
74) Cf. Daube, Testament, 237f.
75) Ibid., 239; Kretschmar, Ordination, 59.
76) See note 53.
77) Cf. Kretschmar, Ordination, 59f.
78) Against Lohse, Ordination, 52; and see Shanks, Title, 342-345.
79) See also Zeitlin, Reply, 348.
80) Lohse, Ordination, 30.
81) Cf. Schlatter, Synagoge, 183.
82) For the relevant text, see Shanks, Title, 337-339; also Dalman, Worte, 272f.
83) Cf. Dalman, Worte, 273; Zeitlin, Reply, 345.
84) Cf. Neusner, Traditions III, 256.
85) Cf. Neusner, Traditions I, 375.
86) Ibid., 14f.; cf. Schlatter, Synagoge, 176-178.

CHAPTER III - HALAKHIC ASSEMBLIES

1) Josephus uses it first in this latter sense in Ant. 14.167ff., according to Zeitlin (Pol. Synedrion, 114).
2) Ibid., 125; cf. Zeitlin, Jud.-Hell. Lit., 312.
3) Zeitlin, Jud.-Hell. Lit., 313: "My theory differs from Büchler's in that I hold that there was no permanent political synedrion. It was called by the ruler only when the need arose."
4) For this latter assembly, see Zeitlin, Pol. Synedrion, 122ff. Before 70 A.D., this religious court (in Zeitlin's view) lacked civil authority and responsibility; first in the period after 70, when it took over from the councils of the high priests some responsibility in civil matters, was it called Sanhedrin (= synedrion) (Pol. Synedrion, 126, cf. Synedrion, 198). The religious Bet Din of the earlier period decided religious law as well as cases of criminal law; still, "political offences were tried by a state synedrion which was summoned for this purpose" (Jud.-Hell. Lit., 313).
5) Hoenig, Synedrion, 179-187; Sanhedrin, 3-11.
6) Hoenig, Sanhedrin, 3-11, 40.
7) In addition to Hoenig, see Mantel, Studies, 1 n. 1; Wolfson, Synedrion, 303-306 and Notes, 87.
8) Note the repeated use of συνέδριον with the definite article, Mk. 14:55 par.; Mt. 15:1; Acts 5:21 (on this verse, see Schürer, Geschichte II, 245 n. 17); 22:30, etc. Cf. Jos. Ant. 14.167ff., where τὸ συνέδριον is a clearly defined institution which must condemn a man before he can be legally executed, before which others have been summoned but none has appeared with the show of strength displayed by Herod (172), and which was liable to summon Herod again (178). Clearly τὸ συνέδριον here is neither a temporary council, nor a court constituted to deal with a particular occa-

sion. Cf. Alon, Jews, 105.

9) This was true especially under the Hasmoneans and Herod. Probably Jos. Ant. 13.408ff. indicates Pharisaic dominance of the Sanhedrin during the reign of Alexandra; notice the change from the time of Hyrcanus, 13.408. Cf. Alon, Jews, 78f. Herod drastically altered the make-up of the Sanhedrin, Ant. 14.175.

10) For the use of the plural to include former high priests and members of their families, see Smallwood, Priests, 16.

11) "Scribes" and "elders" are sometimes kept separate (Mk. 15:1; Acts 4:5, etc.; "elders" then refers to the lay nobility, cf. Jeremias, Jerusalem, 222ff. and Safrai, Self-Government, 384f.), sometimes spoken of together as "elders" (Acts 4:8, 23, etc.; cf. Jeremias, Jerusalem, 222 n. 1).

12) Cf. Acts 5:34; also John 3:1 and 7:45-52; Ant. 14.172 and 15.3f.

13) Cf. Safrai, Self-Government, 383-385.

14) Especially Büchler, Synedrion, but he has many more recent followers. Zeitlin, as we have seen, does not speak of one political, judicial sanhedrin, but does distinguish the occasional councils summoned by the high priests or kings to deal with political offences from the religious Bet Din (Pol. Synedrion, 122-125). Similarly, Hoenig (Sanhedrin, 40) distinguishes "the Great Sanhedrin, which was only an interpretive or legislative body and judged only religious acts," from "the inferior trial courts" of Josephus and the N.T. Mantel (Studies, 92-101) thinks Büchler was right in distinguishing the Great Court in the Hall of Gazit (which, since Herod, had lost all political authority; it was chiefly a legislative body) and the political court of the kings and high priests. A. Guttmann (Judaism, 18), too, distinguishes the high priestly sanhedrin from the sanhedrin of scholars, though he suggests the designations "political" and "religious" are not precise.

15) Cf. Hoenig, Sanhedrin, 85; Mantel, Studies, 63; Moore, Judaism I, 261; Safrai, Self-Government, 381f. Certain specially serious matters were reserved for the supreme Sanhedrin (M. Sanh. 1.5), but otherwise any case brought before a lesser sanhedrin could be referred to the higher instance if the former knew of no precedent by which to judge it (T. Sanh. 7.1).

16) E.g. Mantel, Studies, 94, 288; Zeitlin, Pol. Synedrion, 130-135.

17) Cf. Urbach, Class-Status, 51f.
It seems best to identify τὸ συνέδριον in Jos. and the N.T. with "the Great Court in the Hall of Gazit, whence Torah goes forth to all Israel" (M. Sanh. 11.2); this in turn is the same as the Great Sanhedrin of 71 mentioned in M. Sanh. 1.6 (M. Mid. 5.4 says that it was the "Great Sanhedrin of Israel" which sat in the Hall of Gazit), the assembly whose end, according to M. Sot. 9.11, brought an end to singing at wedding feasts, etc. Some of the other traditions about the Sanhedrin reflect, on the one hand, what was true of a separate Pharisaic assembly of the period before 70 or of the rabbinic assemblies of the later period (e.g. that it was made up exclusively of disciples of the sages, M. Sanh. 4.3f.; cf. Bacher, Sanhedrin, 398), and, on the other hand, a measure of idealization (e.g. the judging of tribes and the waging of wars in M. Sanh. 1.5; the appointment of kings and high priests, T. Sanh. 3.4; cf. A. Guttmann, Judaism, 22f.; Safrai, Self-Government, 393).

18) Kennard, Assembly, 25-51.

19) Kennard calls it the Jewish "Commonality" (κοινόν) or "Ethnic Assembly" (Assembly, 27).

20) Ibid., 35f.

21) Ibid., 41-43, 48.

22) Urbach, Class-Status, 52; cf. Sages I, 580.

23) Cf. Kennard, Assembly, 27-30; Safrai, Self-Government, 377.

24) Jos. War 2.117; cf. Schürer, History I, 357, 360 n. 35.

25) Cf. Schürer, Geschichte II, 259.

26) Cf. the reading of the Western (and Received) text of Acts 24:6f.;

Safrai, Self-Government, 398; Schürer, History I, 377f.

27) For the letter, see Schürer, History I, 456.

28) Schürer (Geschichte II, 262) suggests this text means "dass der Hohe-priester nicht das Recht hatte, ein souverän verfahrendes Gericht abzuhalten in Abwesenheit und ohne Genehmigung des Prokurators".

29) Cf. Schürer, Geschichte II, 236.

30) Cf. Safrai, Self-Government, 377; also his Relations, 204-207.

31) For the letters, see Neusner, Traditions I, 356-358; cf. the letters with instructions sent from Jerusalem to Egypt in 2 Macc. 1:1-2:18.

32) Cf. Safrai, Self-Government, 377. Admittedly, the Sanhedrin did have police at their disposal (cf. Mk. 14:43 par.; Acts 4:3; 5:17f.; Jeremias, Jerusalem, 180; Mantel, Studies, 70f. n. 95) and thus some powers of enforce-ment, but they do not seem to have been invoked in any consistent way. The Qumran sect, whose (solar) calendar differed from that of the Jewish authorities, was confronted with a show of force on their day of atonement (1QpHab. 11.2-8; cf. Talmon, Reckoning, 167); but that incident probably took place under Hasmonean times, when conditions for enforcement were specially favourable.

33) The Sanhedrin's rulings are thus akin to "subordinate" legislation of other legal systems. The constitution, the supreme legislation, of Jewish law was the written Torah; "subordinate" legislation was issued by bodies designated to do so by the supreme legislation, in this case the "priests and elders" operating in the city chosen by God for the issuing of Torah. Cf. Elon, Takkanot, 713.

34) This view is reflected in M. Sanh. 1.6; Sifre to Num. 11:16.

35) Cf. Neusner, Traditions I, 117-119 and the comments there. Mantel (Studies, 57) thinks this "was actually the case"; Hoenig (Sanhedrin, 58) thinks it doubtful, noting that the scholion is post-talmudic and the only witness for such an event.

36) So also Alon, Jews, 34.

37) Cf. Bacher, Sanhedrin, 400f.; Urbach, Class-Status, 41.

38) Cf. Neusner, Traditions, I, 11; Schürer, Geschichte II, 257.

39) Cf. Bacher, Tradition, 49. Hillel is an exception (cf. T. Pes. 4.14), but the tradition that he was appointed nasi perhaps applies only to the sons of Bathyra (Urbach, Class-Status, 49; Sages I, 580), more probably is unhistorical (Cf. Neusner, Traditions I, 231-235).

40) Cf. Safrai, Self-Government, 386f.

41) Note that ἄρχων, used in Acts 23:5 of the high priest, is frequently used in the LXX for nasi.

42) So Mantel, Studies, 67f., 97; cf. Safrai, Self-Government, 380.

43) Hoenig (Sanhedrin, 47, 51f.) argues that the nasi was head of the majority party (liberal Hillelites), the av bet din head of the minority party ("constructionist" Shammaites), and that the latter office disappeared as the Hillelites became completely dominant. But this is surely assigning Hillelite dominance to too early a period (cf. J. Sot. 3.4).

44) Cf. Bacher, Sanhedrin, 400; Lauterbach, Essays, 204f.; Neusner, Tradi-tions III, 276; Urbach, Class-Status, 41.

45) Cf. Smallwood, Priests, 14-34.

46) Cf. Meyer, Tradition, 66-71.

47) In this connection, see Gerhardsson, Tradition, 20.

48) Cf. Neusner, Traditions III, 273; also I, 375f.

49) Cf. Safrai, Self-Government, 394.

50) Cf. Bacher, Tradition, 49; Hunzinger, Institutionen, 147-156; Kennard, Assembly, 35-39.

51) E.g. 1QS 6.8ff. Cf. Rabin, Studies, 103-108.

52) Cf. Forkman, Limits, 99f.; also Finkelstein, Pharisees I, 77-80; Hunzinger, Institutionen, 149-156.

53) Cf. Moore, Judaism I, 81.

54) For the following, cf. Gerhardsson, Memory, 246-249, 254-256; Schiffman, Halakhah, 68-75.
55) Cf. Gerhardsson, Memory, 248, 256.
56) Cf. Hunzinger, Institutionen, 154f.
57) Cf. Neusner, Traditions III, 17.
58) Cf. Bacher, Tradition, 61f.
59) Ibid., 51; A. Guttmann, Judaism, 120; M. Guttmann, Einleitung, 36-42.
60) Cf. M. Guttmann, Einleitung, 43, 82.
61) Cf. Neusner, Traditions III, 278-280.
62) Ibid., 278f.
63) Ibid., I, 375f.
64) Ibid., III, 275f.
65) Ibid., 276.
66) Ibid., 279.
67) Ibid., II, 4.

CHAPTER V - TITHING

1) Cf. Neusner, Traditions III, 286-300.
2) Cf. Weinfeld, Tithe, 1157f.
3) Ibid., 1161.
4) In point of fact, priests and not Levites seem to have been the usual recipients in our period; cf. Judith 11:13; Philo, Virtues, 95; Jos. Life 63, 80; Ant. 20.181, 206f.; and the discussion in Belkin, Philo, 67-78; Oppenheimer, 'Am Ha-Aretz, 38-42.
5) Cf. Tob. 1:8 in Vaticanus; Jos. Ant. 4.240; perhaps also Jub. 32:11 (on this text, see Albeck, Buch, 31f.). See Finkelstein, Examples, 33f. n. 30; Strack-Billerbeck IV, 680-682.
6) On this text, see Albeck, Buch, 30f.
7) Cf. Oppenheimer, 'Am Ha-Aretz, 69-79.
8) Cf. Neusner, Fellowship, 136-142.
9) According to B. Sot. 48a, this practice of the haverim originated with a ruling of Yohanan the high priest; but Meyer (Demaj, 124-131), noting parallel texts to B. Sot. 48a which do not mention doubtful produce (demai) purchased from an am ha-arez but speak quite generally of the necessity of paying tithes, suggests that the original ordinance (which he dates from the first century A.D.) was not sectarian (i.e. a regulation for the haverim) but actually issued by the Jerusalem priesthood for the nation as a whole, insisting on the payment of priestly revenue. For priestly aggressiveness on this point, cf. Ant. 20.206f. See also Oppenheimer, 'Am Ha-Aretz, 34f., 73-76. In that case, B. Sot. 48a has been adapted to the practice of the haverim.
10) Cf. Oppenheimer, 'Am Ha-Aretz, 164.
11) This is perhaps one of the few cases where we may speak of a virtual consensus of scholarly opinion in favour of authenticity (see, however, Fiedler, Jesus, 228-233): partly because the parables in general are recognized as a characteristic medium of Jesus' message (criterion of style), partly because this parable in particular reverses the religious values of Jesus' day (criterion of dissimilarity), and that in a way consistent with Jesus' association with notorious sinners (to be dealt with in Ch. VI; criterion of coherence). We are here speaking of vv. 10-14a. V. 14b was apparently an isolated saying in the gospel tradition (cf. 14:11 and Mt. 23:12), and may well have been attached here secondarily.
12) Jeremias (Gleichnisse, 141) argues for an exclusive sense, "This one was justified and not the other;" but, as Jeremias himself admits, the sense "more justified than the other" is also grammatically possible. The point of the parable appears to be simply that God reverses human evaluations; hence we should be cautious about making of it an absolute statement

about the justification or condemnation of the Pharisee. Cf. also Kruse, Negation, 392.

13) Cf. Jeremias, Gleichnisse, 140; Rengstorf, Luk., 207.

14) Cf. Baumbach, Jesus, 92f.

15) Haenchen, Matth. 23, 51f.

16) In Mt. 23, v. 24 is closely connected with v. 23; but it is lacking in Lk., so that the combination in Mt., while certainly appropriate, may well be secondary.

17) Cf. Strack-Billerbeck IV, 650.

18) So Mt. and Lk. It is clear from M. Shev. 7.1 that its leaves were used for food.

19) So Mt. According to M. Ma'as. 4.5, the sages agreed that its pods must be tithed, though Eliezer held (against the others) that the "seeds and plant" must be tithed as well. Cf. also B.A.Z. 7b; Neusner, Eliezer I, 71. Lk. has "rue" which, according to M. Shev. 9.1, was not subject to tithing. Correns (Verzehntung, 110-112) argues that "rue" in M. Shev. 9.1 refers to the uncultivated plant (as is the case for the other items in the list), whereas Lk. means cultivated rue which, according to the rule in M. Ma'as. 1.1, would be subject to tithing. We have in any case to account for the difference from "dill" in Mt. Nestle ('Anise', 528) suggests the Lukan reading depends on the confusion of an Aramaic term; but see Correns, Verzehntung, 111.

20) So Mt.; liable to tithing according to M. Dem. 2.1. Lk. generalizes: "every kind of garden herb".

21) The point of the verse is of course not affected by the variants in herbs mentioned in Mt. and Lk. I have here followed Mt., but it should be noted that this is not a self-evident choice, nor is it certain that Luke's list shows an ignorance of scribal law. Correns has shown that Luke's reading at each point can be defended; and Baer (Aspects, 125) points out the surprising fact that Luke's list has an exact Mishnaic parallel in M. Uk. 1.2: "mint, rue, and herbs". Baer even suggests on the basis of this parallel that Lk. has here taken over the phrase from the rabbinic schools!

22) Cf. Jeremias, Jerusalem, 252-254.

23) Cf. Barth, Gesetzesverständnis, 74.

24) Cf. Gerhardsson, Program, 140.

25) So Klostermann (Matth., 186).

26) Cf. Barth, Gesetzesverständnis, 74f.

27) This is not noted by those who see the whole verse simply as a radicalization of the Mosaic law which makes both meticulous tithing and moral virtue the necessary ingredients of piety. Cf. Schulz, Q, 101-104; also Haenchen, Matth. 23, 39f.

28) Cf. Kümmel, Weherufe, 142f., 145.

29) Cf. Klausner, Jesus, 367.

30) Cf. Branscomb, Jesus, 210-213.

31) The omission of the concluding phrase in D and Marcion in Lk. 11:42 is too weakly attested to be accepted, especially since the reading can be accounted for by the theological bias of those sources; see Branscomb, Jesus, 208, and especially Epp, Tendency, who establishes the "anti-Judaic" tendency of D in Acts, including the tendency to diminish "the value of the customs and practices of Judaism" (115).

32) Cf. Banks, Jesus, 179f.

33) For the following, see the fine discussion in Urbach, Sages I, 342-365.

CHAPTER VI - RITUAL PURITY

1) Cf. Alon, Jews, 233; Neusner, Idea, 27f., 32-71.

2) Cf. Paschen, Rein, 55-64; von Rad, Theologie I, 271-278.

3) Contrast the approach of B.A. Levine (Presence, 77-91) and Paschen (Rein,

55-64). Cf. Neusner, Idea, 8ff.

4) Cf. Alon, Jews, 232f.; Oppenheimer, 'Am Ha-Aretz, 52f.

5) Cf. Lev. 11:32ff.; 15:12; Num. 19:15; and note the ideal of Zech. 14:21.
In the light of these texts, Neusner appears to draw too sharp a line between scripture and Pharisaic practice, e.g. when he writes (History III,
383f.) that, during the period "from ca. 20 to ca. 70... the most fundamental
and original conception of all took shape: utensils not in the Temple and
not used for the cult to begin with should be subject to uncleanness....
And neither Scriptures nor exegesis of Scriptures will have generated such
an original and revolutionary conception."

6) Büchler, Types, 132.

7) Büchler, 'Am-ha'Ares, 85, 211f.

8) Ibid., 127, 337.

9) So possibly in the case of handwashing; cf. C.G. Montefiore, Gospels I,
141.

10) See the discussion in Beilner, Christus, 75-77.

11) Margoliouth, Traditions, 262.

12) Burkitt, Jesus, 396.

13) C.G. Montefiore, Gospels I, 144.

14) Cf., in connection with Mk. 7, Carlston, Things, 94, especially n. 4;
Haenchen, Weg, 263 n. 1; Lohmeyer, Mark., 139.

15) This is largely due to two articles of Alon, originally published in
Hebrew in Tarbiz (1937-1938) and recently made available in English (Jews,
146-189, 190-234). Neusner (Fellowship, 125 n. 2) speaks of Büchler's thesis
being "demolished" by Alon, and writes elsewhere (Idea, x): "Perhaps the
most valuable service of Büchler was to provoke G. Allon to his brilliant,
if methodologically very primitive, critique." That the Pharisees were concerned with observing purity in daily life has since been abundantly shown
by the works of Neusner himself; cf. e.g. Traditions III, 294-297. See also
Burgsmüller, 'Am ha'ares, 62-84; Rabin, Studies, 16; Safrai, Religion, 802,
828-832; and now Oppenheimer, 'Am Ha-Aretz, 51-66, 83-96.

16) But the evidence is very limited; see Alon, Jews, 233; Le Moyne,
Sadducéens, 268f., 279f., 370.

17) Cf. Alon, Jews, 211, especially n. 61; Meyer, 'Am hā-'Āres, 184.

18) Cf. Neusner, Idea, 29f.

19) Cf. Stein, Laws, 141-154.

20) Alon (Jews, 146-189) proves at length the antiquity of this view against
those who held that the "uncleanness of Gentiles" was first introduced as
one of the 18 measures shortly before the destruction of the temple. Cf.
Jub. 22:16; Ant. 12.120; 14.285; 18.94f.; John 18:28; M. Pes. 8.8; M. Kel.
1.8; M. Oho. 18.7. See also Safrai, Religion, 829.

21) As Alon (Jews, 222) notes, the observance of this relatively uncompli-
cated practice need not imply full-fledged observance of all the Pharisaic
purity regulations. T. Dem. 2.11 appears to place the duty of handwashing
(so at least the traditional rendering of כנפים) on the prospective haver
before other, more difficult demands. The origin of this practice is obscure,
but it is quite possible that it was not a Pharisaic innovation, but a more
widespread custom perhaps introduced into Palestine by Hellenistic influences;
cf. Lévy, Légende, 257 (but note the caveat of Neusner, Idea, 71 n. 1: the
source need not have been specifically Pythagorean); also Brandt, Reinheitslehre, 27-29. Hart (CORBAN, 627) suggests the practice arose in the time of
Antiochus Epiphanes, on, admittedly, very slight evidence; but the impulse
may be correct. In this case, the Pharisees would merely have adopted (at
the time of Shammai and Hillel? cf. B. Shab. 14b) a widespread custom
(minhag) as halakhah.

22) For Essene-Qumran observances of ritual purity, see Buchanan, Role,
397-406; Gnilka, Gemeinschaftsmahl, 39-55; Neusner, Idea, 50-58; Paschen,
Rein, 85-152; van der Ploeg, Meals, 163-175.

23) Cf. Gnilka, Gemeinschaftsmahl, 44-47; Rabin, Studies, 7f.
24) Cf. especially Alon, Jews, 205-223. Of course, here, too, allowance had to be made for temporary, unintentional defilements; cf. T. Shab. 1.15.
25) See e.g. the comments of Neusner in History V, 243; XIV 173f., 180f.
26) Cf. Alon, Jews, 216.
27) Ibid., 216ff.
28) A concern for the purity of food is also witnessed by the House debates in M. Makhsh. 1.2-4; M. Uk. 3.6, 8, 11.
29) Here it is the O.T. purity laws which are at stake, not simply scribal ordinances. Still, Jesus' attitude towards the biblical laws provides the background for a study of his view of the later ordinances and the subject of purity in general.
30) Cf. Braun, Radikalismus II, 65f. n. 7.
31) Neusner, Idea, 60.
32) It seems clear that we are meant to understand that the girl was really dead, despite Jesus' words that she was only "sleeping"; cf. Mk. 5:35 par.; Mt. 9:18; Lk. 8:55.
33) Cf. Neusner, History IV, 4. Note also Lk. 7:14: touching a coffin certainly brought uncleanness; cf. Num. 19:22.
34) We use the traditional term. For the nature of the disease, cf. van der Loos, Miracles, 465-468.
35) Mk. 1:44 par.; cf. Lk. 17:14. This was to be done "as a witness to them". The phrase cannot be interpreted with certainty. Does the "witness" concern Jesus' faithful observance of the law? the completeness of the cure? Or is it to be a "witness against them", i.e. against their unbelief in the face of a demonstration of divine power? See van der Loos, Miracles, 487-489.
36) Cf. Neusner, History VIII, 3; Idea, 60f.
37) Rabbinic law leaves no doubt on this point: a leper, by entering a house, rendered it, and even the utensils within it, unclean (M. Kel. 1.4; T. Neg. 7.11).
38) Cf. van der Loos, Miracles, 479 n. 1.
39) Cf. Mk. 2:14-17 par.; Mt. 11:19 par.; Lk. 15:2; 19:1ff. This remains true, even if Mk. 2:15f. par. and Lk. 15:2 are secondary, part of a frame created for logia originally transmitted independently; cf. Bultmann, Geschichte, 16, 209; Schürmann, Luk., 292f. Note especially Mt. 11:19 par., where "a friend of tax collectors and sinners" apparently represents a typical way of referring to Jesus among those unsympathetic to him. Also Mt. 21:31, the radicalness of which matches that of Lk. 18:14a, both indicating the revolution of values brought by Jesus. Furthermore, Jeremias has effectively shown how a good number of the parables have their original setting in Jesus' vindication of his dealings with the disreputable (Gleichnisse, 124-145; Theologie I, 119-123). See also Hofius, Tischgemeinschaft, 5-25; Pesch, Zöllnergastmahl, 78.
40) Cf. Jeremias, Theologie I, 123: "Denn das nachösterliche Skandalon war der Fluchtod Jesu am Kreuz - die Tischgemeinschaft mit den Sündern ist das vorösterliche Skandalon."
41) Cf. Oppenheimer, 'Am Ha-Aretz, 118-169.
42) Of course, there were other factors as well. If a meal without Torah was an abomination (cf. M. Avot 3.3), it is clear that one must be selective in one's company for that reason as well. Cf. Abrahams, Studies I, 55f.; Branscomb, Jesus, 133-135.
43) Cf. M. Dem. 2.2f.; T. Dem. 2.2; also Neusner, Fellowship, 134f.; Oppenheimer, 'Am Ha-Aretz, 164-166; Rabin, Studies, 16.
44) Cf. Neusner, Fellowship, 129.
45) But apparently exceptions were made; cf. T. Dem. 3.7; 8.4f.; M. Dem. 7.1f.; Oppenheimer, 'Am Ha-Aretz, 164-166.
46) See especially Jeremias, Jerusalem, 303-312; Zöllner, 293-300; also Abrahams, Studies I, 55; Burgsmüller, 'Am ha-'ares, 118-134.

47) For tax collectors, see Donahue, Collectors, 39-61. Note that he finds the translation "toll collectors" preferable, though "tax collectors" may be used in the general sense "referring to anyone who had any role in the collection of taxes" (54); but see Schalit, Herodes, 296. Jeremias (Theologie I, 112f.) urges a careful distinction between tax collectors and toll collectors. In fact, both, as outsiders to the havurah, i.e. ammei ha-arez, would be suspected of ritual uncleanness by the haverim (M. Toh. 7.6, seen in the context of 7.1-6, need imply no more), but their notoriety was the result primarily of their reputation for dishonesty (cf. Lk. 3:12f.; 19:8; Jeremias, Jerusalem, 310f.). In the discussion which follows, "tax collectors" is used in a general sense without any attempt at distinguishing them from toll collectors, since their only significance here is the fact that they represent notorious sinners.

48) Cf. the literature in n. 46.

49) Note the (rather unusual) precision of Mk. 2:16: "scribes belonging to the (party of the) Pharisees", i.e. their professional leaders; cf. also Lk. 15:2.

50) Cf. Jeremias, Theologie I, 120.

51) The parallels from Greek and Latin authors to Mk. 2:17 (see Jülicher, Gleichnisreden II, 176f.) do not of course mean that the verse cannot go back to Jesus. He himself may have applied a well-known proverb to the situation, though in the case of such an obvious metaphor no dependence is required. Cf. Pesch, Zöllnergastmahl, 81f.; Schürmann, Luk., 293. The point here made is in any case clear from such passages as Lk. 7:41f.; 15:11ff., in which Jesus, defending his dealings with the disreputable, tells parables involving the forgiveness of very great transgressors. Jesus, too, reckons with the sinfulness of "sinners".

52) Cf. Jeremias, Theologie I, 119-123.

53) Mk. 7:1-23 will here be considered in its entirety, in spite of the probability that Mk. has here combined originally independent units of tradition. See the discussion below.

54) Note that Mt., who elsewhere always (10 times) has the order "scribes and Pharisees", in v. 1 speaks of "Pharisees and scribes", apparently following Mk. (7:1, 5). Note also the evidence for Matthaean redactional improvements in the next note.

55) Note τότε (Mt. 15:1, 12) for Markan καί (7:1, 17), typical of Matthaean redaction; προσέρχομαι (15:1, a favourite Matthaean word) for Markan συνάγομαι πρός (7:1); omission of Markan πάλιν (7:14) at the beginning of a pericope (15:10); the omission of unnecessary introductory formulas (Mk. 7:9, 20), etc.

56) Cf. Davies, Setting, 458.

57) Cf. Lohmeyer, Matth., 244.

58) Cf. Daube, Responsibilities, 8f.

59) κοινός in the sense of "ritually unclean" (first attested in 1 Macc. 1:47, 62) is limited to Jewish and Christian Greek, though connected with a usage in profane Greek meaning "ordinary", "common" in a derogatory sense. Cf. Paschen, Rein, 165-168.

60) Cf. Berger, Gesetzesauslegung, 462f.; Dibelius, Formgeschichte, 222f.; Horst, Worte, 433.

61) Büchler, 'Am-ha'Ares, 130ff.

62) The reason given in rabbinic texts for considering the hands to be unclean is that they are "fidgety", i.e. liable to touch that which is unclean; cf. M. Toh. 7.8; B. Shab. 14a; B. Suk. 26b.

63) In fact, according to the careful distinctions worked out in the Mishnah, hands are unclean only in the "second degree" (M. Yad. 3.1), and as such can defile hallowed things (kodashim) and heave-offering (terumah), but not ordinary food (hullin) (M. Zav. 5.12; cf. M. Par. 11.5). It is debated as to whether or not they defile second tithe (M. Par. 11.5). These careful

distinctions were apparently not worked out before the Yavnean period. Note the disagreements among Yavnean scholars in M. Sot. 5.2; M. Toh. 2.2; M. Yad. 3.1; cf. also Hübner, Gesetz, 161-164; Neusner, History XI, 43; XII, 202ff.
64) Aristeas 305f; note also Jos. Ant. 12.106. Possibly the uncleanness of hands is referred to in Judith 11:13 as well. Cf. Brandt, Baptismen, 42f., 56, 138; Lévy, Légende, 228f.
65) Admittedly, B. Shab. 15a suggests they meant that hands were considered unclean only for the eating of terumah; but this seems to be an attempt to reconcile traditions assigning the innovation to different periods with later rabbinic distinctions of the degrees of purity required for various types of food. That B. Shab. 14b also suggests the schools of Hillel and Shammai ruled concerning the uncleanness of hands as one of the 18 measures certainly need not represent an innovation on their part; it may indicate that an early practice, perhaps already enjoined by Hillel and Shammai, was reinforced by being adopted at a convocation of sages from the schools. Cf. Alon, Jews, 156-159.
66) E.g. Cohon, Place, 99.
67) Cf. n. 21 above.
68) See, recently, Hengel, Geschichte, 182-198; McHardy, Reference, 119; Reynolds, Note, 295f. and Hand, 87f.; and Ross, Fist, 374f.
69) E.g. Brandt, Reinheitslehre, 2; Horst, Worte, 432.
70) Cf. Black, Approach, 8f.; Weis, Note, 233-236.
71) Cf. Hengel, Geschichte, 182-198.
72) Cf. Reynolds, Note, 295f. and Hand, 87f.
73) Büchler, Law, 35, 38.
74) Brandt, Baptismen, 40f.; Reinheitslehre, 36-41.
75) Cf. Black, Approach, 9, 54; Brandt, Reinheitslehre, 34-36.
76) Horst, Worte, 434 n. 2.
77) Cf. Berger, Gesetzesauslegung, 486; Haenchen, Weg, 262, etc.
78) Cf. Beilner, Christus, 77f.; Pesch, Mark. I, 372f.; V. Taylor, Mark, 337f. Note also Stendahl, School, 58.
79) Cf. Dodd, Scriptures, 83f.
80) Cf. Falk, Vows, 309-312. It is usually held that the son was not in fact bound to bring an offering to the temple, the vow meaning no more than that what was vowed was as unavailable to the parents as if it were a korban offering. This is clearly the case in the vows listed in M. Ned. 1.3f.; M. Naz. 2.1-3. Recently, however, Derrett (KORBAN, 365) has argued that he was so bound as long as the temple stood. For an ossuary inscription providing a nearly contemporary example of a korban text, see Fitzmyer, Inscription, 60-65. On korban, see, in addition to the works cited in the notes below, Buchanan, Formulas, 319-326; Hart, CORBAN, 615-650; Hommel, Wort, 132-149; Rengstorf, Korban, 860-866; Zeitlin, KORBAN, 160-163.
81) C.G. Montefiore, Gospels I, 149.
82) So Falk, Binding, 93; cf. Taubes, Auflösung, 43.
83) Cf. Taubes, op.cit., 34-42.
84) Cf. p. 275 n. 5 in Danby's translation of the Mishnah; and note M. Ned. 9.9.
85) Cf. Hübner, Gesetz, 150-152.
86) Cf. Neusner, Eliezer II, 110.
87) Ibid., 311; cf. Taubes, Auflösung, 45.
88) Cf. also Baer, Aspects, 120f. Baer, recognizing the accuracy of what is said about the halakhah, denies that such a learned argument can go back to Jesus himself. But the knowledge of Pharisaic tradition here assumed is not particularly extensive (cf. Davies, Setting, 424), nor was the "teacher" from Nazareth as uninformed as Baer supposes (for the opposite extreme, see Flusser, Jesus, 20).
89) For the following, see Hübner, Gesetz, 152-155.
90) Cf. Falk, Binding, 92.

91) See Chapter VII below.
92) It may well be that v. 13b was added to Jesus' answer in an attempt to broaden its scope; cf. v. 4 and the longer reading in v. 8.
93) Cf. Gerhardsson, Memory, 21f. n. 5.
94) Cf. Branscomb, Jesus, 173; Schoeps, Jesus, 49ff.
95) Note the importance of the letter of the vow in M. Ned. 5.3; 6.7-9, etc.
96) Cf. Horst, Worte, 434f.
97) Cf. Hubaut, Jésus, 407f.; Hübner, Gesetz, 142ff.
98) Merkel, Jesuswort, 341-350 provides a helpful history of the interpretation of the verse.
99) Cf. Käsemann, Problem, 207f.
100) Berger, Gesetzesauslegung, 465ff.; cf., however, Fiedler, Jesus, 250-252. Note that Merkel, Jesuswort, 354-359 uses the same principle to accept v. 15a as genuine, but deny the authenticity of v. 15b.
101) Hübner, Gesetzesverständnis, 339.
102) See also Kümmel, Reinheit, 40f.; McEleney, Criteria, 440-442, 455-457.
103) Cf. Branscomb, Jesus, 177ff.; Kümmel, Reinheit, 41f.
104) C.G. Montefiore, Gospels I, 132f.
105) Cf. Gerhardsson, Anfänge, 48f.
106) Cf. Jeremias, Theologie I, 24-30.
107) Cf. Gerhardsson, Anfänge, 50f.
108) Cf. Paschen, Rein, 177.
109) That Mt. records the mashal in a slightly different form is probably not an indication that the words of Jesus were recreated freely, but rather that Mt. has restated the logion in a less ambiguous manner. Cf. Allen, Mt., 165; Gerhardsson, Anfänge, 59ff.; Kümmel, Reinheit, 36.
110) Cf. Gerhardsson, Memory, 315-317.
111) Reading καθαρίζων, and understanding Jesus as the subject (as for λέγει, v. 18). Note that Banks, Jesus, 144f. thinks Mk. with this addition does not refer to the food laws of Lev., but rather applies the words of Jesus to the specific early church problem of eating food offered to idols.
112) Cf. Dodd, Studies, 144: "The use of the form Κύριος Ἰησοῦς, however, suggests the intention of referring to the historic Person, as in I Thess. ii. 15, I Cor. xi. 23." That Paul speaks only of what he is "persuaded in the Lord Jesus", and mentions no specific command of the Lord (as in 1 Cor. 7:10; 9:14) may be because he is drawing an halakhic conclusion not made explicit in the logion itself. See below.
113) So Haenchen, Weg, 266.
114) Cf. Carlston, Things, 95; Percy, Botschaft, 118.
115) Cf. Hübner, Gesetz, 164f. It is frequently said that vv. 1-13 and 14-23 cannot be treated together because the subject matter is different (handwashing, then food laws; e.g. Bultmann, Geschichte, 15; Dibelius, Formgeschichte, 222). But v. 15 is better interpreted as a general statement on the true nature of impurity than as a specific attack on the food laws. Mk. uses προσκαλεσάμενος elsewhere to introduce general considerations placing a subject under discussion or observation in its true perspective (3:23; 10:42; 12:43). Still, form and redactional considerations have been advanced for treating the sections separately; cf. Marxsen, Erklärung, 259ff.; Paschen, Rein, 155ff.
116) Cf. Pesch, Mark. I, 367.
117) Cf. Cohon, Place, 104; Merkel, Jesus, 205f.; against Klausner, Jesus, 319; Winter, Trial, 133.
118) Cf. Kruse, Negation, 385-400.
119) Cf. Braun, Radikalismus II, 7-14.
120) Cf. Dodd, Studies, 24-26.
121) Against Dibelius, Formgeschichte, 222.
122) Ibid., 222; Lohmeyer, Mark., 142; Merkel, Jesuswort, 352.

123) Only 4 of these are found in Mt. as "woes", and only 3 of these are in the same order as in Lk. Cf. Manson, Sayings, 94ff. Manson concludes that Mt. 23 is largely drawn from M, perhaps at places conflated with Q (better represented by Lk.); "the coincidences in order between Mt. and Lk. will then be coincidences between M and Q and point to a stage in the tradition anterior to these two sources" (96).
124) Cf. Bultmann, Geschichte, 158; Schulz, Q, 94.
125) Cf. Grundmann, Matth., 493f.; Manson, Sayings, 237.
126) This is perhaps a more natural way of rendering ἐκ (note that γέμουσιν is followed directly by the genitive in v. 27 where the sense "full of" is required), though γέμουσιν ἐκ could simply mean "full of" (cf. John 12:3).
127) Cf. Allen, Mt., 247f.; McNeile, Mt., 336.
128) Cf. Manson, Sayings, 269.
129) So Manson, Sayings, 268; but see Schulz, Q, 95f.
130) Cf. Bultmann, Geschichte, 359.
131) Cf. Jeremias, Jerusalem, 252-254.
132) Cf. Wellhausen, Einleitung, 36.
133) Cf. Dalman, Worte, 372.
134) Cf. Bultmann, Geschichte, 139. Mt. may have understood the text in the sense suggested in the first alternative in (iii) above; see n. 126.
135) Cf. Black, Approach, 2; Wellhausen, Einleitung, 37; but see Dalman, Worte, 50, 372; Moule, Idiom-Book, 186.
136) Cf. Haenchen, Matth. 23, 42 n. 1.
137) Cf. Neusner, History III, 249ff., 355ff.
138) Ibid., III, 369.
139) Cf. Neusner, Inside, 487.
140) For the following, cf. Neusner, Inside, 492f.
141) Ibid., 494.
142) It is of course possible that the reference to a "cup" in v. 26 merely continues the metaphor of v. 25, and here, without any thought for the distinction the schools drew between the outside and inside of vessels, represents the individual whose heart is to be cleansed. Cf. Grundmann, Matth., 494; Haenchen, Matth. 23, 40.
143) Cf. Haenchen, Matth. 23, 52; note also Schulz, Q, 98-100.
144) Cf. Bultmann, Geschichte, 158.
145) Cf. Vermes, Jesus, 35.

CHAPTER VII - SABBATH

1) Cf. Finkelstein, Examples, 28f. Note also Philo, Migr. Abrah. 91.
2) E.g. M. Shab. 7.2. Cf. Finkelstein, Examples, 29-32, who argues that R. Judah was the authority behind the view that there were 39 categories of forbidden activities (29 n. 15). It is, in any case, going beyond the evidence to speak of the 39 categories as a fixed list already in the time of Jesus.
3) Cf. Moore, Judaism II, 32.
4) CD 10.21; 11.5-7. The 1000 cubits was derived from Num. 35:4. Cf. Schiffman, Halakhah, 91ff., 111ff.
5) Ibid., 96.
6) Ibid., 96.
7) Cf. Zeitlin, Takkanot, 353.
8) Ibid., 351-357. Cf. also Zucrow, Adjustment, 83.
9) Note also Mk. 1:32 par.: it is first "at evening, when the sun had set (i.e. when the sabbath (v. 21) was over)" that people "carried to him all who were sick..."
10) Cf. M. Shab. 7.2. That the rule was derived from a prophetic text rather than from Torah was no hindrance to its adoption by the Pharisees since, at least in the early period, prophetic texts were commonly the source of

halakhot. Cf. Urbach, Halacha, 1-27, and note B. Hor. 4a. It may, however, have been the reason why various Amoraim attempted to derive the rule from Torah; cf. Schiffman, Halakhah, 114.

11) Note how various aspects of the matter are discussed by the schools of Shammai and Hillel, M. Er. 1.2; 6.4, 6, etc.; and see the ma'aseh from pre-70 Jerusalem in M. Er. 6.2. Cf. Zeitlin, Takkanot, 357-360. Schiffman, Halakhah, 109 n. 167 argues against reading CD 11.4 as a prohibition of eruvin.

12) Cf. Jub. 50:10f.; CD 11.17f.; Jos. Ant. 3.237; Mek. to Ex. 12:16 and to 21:14, etc.

13) Cf. John 7:22f. and Mek. to Ex. 31:13; B. Shab. 132a; also M. Shab. 18.3; M. Ned. 3.11, etc.

14) E. Levine (Controversy, 480-483) correctly points out that the omer (cf. Lev. 23:10ff.) could, according to Pharisaic law, be reaped on the sabbath (M. Men. 10.1, 3; cf. Daube, Testament, 67), without, however, convincing in his attempt to show that Mt. 12:5 refers to this practice.

15) Cf. Jos. War 1.146; Ant. 12.276f.; 14.63. See also Safrai, Religion, 805. Shammai (or Hillel) is said to have ruled that a siege begun by Jews before the sabbath might be carried on till the city fell, without regard to the sabbath (T. Er. 3.7).

16) Abrahams, Studies I, 130; cf. Moore, Judaism II, 30.

17) Here Simeon b. Yohai (mid-second century) is the only authority cited, though the basic principle must have been accepted before his time. Cf. also T. Shab. 12.8-14.

18) According to Flusser (Jesus, 47), in cases where life was not in danger, "mechanical" means of healing were forbidden on the sabbath; on the other hand, healing by the spoken word was explicitly permitted whether life was in danger or not. Hence Jesus' healings in the synoptics were not against Pharisaic law. Cf. also Safrai, Religion, 805. In this he is following Epstein (Introduction, 280f.). The basis of the statement that healing by the spoken word was permitted in all cases on the sabbath is a rabbinic tradition according to which magical incantations are permitted on the sabbath in certain specifically named cases: according to B. Sanh. 101a, they could be used against snakes and serpents; T. Shab. 7.23 permits their use for the "eye" (i.e., presumably, for protection against the "evil eye") as well; J. Shab. 14.3, for the intestines (cf. Epstein, Introduction, 281). That incantation formulas were in use cannot be doubted, though various rabbis attempted to "judaize" the practice by substituting verses of scripture (cf. Blau, Zauberwesen, 68). Even this met with opposition: Akiva said that the one who utters a charm over a wound and recites scripture has no place in the world to come (M. Sanh. 10.1); according to B. Shevu. 15b, R. Joshua b. Levi said that it was prohibited to use words of Torah in this way to heal oneself, though one might use them as protection from possible afflictions. The suggestion of Epstein and Flusser must therefore be rejected. (i) Aside from the general methodological problem raised by using a rabbinic tradition without reservations for the Pharisaic halakhah of the time of Jesus (and that in opposition to the witness of the gospels; Epstein suggests that the Pharisees and synagogue official who there protest against healings on the sabbath were not experts in the halakhah!), we have in this case evidence that the practice cited by that tradition was viewed as dubious at least by some rabbis long afterwards. (ii) The relevance of that tradition for the healings of Jesus is questionable in any case. His words (e.g. "Stretch out your hand!" "Woman, you are rid of your infirmity!") can scarcely be classified as magical incantations. (iii) The tradition cited is not a general permission for healing through the spoken word whether life was in danger or not, but a permission for incantations to be used in specifically mentioned cases; moreover, the cases mentioned in T. Shab.

7.23 and B. Sanh. 101a represented very definite threats to life.
19) Note also B. Shab. 30a; and see Schoeps, Jesus, 47f.
20) Cf. Moore, Judaism II, 27.
21) This remains true even though the Shammaites, whose rulings were stricter than the Hillelites, were dominant at the time of Jesus, and even though the rabbinic halakhah of a later period was often still more liberal than the Pharisaic halakhah at this time. Cf. Abrahams, Studies I, 129-135; Bietenhardt, Sabbatvorschriften, 53-61; Finkelstein, Book, 45-51 and Examples, 29f.; Kimbrough, Concept, 483-502; Moore, Judaism II, 27.
22) Cf. Moore, Judaism II, 34ff.; also Bowman, Mark, 118f.
23) On the other hand, we cannot regard the phrase peculiar to Mt. (24:20; cf. Mk. 13:18), according to which the disciples in the time of tribulation are to pray that their flight not be "on the sabbath", as indicating that Jesus would have prohibited such a "journey" on the sabbath! Even the Pharisees would permit a journey to save one's life. The thought (whether or not we attribute it to Jesus) is rather that, by fleeing on the sabbath when others made no journey, the disciples would be easily recognized, and their lives thus endangered. Cf. Barth, Gesetzesverständnis, 85f.; Grundmann, Matth., 506.
24) The recent article of Neirynck (Jesus, 227-270) provides a helpful history of the exegesis of this pericope. For further bibliography, see Pesch, Mark. I, 187.
25) For those holding this view, see Neirynck, Jesus, 231f. n. 8; add Pesch, Mark. I, 178f.
26) For this view, see Neirynck, Jesus, 235-237.
27) See Cranfield, Mark, 116-118; Hultgren, Formation, 38ff.; and those cited by Neirynck, Jesus, 242-246.
28) For this as the first century form of the Aramaic phrase, see Fitzmyer, Methodology, 92f.; Jeremias, Theologie I, 248 n. 19.
29) Manson, Mark ii. 27f., 138-146; cf. Neirynck, Jesus, 237-241.
30) Cf. Beare, Sabbath, 132; Benoit, Epis, 234; Gils, Sabbat, 522.
31) Cf. Hübner, Gesetz, 120f.; Käsemann, Problem, 207; Kuhn, Sammlungen, 75; Lohse, Worte, 84f.; Neirynck, Jesus, 232 n. 11; Rordorf, Sonntag, 63ff., etc.
32) For arguments against the view (most recently represented by Benoit, Epis, 236-238; cf. Murmelstein, Gang, 111-120) that Mark represents the charge as the making of a path on the sabbath, see Neirynck, Jesus, 254ff.
33) Reaping is one of the 39 categories prohibited by M. Shab. 7.2. The rabbis later debated whether or not rubbing the ears of corn in the hands (cf. Lk. 6:1) constituted threshing (B. Bez. 12b), another forbidden category (M. Shab. 7.2). Cf. Moore, Judaism II, 29 n. 2; III, 171. But whether or not the disciples were rebuked on this point, there can be no doubt that picking the ears was seen as reaping and condemned. Cf. also Banks, Jesus, 114 n. 2 against Flusser's reading of the passage (Jesus, 44).
34) Cf. Pesch, Mark. I, 179.
35) Mt. 12:1 states explicitly that the disciples were hungry. This is probably not to be understood as an attempt on Matthew's part to provide an halakhic justification for what follows, since hunger in itself was scarcely sufficient grounds for breaking the sabbath. His intention seems to have been simply to better motivate the disciples' actions and better prepare for the parallel with David. Cf. Banks, Jesus, 113; Hummel, Auseinandersetzung, 41.
36) Cf. Kuhn, Sammlungen, 77; Schweizer, Mark., 39.
37) Cf. Daube, Testament, 68-71; Merkel, Jesus, 204; Rordorf, Sonntag, 60.
38) Cf. B. Men. 95b-96a; Strack-Billerbeck I, 618f.
39) Cf. Abrahams, Studies I, 134; Lohmeyer, Mark., 65.
40) Cf. Hay, Son, 74.

41) It has been suggested that Mt. 12:5f. is also more satisfying from a
halakhic viewpoint; cf. Daube, Testament, 70f. But Mt. 12:7 should make us
wary of distinguishing too sharply between the non-halakhic approach of
Jesus and Matthew's supposed legalism. Cf. Barth, Gesetzesverständnis, 77f.
42) Cf. Banks, Jesus, 116f.; Guelich, Law, 51; Hübner, Gesetz, 124f.;
Hummel, Auseinandersetzung, 42. The neuter μεῖζον (Mt. 12:6) presumably
contains a veiled reference to the Messiah; cf. Grundmann, Matth., 321.
Alternatively, the kingdom of God may be meant (Manson, Sayings, 187).
43) Against Benoit, Epis, 238f.; Hübner, Gesetz, 124; Pesch, Mark. I, 182;
Roloff, Kerygma, 57f., etc.
44) Cf. Cranfield, Mark, 115; Schlatter, Mark., 22; Matth., 394f. Note also
Kümmel, Jesus, 28; Lohmeyer, Mark., 64f.
45) Since, as we have argued, vv. 25f. can scarcely have existed independently of vv. 23f., the basic historicity of vv. 23f. seems assured as well.
Cf. Haenchen, Weg, 122f.; Pesch, Mark. I, 183; note also Banks, Jesus, 114;
Daube, Responsibilities, 4-8; V. Taylor, Mark, 214f. The arguments against
this position (Bultmann, Geschichte, 14; also Beare, Sabbath, 133; Hultgren,
Formation, 41f.; Schweizer, Mark., 38, etc.) are not conclusive: that the
journey in itself constituted a violation of the sabbath laws is not certain,
since it need not have been a long one (cf. Abrahams, Studies I, 134); it
need occasion no surprise that there were Pharisees among those who at this
time crowded about Jesus wherever he went; nor that Jesus himself is not
said to pick the corn, since he may well have been otherwise occupied; nor
that he is held responsible for the conduct of his disciples, since this
was a common view.
46) Mt. and Lk. either omitted the verse, or perhaps followed a version of
the tradition in which that verse had not yet been added. Cf. Barth,
Gesetzesverständnis, 85 n. 1; Hübner, Gesetz, 115ff.; and the discussion in
Staudinger, Sabbatkonflikte, 178-190.
47) Cf. Cranfield, Mark, 118; Kuhn, Sammlungen, 73; Staudinger, Sabbatkonflikte, 200f.; V. Taylor, Mark, 220, etc.
48) Cf. Jeremias, Theologie I, 95.
49) Mk. 1:23-28 par., 29-31 par.; 3:1-6 par.; Lk. 13:10-17; 14:1-6 in the
synoptics. The two narratives peculiar to Luke are usually taken to be
secondary compositions (Bultmann, Geschichte, 10; Lohse, Worte, 81; Roloff,
Kerygma, 66, etc.; but see Staudinger, Sabbatkonflikte, 89ff.); still the
authenticity of Jesus' defence in these passages (13:15f.; 14:5) must be
judged independently of their setting. See below. The historicity of Mk.
3:1-6 (1-5?) is often assessed more positively (cf. Lohse, Worte, 84; Pesch,
Mark. I, 195f.; Roloff, Kerygma, 63f.). Furthermore, it should be noted that
sabbath healings and controversies are also to be found in John's gospel
(5:9ff.; 7:22f.; 9:14, 16). In John 5, Jesus' defence is a christological
one, in a typically Johannine strain: "My Father goes on working, and so do
I" (5:17). John 7:22f. contains a curiously halakhic argument, with close
parallels in rabbinic texts (Mek. to Ex. 31:13; B. Yom. 85b). See Cullmann,
Worship, 84-93; Lohse, Worte, 79f.; Roloff, Kerygma, 80-85.
50) Cf. Bultmann, Geschichte, 158; Hübner, Gesetz, 128; Lohse, Worte, 85f.
51) Cf. Lk. 13:14, in which, according to Abrahams (Studies I, 134), the
Pharisaic view is presented "precisely".
52) This seems the most natural interpretation of the verse; cf. Beilner,
Christus, 33; Bietenhardt, Sabbatvorschriften, 63; Kümmel, Jesus, 28, etc.
Another view refers "doing evil" and "destroying life" to the Pharisees'
plots against Jesus (vv. 2, 6), and understands Jesus as asking if it is
his activity in healing or theirs in plotting to kill him which is "unlawful" (cf. Lohmeyer, Mark., 68f.; Pesch, Mark. I, 192f.; Roloff, Kerygma,
65; V. Taylor, Mark, 222).
53) Cf. Schoeps, Jesus, 48.

54) Literally, "Who among you has one sheep...?", but the numeral is probably used for the indefinite article; cf. Jeremias, Gleichnisse, 198.
55) Admittedly, in Mt. 12:11f., Jesus is speaking to the issue if it is
"lawful" to heal on the sabbath (12:10), a question he himself puts in
Lk. 14:3. But, apart from the question whether the settings have been shaped
secondarily to fit a saying first transmitted in isolation, the fact remains
that Jesus' answer appeals rather to practice and compassion than to legal
definition.
56) Cf. Banks, Jesus, 126; Manson, Sayings, 188f.; Roloff, Kerygma, 78f.;
Schiffman, Halakhah, 122.
57) See Lohse, Worte, 87; Staudinger, Sabbatkonflikte, 83ff. for a summary
of the discussions of Black and Jeremias about the original form of the
saying which gave rise to Matthew's "sheep" and Luke's "son or ox" (but the
text is doubtful).
58) To judge by the evidence, the Pharisees would have held it lawful to
draw up a son whose life was in danger, but not an animal (cf. T. Shab.
14.3). Later halakhah did, however, introduce ways of assisting an animal
under these circumstances; cf. B. Shab. 128b; Schiffman, Halakhah, 122.
Note that CD 11.13f. does not permit assisting such an animal; the regulation concerning assistance for people (CD 11.16f.) is difficult to interpret;
cf. Schiffman, Halakhah, 125-128.
59) Lohse (Worte, 81) sees 13:15f. as a secondary formulation of the authentic saying in Mt. 12:11-12a par. See also Roloff, Kerygma, 67f.
60) Rabbinic law prohibited as a rule the tying and untying of knots on the
sabbath (M. Shab. 7.2), but exceptions were made, which included the tying
of cattle (M. Shab. 15.2; cf. B. Shab. 113a). Careful regulations for
watering cattle were given, cf. B. Er. 20b-21a. Note also the regulations
for cattle "going out" on the sabbath in M. Shab. 5.1-4; and compare CD
11.5-7. Again, it must be emphasized that the legality of the practice is
not the point of Lk. 13:15f.
61) Cf. Lohse, Worte, 86f.

CHAPTER VIII - OATHS

1) Cf. Blank, Curse, 78; Crawley, Oath, 430f.; Pedersen, Eid, 82ff.; Silving,
Oath, 1330.
2) Cf. Crawley, Oath, 432; Pedersen, Eid, 104-106.
3) Cf. Crawley, Oath, 432; Pedersen, Eid, 155; Silving, Oath, 1330.
4) Cf. Pedersen, Eid, 156; Silving, Oath, 1331.
5) Cf. Blank, Curse, 89; Crawley, Oath, 432; Pedersen, Eid, 158.
6) Cf. Pedersen, Eid, 160; Silving, Oath, 1336; and note Philo's definition
of an oath as "the invoking of God as a witness on matters in question"
(Dec. 86; cf. Spec. Laws 2.10).
7) For this rendering of the O.T. phrase יהוה חי, see Pedersen, Eid,
141; and especially Greenberg, Particle, 34-39.
8) Cf. Pedersen, Eid, 147f. for the essential equivalence of such oaths and
an oath by God himself.
9) Cf. Pedersen, Eid, 134f. Similarly, one can add weight to one's words by
swearing "by my life", "by my head", etc. Again, something essential to
one's well-being is put at stake. Cf. Pedersen, Eid, 136f.
10) Cf. Pedersen, Eid, 196; Silving, Oath, 1332; Urbach, Sages I, 124.
11) Ex. 20:7. Cf. Jos. Ant. 2.276; Philo, Moses 2.114; B. Ned. 10a-b;
Strack-Billerbeck I, 330-332; Urbach, Sages I, 127ff.
12) Note already Dan. 12:7; cf. also 1QapGen. 2.4, 7, 14.
13) Cf. Lieberman, Oaths, 115ff.; Mann, Oaths, 261ff.; and note Philo,
Dec. 92; Spec. Laws 2.8.
14) For the prohibition of oaths among non-Jews, see Stählin, Gebrauch, 116
n. 2a. For Philo's views, see Belkin, Philo, 140-178.

15) Cf. also CD 15.1ff.; 16.1ff. But the evidence is difficult to assess; cf. Davies, Setting, 241-244.
16) Cf. Strack-Billerbeck I, 328ff. Belkin (Philo, 140) distinguishes between the haggadic teaching of the rabbis, which was opposed to swearing, and the halakhic, which legislated for the necessary evil. Cf. also C.G. Montefiore, Gospels II, 69.
17) Cf. Lieberman, Oaths, 115ff.
18) Cf. Lieberman, Oaths, 134. Lieberman does, however, note that certain rabbis were prepared to go further than others in approving popular usage (137). And the fact remains that the rabbis themselves often used oaths which would not be binding by the definitions given here. See Strack-Billerbeck I, 332ff. for examples. Possibly the strict rules of M. Shevu. 4.13 were only applied in court; cf. Strack-Billerbeck I, 331; also Cohen, Law II, 751 n. 72; Mann, Oaths, 263. On the use of oaths in court, see Falk, Introduction, 129-132.
19) Cf. Guelich, Law, 150f.; Pedersen, Eid, 123.
20) See Lieberman, Oaths, 117 for examples. Philo confuses oaths and vows in Spec. Laws 2.12f., 24; cf. Belkin, Philo, 157. And see CD 16.6ff., where O.T. texts concerning vows (Num. 30; Deut. 23:24(23)) are cited in regulations regarding oaths.
21) Cf. Lieberman, Oaths, 130ff. The rabbis did not, however, regard such oaths as valid since korban, though holy, was not a substitute for the divine name.
22) See H. Freedman's note to B. Ned. 15b in the Soncino edition, Ned., p. 42 n. 2.
23) Against Manson, Sayings, 158; cf. Davies, Setting, 240.
24) Guelich, Law, 285 n. 1 suggests quite plausibly that the oath intended in Mt. 5:34b-35a is one "by heaven and earth", but that the terms have been divided so that the O.T. text (Isa. 66:1) might be fitted in. Philo, Spec. Laws 2.5 may, however, imply that "earth" and "heaven" were used separately in oaths.
25) For examples of these oaths, see Strack-Billerbeck I, 332ff. Lieberman, Oaths, 132f. finds in T. Ned. 1.3 proof that Jerusalem was used in oaths.
26) The repetition "yes, yes", "no, no" seems to serve only as emphasis. James provides us with an alternative, perhaps more original form of the saying: "Let your yes mean yes, your no mean no" (5:12). Cf. Dibelius, Jak., 230f.; Manson, Sayings, 159; C.G. Montefiore, Gospels II, 69. At any rate, the evidence for "yes, yes" as a possible oath from later rabbinic literature is scarcely sufficient grounds for arguing that it is to be so understood here. Cf. Banks, Jesus, 195; Guelich, Law, 157 n. 1; Mann, Oaths, 263f.; Meier, Law, 153f.; Percy, Botschaft, 147 n. 4; Stählin, Gebrauch, 118-120. Note that "Yes, yes" and "No, no" in 2 Cor. 1:17 are not to be understood as oaths.
27) ἐκ τοῦ πονηροῦ ; alternatively, "from the Evil One"; cf. John 8:44.
28) This may well be the force of the antithetical form, "You have heard... but I say..." Daube (Testament, 55-62) has shown how these formulas may be used to contrast a possible interpretation of a text with the proper one. So, in the antitheses, a statutory understanding of O.T. commands, which sees the will of God as fulfilled when the literal wording of the text has been observed, is contrasted with Jesus' radical interpretation of the will of God. The antithetic formulation is thus an admirable expression of Jesus' intent, whether or not its use in each individual case goes back to Jesus. Appropriately, too, 5:21-48 is introduced by 5:20, in which a righteousness deeper than that of the scribes and Pharisees is required.
29) Cf. Braun, Radikalismus II, 80f.
30) Cf. Allen, Mt., 53; Dietzfelbinger, Antithesen, 33; Minear, Yes, 2f.; Percy, Botschaft, 148.

31) Cf. Bultmann, Geschichte, 143; Guelich, Law, 283ff. Minear (Yes, 1ff.) suggests on the basis of the form of the saying in Justin Martyr (Apology I, 16, 5) that the original saying may not have mentioned any examples of oaths, and that those of vv. 34b-36 were added (in two stages) somewhat later; cf. also Dietzfelbinger, Antithesen, 33. But on this view the form in James is difficult to explain: what would be the point of adding these examples ("by heaven", "by earth") without the explanations? Cf. Wrege, Überlieferungsgeschichte, 74.

32) Cf. Haenchen, Matth. 23, 38f.; Manson, Sayings, 234; McNeile, Mt., 334.

33) Cf. Baumbach, Jesus, 63.

34) It should be pointed out that the mention of swearing by the temple or altar is in itself no proof that the passage precedes 70 A.D., as Haenchen (Matth. 23, 42) and Minear (Yes, 6) suppose. Such oaths and vows were in use long after the destruction of the temple; cf. Alon, Jews, 198 n. 24.

35) Cf. Strack-Billerbeck I, 931.

36) Lieberman, Oaths, 128-135.

37) Cf. T. Ned. 1.3. Lieberman (Oaths, 132) discusses the readings he adopts for this text.

38) Cf. Lieberman, Oaths, 129.

39) Ibid., 134. According to Mt. 27:6; Jos. War 2.175, the term korban was used for the temple treasury; hence, if by "gold of the temple" is meant that of the treasury, korban could well be considered its equivalent. Korban can also be used as a general word for any offering brought to the temple; hence it could well be considered an equivalent of "gift on the altar".

40) This is the suggestion of McNeile, Mt., 334; but the criticism of vv. 17, 19 would be pointless if Jesus was attacking his own caricature.

41) Misrepresentation is implied by Baer, Aspects, 123; Mann, Oaths, 266.

42) Belkin (Philo, 169f.) offers an alternative explanation. Taking these verses to refer to vows, he says that, strictly, a vow could not be by something forbidden or consecrated by law (e.g. the temple or altar), but only "by something which has itself become sacred or prohibited through a vow" (e.g. korban; cf. M. Ned. 2.1; B. Ned. 14a). Still, the Pharisees accepted vows by the temple or altar when made by Judaeans, who naturally "associated the Temple, the altar, and Jerusalem with the sacrifices offered there"; they did not, however, accept such vows on the part of Galileans, for whom the association was not so natural (cf. M. Ned. 2.4; Vermes, Jesus, 54). "Hence the criticism of Jesus." Other explanations are supplied by Haenchen (Matth. 23, 39 n. 1) and Minear (Yes, 4).

43) Bultmann, Geschichte, 141f.; cf. 158; also Guelich, Law, 289f.

44) Cf. Bultmann, Geschichte, 142; Haenchen, Matth. 23, 38.

CHAPTER IX -DIVORCE

1) Cf. Amram, Law, 38; Percy, Botschaft, 145.

2) Cf. Amram, Law, 26.

3) Cf. Schubert, Ehescheidung, 23-27.

4) Note that Sir. 7:26 appears to advise against divorce.

5) The meaning of this text is, however, uncertain. See the discussion in Isaksson, Marriage, 27-34.

6) Allusions to such a contract may be found in Mal. 2:14; Prov. 2:17. Cf. de Vaux, Institutions I, 58.

7) Cf. Lövestam, Äktenskapet, 120f.; Vermes, Studies, 65-67.

8) Cf. Vermes, Studies, 65.

9) Cf. Belkin, Philo, 230f.

10) Cf. Abrahams, Studies I, 74f.; also Amram, Law, 63-77. Not without reason, Abrahams speaks of the husband's consent in such a case as a "legal fiction".

11) Cf. Amram, Law, 48f.

12) Cf. Schubert, Ehescheidung, 26f.

13) For the definition of <u>ketubbah</u>, see Cohen, Law I, 353f.

14) Cf. A. Guttmann, Judai<u>sm</u>, 44; Neusner, Traditions I, 104.

15) Cf. Blinzler, Strafe, 45 n. 2; Holzmeister, Streitfrage, 135; Lövestam, Bedeutung, 22.

16) Cf. Derrett, Law, 160f., 171.

17) Cf. Bulz, Divorce, 72f.; Nembach, Ehescheidung, 164f.; Neufeld, Laws, 167 n. 1.

18) For the various alternatives and their supporters, see Vermes, Studies, 50-56.

19) Unfortunately the text of the Temple Scroll was not available at the time of writing. This brief section of the document was, however, brought to light by Yadin already in 1972 (L'attitude, 98f.).

20) For ἀπολύειν as a technical term for divorce, see Lövestam, Skilsmässoterm, 132-135.

21) Note that Schaller (Adultery, 107f.; Sprüche, 239ff.) suggests the rendering "with her (i.e. his second wife)". In either case the words imply that marriage must be monogamous and indivisible; the husband has the same responsibility to be faithful to his wife as she has to be faithful to him. As we shall see, this does correspond to the views of Jesus (cf. Hoffmann, Saying, 53) and may well be original; it does not, however, correspond with the usual Jewish view, so that Mt. may have omitted the words as apt to confuse.

22) Cf. Daube, Testament, 363f.; Delling, Logion, 266.

23) The slight evidence collected by Bammel (Eherecht, 95-101) for Palestinian practice does not really alter this picture. Cf. Fitzmyer, Texts, 205.

24) This remains true whichever of the variant readings we adopt for the verse. Even if the wife is said to "leave" (ἐξέλθη) rather than divorce her husband, the further statement that she marries another is opposed to Jewish usage, where the man is said to marry the woman, not the reverse; cf. Kuhn, Sammlungen, 162f. For a discussion of the readings, see Dupont, Mariage, 61-63.

25) Cf. Abrahams, Studies I, 66; Daube, Testament, 365 for this possibility; against it, see Haenchen, Weg, 341.

26) Daube (Testament, 143f.) treats vv. 2-12 as a formal unit, vv. 10-12 being the private explanation to the disciples of a mystifying answer given in public (vv. 2-9). But vv. 2-9 can scarcely be classified as a mystifying answer meant only to silence opponents, and which the following verses then "clarify". Cf. Kuhn, Sammlungen, 165f. Moreover, the fact that v. 11 seems to reflect the saying we find in Mt. 5:32 par. Lk. 16:18 suggests as well that Mk. has combined originally separate units of tradition because of their common theme.

27) Cf. Bultmann, Geschichte, 143; Guelich, Antitheses, 446f.

28) Similarly, the attempt (cf., among others, Diderichsen, Skilsmisseperikope, 91f.; Nepper-Christensen, Utugtsklausulen, 132; Schaller, Sprüche, 238ff.) to see two different viewpoints behind Mk. 10:2-9 (condemning divorce) and 10:10-12 (condemning divorce and remarriage) is forced. See Delling, Logion, 272; Lövestam, Bedeutung, 23f. n. 18.

29) That the original saying did mention remarriage is supported by Mk. 10:11 par. Mt. 19:9.

30) Note that Sickenberger (Unzuchtsklausel, 196) suggests that the man's remarriage is not mentioned because it is not mentioned in Deut. 24:1 to which Mt. 5:32 serves as an antithesis (cf. 5:31).

31) Cf. Dietzfelbinger, Antithesen, 25; Jervell, Skilsmisse, 201; Schaller, Sprüche, 232ff.

32) We cannot enter at length into the debate surrounding these words. That they were not spoken by Jesus appears the proper conclusion to be drawn from

the fact that Paul, Mark, and Luke know of no such exception. That a real exception is meant has been adequately shown by many, perhaps most clearly by Dupont (Mariage, 102-106); there is no need to repeat his argument here. It is true that the Greek πορνεία (as well as the Hebrew זנות) can be used of marriages which violate the rules of Lev. 18 prohibiting intercourse between near relatives (the principle spokesmen for this interpretation are Bonsirven, Divorce, 38-60; and Baltensweiler, Ehe, 87-102; cf. recently Fitzmyer, Texts, 220f.; Meier, Law, 147-150); still it is unlikely that that technical meaning could be indicated or understood without further ado by the quite general word πορνεία (cf. Dupont, Mariage, 110-114; Lövestam, Äktenskapet, 137-139; Schneider, Wort, 81).

33) πορνεία is a broader term than μοιχεία (cf. Mt. 15:19), since it can be used of "every kind of unlawful sexual intercourse" (Bauer-Arndt-Gingrich, 699; cf. Fjärstedt, Fråga, 130); when, however, used of a wife's extramarital intercourse, it is essentially an equivalent of μοιχεία (note Hos. 2:2(4)LXX; Sir. 23:23; cf. Lövestam, Bedeutung, 20f.; Schaller, Sprüche, 235; Sickenberger, Unzuchtsklausel, 195; Wrege, Überlieferungsgeschichte, 68f.). It is not impossible that παρεκτὸς λόγου πορνείας in Mt. 5:32 represents an interpretation of ערות דבר in Deut. 24:1 (cf., among others, Dupont, Mariage, 87; Schillebeeckx, Marriage I, 214; Stendahl, School, 137; but see Lövestam, Äktenskapet 141f.; Meier, Law, 143f. for the contrary view); even so, it does not simply restate the Shammaite position. The Shammaites interpreted ערות as referring to shameful activity of various kinds, including extramarital intercourse; πορνεία refers to the latter. Cf. Hübner, Gesetz, 51-54.

34) This understanding is now quite common; see e.g. Hübner, Gesetz, 49ff.; Lövestam, Bedeutung, 26; Schaller, Sprüche, 234f.; Wrege, Überlieferungsgeschichte, 68.

35) Cf. Lövestam, Bedeutung, 27f.; Schneider, Wort, 65.

36) Cf. Dungan, Sayings, 81ff.

37) That the casuistic form of the saying does not militate against this conclusion will be shown below under C. CONCLUSIONS.

38) Cf. Schmid, Markus, 177; Sickenberger, Unzuchtsklausel, 190f.

39) Markan priority is argued effectively and at length by Catchpole (Material, 92ff.); only a part of the argument can be given here.

40) Cf. Fitzmyer, Texts, 221-223.

41) Cf. Beilner, Christus, 127.

42) Cf. Baltensweiler, Ehe, 84; Catchpole, Material, 95.

43) Cf. Pesch, Weisung, 211f. Note, too, that the substance of Mt. 19:4-8 does not correspond as well to the altered form of the question in v. 3; cf. Catchpole, Material, 94f.; Hübner, Gesetz, 55.

44) Cf. Catchpole, Material, 101f., where this is illustrated in more detail.

45) Cf. Baltensweiler, Ehe, 83f.; Schaller, Sprüche, 230 n. 10; Schmid, Markus, 177ff.

46) It was, of course, of special interest for Mt. to show that Jesus did not violate the Mosaic law; this point could be better maintained if Deut. 24:1 was seen as a concession than as a command. For "concessions to sinfulness" as an element of Jewish law, cf. Daube, Concessions, 1-13.

47) Cf. Bauer-Arndt-Gingrich, 717. Greeven (Ehe, 377f.) interprets πρὸς here as final: divorce was permitted "in order to demonstrate your hardheartedness". But see Bornkamm, Ehescheidung, 57 n. 5.

48) Cf. Hübner, Gesetz, 61; Schelkle, Ehe, 185f.

49) Cf. Soulen, Marriage, 442.

50) Cf. Haacker, Ehescheidung, 31. The quotations from Gen. 1:27 and 2:24 follow the LXX, but the argument does not seem specially dependent on that version (against Berger, Gesetzesauslegung, 508, 548f.); Jesus may well have cited a Hebrew text which has been assimilated in the tradition to the

156

LXX (cf. Catchpole, Material, 116f.). In particular, it has been argued that the words οἱ δύο in v. 8, drawn from the LXX but not found in the M.T., are critical to the argument; this does not, however, appear to be necessary, and in any case we must allow for the possibility that a Hebrew variant corresponding to the LXX did exist; cf. the critical apparatus to Gen. 2:24 in BHS; Stendahl, School, 59f. The quotations are thus not a sufficient reason for classifying the argument as secondary.

51) The argument appears complete and satisfactory without introducing (as does Daube, Testament, 71ff.) a reference to the myth of the androgynous man.

52) Cf. Catchpole, Material, 114ff.; Dungan, Sayings, 125; Hübner, Gesetz, 61; Isaksson, Marriage, 113-115. Against Diderichsen's reasons for seeing the pericope as secondary (Skilsmisseperikope, 116ff.), see Baltensweiler, Ehe, 52f.

53) Cf. Jervell, Skilsmisse, 198.

54) Note, too, that many of Jesus' commands are stated in poetic, even hyperbolic language (Mt. 5:29f., 39ff.; 6:3, 6, etc.; cf. Dodd, Gospel, 52ff.). Clearly in these cases his intention was not that his words be understood as statutes and literally observed, but that they be understood as indicating the kind of attitude God desires.

CHAPTER X - JESUS AND THE SAGES OF THE HALAKHAH

1) Cf. Branscomb, Jesus, 125ff.; Cohon, Place, 94; Schoeps, Jesus, 43.

2) Cf. Safrai, Synagogue, 918.

3) Cf. Jeremias, Words, 41-62.

4) Cf. H. Montefiore, Jesus, 60-71.

5) For the "seat of Moses" as a symbolic reference to the legal and teaching authority of the "scribes and Pharisees", see Renov, Seat, 262-267.

6) Cf. Braun, Radikalismus II, 7. Note, however, Mk. 8:15 par., a "pregnant" logion which the evangelists have applied in different ways, but in which Jesus apparently warned of the evil tendencies inherent in Pharisaism.

7) Mt. 5:19 is of course difficult to reconcile with Jesus' own conduct in these areas, and is for that reason perhaps better assigned to a Christian community which showed itself zealous in the fulfilment of each detail of the law. Admittedly, the verse is directed against those who teach the annulment of a part of the law, and Jesus himself seems never to have gone that far; still, the concern for upholding every detail of the law which this verse expresses was apparently not characteristic of Jesus. For a suggestive treatment of the verse, see Schürmann, Untersuchungen, 126-136; note especially 135 n. 47 on the possibility of assigning it to Jesus.

Abbreviations and Transliteration

Abbreviations of journals and reference works are based on those found in RGG[3] Vol. VI, xx-xxxi. The abbreviations of Elenchus Bibliographicus Biblicus have been used to supplement those of RGG. The transliteration of Hebrew words follows the General Transliteration Rules of Encyclopaedia Judaica (Vol. I, 90). Note that _alef_ and _ayin_ are not transliterated, though a simple apostrophe is used to separate vowels which are not to be treated as a diphthong.

Bibliography

A. TEXTS AND TRANSLATIONS

Biblia Hebraica Stuttgartensia..., ed. K. Elliger and W. Rudolph. Stuttgart 1968ff. (= BHS)
Septuaginta. Vetus Testamentum Graecum Auctoritate Societatis Litterarum Gottingensis editum.
    I. Band: Genesis, ed. J.W. Wevers. 1974.
    IX. Band, I: Maccabaeorum liber I, ed. W. Kappler. 1936.
    IX. Band, II: Maccabaeorum liber II, ed. W. Kappler and R. Hanhart. 1959.
    X. Band: Psalmi cum Odis, ed. A. Rahlfs. 1931.
    XII. Band, II: Sapienta Iesu Filii Sirach, ed. J. Ziegler. 1965.
    XIII. Band: Duodecim Prophetae, ed. J. Ziegler. 1943.
    XIV. Band: Isaias, ed. J. Ziegler. 1939.
Septuaginta..., ed. A. Rahlfs, I-II. Stuttgart 1935.
Synopsis Quattuor Evangeliorum..., ed. K. Aland. 9. erneut revidierte Auflage. Stuttgart 1976.
Novum Testamentum Graece..., ed. E. Nestle, K. Aland. 25th ed. London 1973.
The Apocrypha and Pseudepigrapha of the Old Testament in English. I-II. Ed. R.H. Charles. Oxford 1913.
Die Texte aus Qumran. Hebräisch und deutsch. Ed. E. Lohse. München 1964.
Josephus with an English Translation by H. St. J. Thackeray, R. Marcus, and L.H. Feldman. I-IX. London 1926-1965.
Philo with an English Translation by F.H. Colson and G.H. Whitaker. I-X. London 1929-1962.
The Genesis Apocryphon of Qumran Cave I. Text, translation and commentary by J.A. Fitzmyer. Rome [2]1971.
Shishshah Sidrei Mishnah, ed. C. Albeck, I-VI. Jerusalem-Tel Aviv 1954-1958.
The Mishnah. Trans. from the Hebrew with Introduction and Brief Explanatory Notes by H. Danby. Oxford 1933.
The Tosefta..., ed. S. Lieberman. I-III (Zera'im-Nashim). New York 1955-1967.
Tosephta..., ed. M.S. Zuckermandel. Jerusalem [2]1937.
Der babylonische Talmud mit Einschluss der vollstaendigen Mishnah. Ed. L. Goldschmidt. Iff. Berlin 1925.
The Babylonian Talmud. Translated into English. Ed. I. Epstein. I-XVIII. London (Soncino Press) 1961.

Talmud Yerushalmi. I-II. Berlin 1929.
Mekilta de-Rabbi Ishmael. Ed. J. Lauterbach. I-III. Philadelphia 1976
   (= 1933-1935).
Sifra..., ed. I.H. Weiss. Wien 1962.
Sifra. Halachischer Midrasch zu Leviticus. Übersetzt von J. Winter.
   Breslau 1938.
Siphre d'be Rab..., ed. H.S. Horovitz. Leipzig 1917.
Sifre zu Numeri. German trans. and notes by K.G. Kuhn. Stuttgart 1933-1955.
Sifre on Deuteronomy. Ed. H.S. Horovitz and L. Finkelstein. New York 1969
   (= 1939).
Sifre zu Deuteronomium. German trans. and notes by G. Kittel. 1:1-11:28.
   Stuttgart 1922.

B. LITERATURE

Abrahams, I., Studies in Pharisaism and the Gospels. I-II. Cambridge
   1917-1924.
Albeck, C., Das Buch der Jubiläen und die Halacha. Berlin 1930.
- Einführung in die Mischna. Berlin 1971.
Allen, W.C., A Critical and Exegetical Commentary on the Gospel according
   to S. Matthew. Edinburgh [2]1907.
Alon, G., Jews, Judaism and the Classical World. Studies in Jewish History
   in the Times of the Second Temple and Talmud. Jerusalem 1977.
Alt, A., "Die Ursprünge des israelitischen Rechts," in Kleine Schriften zur
   Geschichte des Volkes Israel. I, München 1953, 278-332.
Amram, D.W., The Jewish Law of Divorce according to Bible and Talmud with
   Some References to its Development in Post-Talmudic Times. Philadelphia
   1896.
Andrew, M.E., see Stamm, J.J.

Bacher, W., Die exegetische Terminologie der jüdischen Traditionsliteratur.
   I-II. Darmstadt 1965 (= 1899-1905).
- "Sanhedrin," in DB IV, 397-402.
- Tradition und Tradenten in den Schulen Palästinas und Babyloniens. Studien
   und Materialien zur Entstehungsgeschichte des Talmuds. Leipzig 1914.
- "Zur Geschichte der Ordination," in MGWJ 2 (1894) 122-127.
Baer, Y., "Some Aspects of Judaism as Presented in the Synoptic Gospels"
   (Hebrew), in Zion 31 (1966) 117-152.
Baltensweiler, H., Die Ehe im Neuen Testament. Exegetische Untersuchungen
   über Ehe, Ehelosigkeit und Ehescheidung. Zürich 1967.
Bamberger, B.J., "Revelations of Torah after Sinai," in HUCA 16 (1941) 97-113.
Bammel, E., "Markus 10.11f. und das jüdische Eherecht," in ZNW 61 (1970)
   95-101.
Banks, R., Jesus and the Law in the Synoptic Tradition. Cambridge 1975.
Barth, G., "Das Gesetzesverständnis des Evangelisten Matthäus," in G. Born-
   kamm, G. Barth, and H.J. Held, Überlieferung und Auslegung im Matthäus-
   evangelium, Neukirchen Kreis Moers [4]1965, 54-154.
Bauer, W., A Greek-English Lexicon of the New Testament and Other Early
   Christian Literature. Trans. and adapted from the 4th German edition
   by W.F. Arndt and F.W. Gingrich. Chicago 1957.
Baumbach, G., Jesus von Nazareth im Lichte der jüdischen Gruppenbildung.
   Berlin 1971.
Baumgarten, J.M., "The Unwritten Law in the Pre-Rabbinic Period," in JStJud
   3 (1972) 7-29.
Beare, F.W., "The Sabbath was Made for Man?" in JBL 79 (1960) 130-136.
Beilner, W., Christus und die Pharisäer. Wien 1959.
Belkin, S., Philo and the Oral Law. Cambridge, Mass. 1940.
Benoit, P., "Les épis arrachés," in Exégèse et théologie. III., Paris 1968,
   228-242.

Berger, K., Die Gesetzesauslegung Jesu. Ihr historischer Hintergrund im
Judentum und im Alten Testament. I. Markus und Parallelen. Neukirchen-
Vluyn 1972.
Bietenhardt, H., "Sabbatvorschriften von Qumran im Lichte des rabbinischen
Rechts und der Evangelien," in H. Bardtke (ed.), Qumran-Probleme, Berlin
1963, 53-74.
Bikerman, E., "La chaîne de la tradition pharisienne," in RB 59 (1952) 44-54.
Billerbeck, P., see Strack, H.L.
Black, M., An Aramaic Approach to the Gospels and Acts. Oxford [3]1967.
Blank, S.H., "The Curse, Blasphemy, The Spell, and the Oath," in HUCA 23
(1950-1951) 73-95.
Blau, L., Das altjüdische Zauberwesen. Berlin [2]1914.
Blinzler, J., "Die Strafe für Ehebruch in Bibel und Halacha. Zur Auslegung
von Joh. VIII.5," in NTS 4 (1957-1958) 32-47.
Bonsirven, J., Le divorce dans le Nouveau Testament. Paris 1948.
Bornkamm, G., "Ehescheidung und Wiederheiratung im Neuen Testament," in
Geschichte und Glaube. I, München 1968, 56-59.
Bowker, J., Jesus and the Pharisees. Cambridge 1973.
Bowman, J., The Gospel of Mark: The New Christian Jewish Passover Haggadah.
Leiden 1965.
Brandt, W., Die jüdischen Baptismen oder das religiöse Waschen und Baden
im Judentum mit Einschluss des Judenchristentums. (BZAW 18) Giessen
1910.
- Jüdische Reinheitslehre und ihre Beschreibung in den Evangelien. (BZAW
19) Giessen 1910.
Branscomb, B.H., Jesus and the Law of Moses. New York 1930.
Braun, H., Spätjüdisch-häretischer und frühchristlicher Radikalismus. I-II.
Tübingen 1957.
Bruce, F.F., New Testament History. New York 1972.
Buchanan, G.W., "The Role of Purity in the Structure of the Essene Sect,"
in RQum 4 (1963-1964) 397-406.
- "Some Vow and Oath Formulas in the New Testament," in HThR 58 (1965)
319-326.
Büchler, A., Der galiläische 'Am-ha'Ares des zweiten Jahrhunderts. Wien
1906.
- "The Law of Purification in Mark vii. 1-23," in ET 21 (1909-1910) 34-40.
- Studies in Sin and Atonement in the Rabbinic Literature of the First
Century. London 1928.
- Das Synedrion in Jerusalem und das Grosse Beth-Din in der Quaderkammer
des jerusalemischen Tempels. Wien 1902.
- Types of Jewish-Palestinian Piety from 70 B.C.E. to 70 C.E. The Ancient
Pious Men. London 1922.
Budd, P.J., "Priestly Instruction in Pre-Exilic Israel," in VT 23 (1973)
1-14.
Bultmann, R., Die Geschichte der synoptischen Tradition. Göttingen [2]1931.
Bulz, E., Le divorce en droit rabbinique dans ses rapports avec le droit
laïque moderne. La Chaux-de-Fonds 1954.
Burgsmüller, A., Der 'am ha-'ares zur Zeit Jesu. Marburg 1964.
Burkitt, F.C., "Jesus and the 'Pharisees'," in JThS 28 (1927) 392-397.

Carlston, C., "The Things that Defile (Mark VII.14) and the Law in Matthew
and Mark," in NTS 15 (1968-1969) 75-96.
Carmignac, J., "Les éléments historiques des "Hymnes" de Qumran," in RQum
2 (1960) 205-222.
Catchpole, D.R., "The Synoptic Divorce Material as a Traditio-Historical
Problem," in BJRL 57 (1974) 92-127.
Chajes, Z.H., The Student's Guide through the Talmud. New York [2]1960.

Cohen, B., Jewish and Roman Law. I-II. A Comparative Study. New York 1966.
- Law and Tradition in Judaism. New York 1959.
Cohn, H.H., "Secularization of Divine Law," in Scripta Hierosolymitana 16 (1966) 55-103 (= H.H. Cohn (ed.), Jewish Law in Ancient and Modern Israel, New York 1971, 1-49).
Cohon, S.S., "Authority in Judaism," in HUCA 11 (1936) 593-646.
- "The Place of Jesus in the Religious Life of his Day," in JBL 48 (1929) 82-108.
Correns, D., "Die Verzehntung der Raute. Luk xi 42 und M Schebi ix I," in NovTest 6 (1963) 110-112.
Cranfield, C.E.B., The Gospel According to St. Mark. Cambridge 1966.
Crawley, A.E., "Oath: Introductory and Primitive," in ERE IX, 430-434.
Cross, F.M. and Talmon, S. (ed.), Qumran and the History of the Biblical Text. Cambridge, Mass. 1975.
Cullmann, O., Early Christian Worship. London 1973 (= 1953).
Dalman, G., Die Worte Jesu. Darmstadt 1965 (= ^{2}1930).
Daube, D., "Concessions to Sinfulness in Jewish Law," in JJS 10 (1959) 1-13.
- "Exousia in Mark I 22 and 27," in JThS 39 (1938) 45-59.
- The New Testament and Rabbinic Judaism. London 1956.
- "Rabbinic Methods of Interpretation and Hellenistic Rhetoric," in HUCA 22 (1949) 239-264.
- "Responsibilities of Master and Disciples in the Gospels," in NTS 19 (1972-1973) 1-15.
Davies, W.D., Christian Origins and Judaism. London 1962.
- The Setting of the Sermon on the Mount. Cambridge 1964.
Delling, G., "Das Logion Mark. x ii (und seine Abwandlungen) im Neuen Testament," in NovTest 1 (1956) 263-274.
Derrett, J.D.M., "KORBAN, HO ESTIN DŌRON," in NTS 16 (1969-1970) 364-368.
- Law in the New Testament. London 1970.
Dibelius, M., Der Brief des Jakobus. Göttingen 1921.
- Die Formgeschichte des Evangeliums. Tübingen ^{4}1961.
Diderichsen, B.K., Den markianske skilsmisseperikope. Dens genesis og historiske placering. Glydendal 1962.
Dietzfelbinger, C., Die Antithesen der Bergpredigt. München 1975.
Dodd, C.H., According to the Scriptures. The Sub-structure of New Testament Theology. London 1952.
- Gospel and Law. The Relation of Faith and Ethics in Early Christianity. New York 1951.
- More New Testament Studies. Manchester 1968.
Donahue, J.R., "Tax Collectors and Sinners. An Attempt at Identification," in CBQ 33 (1971) 39-61.
Dungan, D.L., The Sayings of Jesus in the Churches of Paul. The Use of the Synoptic Tradition in the Regulation of Early Church Life. Oxford 1971.
Dunn, J.D.G., "Prophetic 'I'-Sayings and the Jesus Tradition: The Importance of Testing Prophetic Utterances within Early Christianity," in NTS 24 (1977-1978) 175-198.
Dupont, J., Mariage et divorce dans l'évangile. Matthieu 19, 3-12 et parallèles. Bruges 1959.

Ehrhardt, A., "Jewish and Christian Ordination," in JEH 5(1954) 125-138 (= The Framework of the New Testament Stories, Manchester 1964, 132-150).
Elon, M., "Takkanot," in EncJud 15, 712-728.
Epp, E.J., The Theological Tendency of Codex Bezae Cantabrigiensis in Acts. Cambridge 1966.
Epstein, J.N., Introduction to Tannaitic Literature. Mishna, Tosephta and Halakhic Midrashim (Hebrew). Jerusalem 1957.

Falk, Z.W., "Binding and Loosing," in JJS 25 (1974) 92-100.
- Introduction to Jewish Law of the Second Commonwealth. I. Leiden 1972.
- "On Talmudic Vows," in HThR 59 (1966) 309-312.
Ferguson, E., "Jewish and Christian Ordination: Some Observations," in HThR 56 (1963) 13-19.
Fiedler, P., Jesus und die Sünder. Bern 1976.
Finkel, A., The Pharisees and the Teacher of Nazareth. Leiden 1974.
Finkelstein, L., "The Book of Jubilees and the Rabbinic Halaka," in HThR 16 (1923) 39-61.
- The Pharisees. The Sociological Background of Their Faith. I-II. Philadelphia ³1962.
- "Some Examples of the Maccabean Halaka," in JBL 49 (1930) 20-42.
Fitzmyer, J.A., "The Aramaic Qorban Inscription from Jebel Hallet Et-Turi and Mark 7.11/Matt. 15.5," in JBL 78 (1959) 60-65.
- "The Languages of Palestine in the First Century A.D.," in CBQ 32 (1970) 501-531.
- "The Matthean Divorce Texts and some New Palestinian Evidence," in ThSt 37 (1976) 197-226.
- "Methodology in the Study of the Aramaic Substratum of Jesus' Sayings in the New Testament," in J. Dupont (ed.), Jésus aux origines de la christologie, Louvain 1975, 73-102.
Fjärstedt, B., "Fråga och svar i Matt. 19, 3-12," in SEÅ 33 (1968) 118-140.
Flusser, D., Jesus in Selbstzeugnissen und Bilddokumenten. Hamburg 1968.
Forkman, G., The Limits of the Religious Community. Expulsion from the Religious Community within the Qumran Sect, within Rabbinic Judaism and within Primitive Christianity. Lund 1972.

Gerhardsson, B., Die Anfänge der Evangelientradition. Wuppertal 1977.
- "Bibelns ethos," in G. Wingren (ed.), Etik och kristen tro, Lund 1971, 15-92.
- "The Hermeneutic Program in Matthew 22:37-40," in R. Hamilton-Kelly and R. Scroggs (ed.), Jews, Greeks and Christians. Essays in Honor of William David Davies, Leiden 1976, 129-150.
- Memory and Manuscript. Oral Tradition and Written Transmission in Rabbinic Judaism and Early Christianity. Copenhagen ²1964.
- Tradition and Transmission in Early Christianity. Lund 1964.
Gerstenberger, E., Wesen und Herkunft des "apodiktischen Rechts". Neukirchen-Vluyn 1965.
Gilat, Y.D., "Soferim," in EncJud 15, 79-81.
Gils, F., "'Le sabbat a été fait pour l'homme et non l'homme pour le sabbat' (Mc, II, 27)," in RB 69 (1962) 506-523.
Gnilka, J., "Das Gemeinschaftsmahl der Essener," in BZ 5 (1961) 39-55.
Greenberg, M., "The Hebrew Oath Particle Hay/He," in JBL 76 (1957) 34-39.
Greene, W., "Extra-legal Juridical Prerogatives," in JStJud 7 (1976) 152-176.
Greeven, H., "Ehe nach dem Neuen Testament," in NTS 15 (1968-1969) 365-388.
Grundmann, W., Das Evangelium nach Matthäus. Berlin 1972.
Guelich, R.A., 'Not to Annul the Law Rather to Fullfill the Law and the Prophets:' An Exegetical Study of Jesus and the Law in Matthew with Emphasis on 5:17-48. Hamburg 1967.
- "The Antitheses of Matthew v. 21-48: Traditional and/or Redactional?" in NTS 22 (1975-1976) 444-457.
Guttmann, A., Rabbinic Judaism in the Making. Detroit 1970.
Guttmann, M., Zur Einleitung in die Halacha. I-II: (In 32. and 36. Jahresber. d. Landes-Rabbinerschule in Budapest.) Budapest 1909-1913.

Haacker, K., "Ehescheidung und Wiederverheiratung im Neuen Testament," in ThQ 151 (1971) 28-38.
Haenchen, E., "Matthäus 23," in Gott und Mensch. Gesammelte Aufsätze, Tübingen 1965, 29-54 (= ZThK 48 (1951) 38-63).

- Der Weg Jesu. Berlin 1966.
Hart, J.H.A., "CORBAN," in JQR 19 (1907) 615-650.
Hay, L.S., "The Son of Man in Mark 2.10 and 2.28," in JBL 89 (1970) 69-75.
Hengel, M., "Mc 7.3 pugme: Die Geschichte einer exegetischen Aporie und der Versuch ihrer Lösung," in ZNW 60 (1969) 182-198.
Herford, R.T., The Pharisees. London 1924.
Hoenig, S., The Great Sanhedrin. Philadelphia 1953.
- "Synedrion in the Attic Orators, the Ptolemaic Papyri and its Adoption by Josephus, the Gospels and the Tannaim," in JQR 37 (1946-1947) 179-187.
Hoffmann, P., "Jesus' Saying about Divorce and its Interpretation in the New Testament Tradition," in Conc No. 6 Vol. 5 (1970) 51-66.
Hofius, O., Jesu Tischgemeinschaft mit den Sündern. Stuttgart 1967.
Holzmeister, U., "Die Streitfrage über die Ehescheidungstexte bei Matthäus," in Bibl 26 (1945) 133-146.
Hommel, H., "Das Wort korban und seine Verwandten," in Philologus 98 (1954) 132-149.
Hooker, M.D., "Christology and Methodology," in NTS 17 (1970-1971) 480-487.
Horst, J., "Die Worte Jesu über die kultische Reinheit und ihre Verarbeitung in den evangelischen Berichten," in ThStKr 87 (1914) 429-454.
Hruby, K., "La notion d'ordination dans la tradition juive," in MaisD 102 (1970) 30-56.
Hubaut, M., "Jésus et la Loi de Moise," in RT Louv 7 (1976) 401-425.
Hübner, H., Das Gesetz in der synoptischen Tradition. Studien zur These einer progressiven Qumranisierung und Judaisierung innerhalb der synoptischen Tradition. Witten 1973.
- "Mark. vii. 1-23 und das 'jüdisch-hellenistische' Gesetzesverständnis," in NTS 22 (1975-1976) 319-345.
Hultgren, A.J., "The Formation of the Sabbath Pericope in Mark 2:23-28," in JBL 91 (1972) 38-43.
Hummel, R., Die Auseinandersetzung zwischen Kirche und Judentum im Matthäusevangelium. München 1966.
Hunzinger, C.-H., "Spuren pharisäischer Institutionen in der frühen rabbinischen Überlieferung," in Tradition und Glaube. Das frühe Christentum in seiner Umwelt. Festgabe für K.G. Kuhn, Göttingen 1971, 147-156.

Isaksson, A., Marriage and Ministry in the New Temple. A Study with Special Reference to Mt. 19.3-12 and 1 Cor. 11.3-16. Lund 1965.

Jackson, B.S., Essays in Jewish and Comparative Legal History. Leiden 1975.
Jeremias, J., Die Gleichnisse Jesu. Göttingen 7 1965.
- grammateus, in ThW I, 740-742.
- The Eucharistic Words of Jesus. Trans. from the 3rd German edition with the author's revisions to July 1964. London 1966.
- Jerusalem in the Time of Jesus. Based on the 3rd German edition with author's revisions to 1967. London 1969.
- Neutestamentliche Theologie. I. Die Verkündigung Jesu. Gütersloh 1971.
- "Presbuterion ausserchristlich bezeugt," in ZNW 48 (1957) 127-132.
- "Zöllner und Sünder," in ZNW 30 (1931) 293-300.
Jervell, J., "Skilsmisse og gjengifte etter Det nye testamente," in NTT 62 (1961) 195-210.
Jülicher, A., Die Gleichnisreden Jesu. I-II. Tübingen 2 1910.

Käsemann, E., "Das Problem des historischen Jesus," in Exegetische Versuche und Besinnungen. I, Göttingen 4 1965, 187-214 (= ZThK 51 (1954) 125-153).
Kennard, J.S., Jr., "The Jewish Provincial Assembly," in ZNW 53 (1962) 25-51.
Kimbrough, S.T., Jr., "The Concept of Sabbath at Qumran," in RQum 5 (1964-1966) 483-502.

Klausner, J., Jesus of Nazareth. His Life, Times, and Teaching. London 1929.
Klostermann, E., Das Matthäusevangelium. Tübingen [2]1927.
Kretschmar, G., "Die Ordination im frühen Christentum," in FreibZ 22 (1975) 35-69.
Kruse, H., "Die 'dialektische Negation' als semitisches Idiom," in VT 4 (1954) 385-400.
Kuhn, H.-W., Ältere Sammlungen im Markusevangelium. Göttingen 1971.
Kummel, W.G., "Äussere und innere Reinheit des Menschen bei Jesus," in Das Wort und die Wörter. Festschrift Gerhard Friedrich zum 65. Geburtsdag, Stuttgart 1973, 35-46.
- "Jesus und der jüdische Traditionsgedanke," in Heilsgeschehen und Geschichte. Gesammelte Aufsätze 1933-1964, Marburg 1965, 15-35 (= ZNW 33 (1934) 105-130).
- "Die Weherufe über die Schriftgelehrten und Pharisäer (Matthäus 23, 13-36)," in W.P. Eckert, N.P. Levinson, and M. Stöhr (ed.), Antijudaismus im Neuen Testament? München 1967, 135-147.

Lauterbach, J.Z., Rabbinic Essays. Cincinnati 1951.
Légasse, S., "Scribes et disciples de Jésus," in RB 68 (1961) 321-345, 481-506.
Leivestad, R., "Das Dogma von der prophetenlosen Zeit," in NTS 19 (1972-1973) 288-299.
Le Moyne, J., Les Sadducéens. Paris 1972.
Levine, B.A., In the Presence of the Lord. A Study of Cult and Some Cultic Terms in Ancient Israel. Leiden 1974.
Levine, E., "The Sabbath Controversy according to Matthew," in NTS 22 (1975-1976) 480-483.
Lévy, I., La légende de Pythagore de Grèce en Palestine. Paris 1927.
Lieberman, S., "The Discipline in the So-Called Dead Sea Manual of Discipline," in JBL 71 (1952) 199-206 (= Texts and Studies, New York 1974, 200-207).
- Hellenism in Jewish Palestine. New York [2]1962.
- "Oaths and Vows," in Greek in Jewish Palestine, New York 1942, 115-143.
Lohmeyer, E., Das Evangelium des Markus. Göttingen 1953 (= 1937).
- Das Evangelium des Matthäus. Göttingen [3]1962.
Lohse, E., "Jesu Worte über den Sabbat," in Judentum, Urchristentum, Kirche. Festschrift für Joachim Jeremias, Berlin 1960, 79-89 (= Die Einheit des Neuen Testaments, Göttingen 1973, 62-72).
- Die Ordination im Spätjudentum und im Neuen Testament. Göttingen 1951.
van der Loos, H., The Miracles of Jesus. Leiden 1965.
Lövestam, E., Äktenskapet i Nya Testamentet. Lund 1950.
- "Apoluein - en gammalpalestinensisk skilsmässoterm," in SEÅ 27 (1962) 132-135.
- "Die funktionale Bedeutung der synoptischen Jesusworte über Ehescheidung und Weiderheirat," in A. Fuchs (ed.), Theologie aus dem Norden, Freistadt 1977, 19-28.

Maher, M., "'Take my yoke upon you' (Matt. xi. 29)," in NTS 22 (1975-1976) 97-103.
Mann, J., "Oaths and Vows in the Synoptic Gospels," in AmerJourTheol 21 (1917) 260-274.
Manson, T.W., "Mark ii. 27f.," in CN 11 (1947) 138-146.
- The Sayings of Jesus. London 1975 (= 1949).
Mantel, H., "Ordination and Appointment in the Period of the Temple," in HThR 57 (1964) 325-346.
- Studies in the History of the Sanhedrin. Cambridge, Mass. 1961.
Margoliouth, G., "'The Traditions of the Elders' (St. Mark VII. 1-23)," in ET 22 (1910-1911) 261-263.

Marxsen, W., "Redaktionsgeschichtliche Erklärung der sogenannten Parabel-
theorie des Markus," in ZThK 52 (1955) 255-271.
McEleney, N.J., "Authenticating Criteria and Mark 7:1-23," in CBQ 34 (1972)
431-460.
McHardy, W.D., "Mark 7.3 - A Reference to the Old Testament?" in ET 87
(1976) 119.
McNeile, A.H., The Gospel According to St. Matthew. London 1965 (= 1915).
Meier, J.P., Law and History in Matthew's Gospel. A Redactional Study of
Mt. 5:17-48. Rome 1976.
Merkel, H., "Jesus und die Pharisäer," in NTS 14 (1967-1968) 194-208.
- "Markus 7,15 - das Jesuswort über die innere Verunreinigung," in ZRGG 20
(1968) 340-363.
Meyer, R., "Der 'Am-ha-'Ares. Ein Beitrag zur Religionssoziologie Palästinas
im ersten und zweiten nachchristlichen Jahrhundert," in Judaica 3 (1947)
169-199.
- "Das angebliche Demaj-Gesetz Hyrkans I," in ZNW 38 (1939) 124-131.
- Tradition und Neuschöpfung im antiken Judentum. Dargestellt an der
Geschichte des Pharisäismus. (Sitzungsberichte der sächsischen Akademie
der Wissenschaften zu Leipzig. Philologisch-historische Klasse Band
110 Heft 2.) Berlin 1965.
Minear, P.S., "Yes or No: the Demand for Honesty in the Early Church," in
NovTest 13 (1971), 1-13.
Montefiore, C.G., The Synoptic Gospels. I-II. London [2]1927.
Montefiore, H., "Jesus and the Temple Tax," in NTS 11 (1964-1965) 60-71.
Moore, G.F., Judaism in the First Centuries of the Christian Era. The Age
of the Tannaim. I-III. Cambridge, Mass. 1927-1930.
Moule, C.F.D., An Idiom-Book of New Testament Greek. Cambridge [2]1959.
Murmelstein, B., "Jesu Gang durch die Saatfelder," in Angelos 3 (1930)
111-120.

Neirynck, F., "Jesus and the Sabbath. Some Observations on Mark II, 27," in
J. Dupont (ed.), Jésus aux origines de la christologie, Louvain 1975,
227-270.
Nembach, U., "Ehescheidung nach alttestamentlichem und jüdischem Recht," in
ThZ 26 (1970) 161-171.
Nepper-Christensen, P., "Utugtsklausulen og Josef i Matthaeusevangeliet,"
in SEÅ 34 (1969) 122-146.
Nestle, E., "'Anise' and 'Rue'," in ET 15 (1903-1904) 528.
Neufeld, E., Ancient Hebrew Marriage Laws with Special Reference to
General Semitic Laws and Customs. London 1944.
Neusner, J., Eliezer ben Hyrcanus. The Tradition and the Man. I-II. Leiden
1973.
- "The Fellowship (havurah) in the Second Jewish Commonwealth," in HThR 53
(1960) 125-142.
- "'First Cleanse the Inside.' The 'Halakhic' Background of a Controversy-
Saying," in NTS 22 (1975-1976) 486-495.
- A History of the Mishnaic Law of Purities. I-XIV (Kelim - Miqvaot). Leiden
1974ff.
- The Idea of Purity in Ancient Israel. Leiden 1973.
- The Rabbinic Traditions about the Pharisees before 70. I-III. Leiden 1971.
Newman, J., Semikhah (Ordination): A Study of its Origin, History and
Function in Rabbinic Literature. Manchester 1950.
Nissen, A., "Tora und Geschichte im Spätjudentum," in NovTest 9 (1967)
241-277.

Odeberg, H., Fariseism och kristendom. Lund 1943.
O'Dell, J., "The religious Background of the Psalms of Solomon," in RQum 3
(1961-1962) 241-257.

Oppenheimer, A., The 'Am Ha-Aretz. A Study in the Social History of the Jewish People in the Hellenistic-Roman Period. Leiden 1977.

Paschen, W., Rein und unrein. Untersuchung zur biblischen Wortgeschichte. München 1970.

Pedersen, J., Der Eid bei den Semiten in seinem Verhältnis zu verwandten Erscheinungen sowie die Stellung des Eides im Islam. Strassburg 1914.

Percy, E., Die Botschaft Jesu. Eine traditionskritische und exegetische Untersuchung. Lund 1953.

Pesch, R., Das Markusevangelium. I-II. Freiburg 1976-1977.

- "Die neutestamentliche Weisung für die Ehe," in BiLeb 9(1968) 208-221.

- "Das Zöllnergastmahl (Mk 2,15-17)," in Mélanges bibliques en hommage au R.P. Béda Rigaux, Gembloux 1970, 63-87.

van der Ploeg, J., "The Meals of the Essenes," in JSS 2 (1957) 163-175.

Rabin, C., Qumran Studies. Oxford 1957.

von Rad, G., Theologie des Alten Testaments. I. München 1957.

Rengstorf, K.H., Das Evangelium nach Lukas. Göttingen [16]1975.

- korban, in ThW III, 860-866.

- manthano, etc., in ThW IV, 392-465.

Renov, I., "The Seat of Moses," in IsrEJ 5 (1955) 262-267.

Reynolds, S.M., "A Note on Dr. Hengel's Interpretation of pugme in Mark 7.3," in ZNW 62 (1971) 295f.

- "Pugme (Mark 7.3) as 'Cupped Hand'," in JBL 85 (1966) 87f.

Rivkin, E., "Defining the Pharisees: the Tannaitic Sources," in HUCA 40-41 (1969-1970) 205-249.

Roloff, J., Das Kerygma und der irdische Jesus. Göttingen 1970.

Rordorf, W.A., Der Sonntag. Geschichte des Ruhe- und Gottesdiensttages im ältesten Christentum. Zürich 1962.

Ross, J.M., "With the Fist," in ET 87 (1976) 374f.

Rössler, D., Gesetz und Geschichte. Untersuchungen zur Theologie der jüdischen Apokalyptik und der pharisäischen Orthodoxie. Neukirchen Kr. Moers 1960.

Safrai, S., "Jewish Self-Government," in CompRerJudNT Section 1 Volume 1, 377-419.

- "Relations between the Diaspora and the Land of Israel," in CompRerJudNT Section 1 Volume 1, 184-215.

- "Religion in Everyday Life," in CompRerJudNT Section 1 Volume 2, 793-833.

- "The Synagogue," in CompRerJudNT Section 1 Volume 2, 908-944.

Sanders, E.P., Paul and Palestinian Judaism. London 1977.

Schalit, A., König Herodes. Der Mann und sein Werk. Berlin 1969.

Schaller, B., "'Commits adultery with her', not 'against her', Mk 10.11," in ET 83 (1971-1972) 107f.

- "Die Sprüche über Ehescheidung und Wiederheirat in der synoptischen Über-lieferung," in E. Lohse, C. Burchard, and B. Schaller (ed.), Der Ruf Jesu und die Antwort der Gemeinde. Exegetische Untersuchungen Joachim Jeremias zum 70. Geburtstag gewidmet von seinen Schülern, Göttingen 1970, 226-246.

Schelkle, K.H., "Ehe und Ehelosigkeit im Neuen Testament," in Wort und Schrift, Düsseldorf 1966, 183-198.

Schiffman, L.H., The Halakhah at Qumran. Leiden 1975.

Schillebeeckx, E., Marriage: Secular Reality and Saving Mystery. I-II. London 1965.

Schlatter, A., Die Evangelien nach Markus und Lukas. Stuttgart 1954 (= 1947).

- Der Evangelist Matthäus. Stuttgart [3]1948.

- Synagoge und Kirche bis zum Barkochba-Aufstand. Stuttgart 1966.

- Die Theologie des Judentums nach dem Bericht des Josefus. Gütersloh 1932.

Schlier, H., haireomai, etc., in ThW I, 179-184.

Schmid, J., "Markus und der aramäische Matthäus," in Synoptische Studien (festsch. A. Wikenhauser), München 1953, 148-183.

Schneider, G., "Jesu Wort über die Ehescheidung in der Überlieferung des Neuen Testaments," in TThZ 80 (1971) 65-87.

Schoeps, H.-J., "Jesus und das jüdische Gesetz," in Studien zur unbekannten Religions- und Geistesgeschichte, Göttingen 1963, 41-61.

Schubert, K., "Ehescheidung im Judentum zur Zeit Jesu," in ThQ 151 (1971) 23-27.

Schulz, S., Q. Die Spruchquelle der Evangelisten. Zürich 1972.

Schürer, E., Geschichte des jüdischen Volkes im Zeitalter Jesu Christi. I-III. (3rd and) 4th ed. Leipzig 1901-1909.

- The History of the Jewish People in the Age of Jesus Christ (175 B.C. - A.D. 135). Revised and edited by G. Vermes and F. Millar. Vol. I. Edinburgh 1973.

Schürmann, H., Das Lukasevangelium. I (1,1-9,50). Freiburg 1969.

- Traditionsgeschichtliche Untersuchungen zu den synoptischen Evangelien. Düsseldorf 1968.

Schweizer, E., Das Evangelium nach Markus. Göttingen 1967.

Shanks, H., "Is the Title 'Rabbi' Anachronistic in the Gospels?" in JQR 53 (1962-1963) 337-345.

- "Origins of the Title 'Rabbi'," in JQR 59 (1968-1969) 152-157.

Sickenberger, J., "Die Unzuchtsklausel im Matthäusevangelium," in ThQ 123 (1942) 189-206.

Silving, H., "The Oath," in Yale Law Journal 68 (1959) 1329-1390.

Smallwood, E.M., "High Priests and Politics in Roman Palestine," in JThS 13 (1962) 14-34.

Smith, M., "The Dead Sea Sect in Relation to Ancient Judaism," in NTS 7 (1960-1961) 347-360.

- "Palestinian Judaism in the First Century," in M. Davis (ed.), Israel: Its Role in Civilization, New York 1956, 67-81.

Soulen, R.N., "Marriage and Divorce. A Problem in New Testament Interpretation," in Interpr 23 (1969) 439-450.

Stählin, G., "Zum Gebrauch von Beteurungsformeln im Neuen Testament," in NovTest 5 (1962) 115-143.

Stamm, J.J. and Andrew, M.E., The Ten Commandments in Recent Research. London 1967.

Starfelt, E., Studier i rabbinsk och nytestamentlig skrifttolkning. Lund 1959.

Staudinger, F., Die Sabbatkonflikte bei Lukas. (U. Graz dissert.). St. Pölten 1964.

Stein, S., "The Dietary Laws in Rabbinic and Patristic Literature," in StPatrist 2 (1957) 141-154.

Stendahl, K., The School of St. Matthew and its Use of the Old Testament. Lund ²1968.

Strack, H.L. and Billerbeck, P., Kommentar zum Neuen Testament aus Talmud und Midrasch. I-IV. München 1922-1928.

Talmon, S., "The Calendar Reckoning of the Sect from the Judaean Desert," in Scripta Hierosolymitana 4 (1958) 162-199.

Taubes, Z., "Die Auflösung des Gelübdes," in MGWJ 73 NF 37 (1929) 33-46.

Taylor, R.O.P., The Groundwork of the Gospels. Oxford ²1946.

Taylor, V., The Gospel According to St. Mark. London ²1966.

Urbach, E.E., "Class-Status and Leadership in the World of the Palestinian Sages," in PrIsrAcSci&Hum 2 (1968) 38-74.

- "Derasha as a Basis of the Halakha and the Problem of the Soferim" (Hebrew), in Tarb 27 (1958) 166-182.

- "Halacha and Prophecy" (Hebrew), in Tarb 18 (1947) 1-27.

- The Sages: Their Concepts and Beliefs. I-II. Jerusalem 1975.
- "The Talmudic Sage - Character and Authority," in CHMond 11 (1968)
  116-147.

de Vaux, R., Les institutions de l'Ancien Testament. I-II. Paris 1958-1960.
Vermes, G., Jesus the Jew. A Historian's Reading of the Gospels. London
  1973.
- Post-biblical Jewish Studies. Leiden 1975.

Weinfeld, M., Deuteronomy and the Deuteronomic School. Oxford 1972.
- "Tithe," in EncJud 15, 1156-1162.
Weingreen, J., From Bible to Mishna. The Continuity of Tradition.
  Manchester 1976.
Weis, P.R., "A Note on pugme," in NTS 3 (1956-1957) 233-236.
Wellhausen, J., Einleitung in die drei ersten Evangelien. Berlin 1905.
Winter, P., On the Trial of Jesus. Berlin 1961.
Wolfson, H.A., "Notes on Proverbs 22.10 and Psalms of Solomon 17.48," in
  JQR 37 (1946-1947), 87.
- "Synedrion in Greek Jewish Literature and Philo," in JQR 36 (1945-1946)
  303-306.
Wrege, H.-T., Die Überlieferungsgeschichte der Bergpredigt. Tübingen 1968.

Yadin, Y., "L'attitude essénienne envers la polygamie et le divorce," in
  RB 79 (1972) 98f.

Zeitlin, S., "The Halaka. Introduction to Tannaitic Jurisprudence," in
  JQR 39 (1948-1949) 1-40.
- "Korban," in JQR 53 (1962-1963) 160-163.
- "The Political Synedrion and the Religious Sanhedrin," in JQR 36 (1945-
  1946) 109-140.
- "A Reply," in JQR 53 (1962-1963) 345-349.
- "Synedrion in the Judeo-Hellenistic Literature and Sanhedrin in the
  Tannaitic Literature," in JQR 36 (1945-1946) 307-315.
- "Synedrion in Greek Literature, the Gospels and the Institution of the
  Sanhedrin," in JQR 37 (1946-1947) 189-198.
- "The Takkanot of Erubin. A Study in the development of the Halaka," in
  JQR 41 (1950-1951) 351-361.
- "The Title Rabbi in the Gospels in Anachronistic," in JQR 59 (1968-1969)
  158-160.
Zucrow, S., Adjustment of Law to Life in Rabbinic Literature. Boston 1928.

Index of authors

Index of references

172